# NOUS SOLIS

BY

ERIK P. ANTONI

Proof Editing By

Laura Hnasko

Cover Artwork By

R.A. Frederickson

Cover Design By

Melissa Williams Design

Noetic Press



ISBN: 979-8-9917387-4-3

1.6.9

Please visit the author's webpage at:

www.songoftheimmortalbeloved.com

Other Books Written by Erik P. Antoni:

Song of the Immortal Beloved

Concerto of the Rising Sun

The Alchepedia

Anthros Galactica (Book Series)

# SECTIONS

## Sources, Quotations, and Interpretive Method

This work engages a wide range of sources drawn from sacred texts, philosophy, psychology, mythology, consciousness studies, and modern speculative thought. In presenting these materials, the author employs a comparative and interpretive methodology intended to illuminate underlying patterns of meaning rather than to offer strictly philological or historical exegesis.

Unless otherwise specified, quotations from primary and secondary sources are reproduced faithfully in meaning. In some instances, passages have been lightly edited for clarity, brevity, or continuity, including the omission of nonessential material, modernization of punctuation, or the consolidation of closely related sentences. Such edits do not alter the substantive intent of the original authors. Where quotations reflect paraphrase, summary, or interpretive condensation, this is done deliberately to preserve conceptual coherence within the broader philosophical framework of this book.

Biblical passages are cited from established translations (e.g., King James Version, New International Version) and are reproduced substantially verbatim, with formatting adjustments only. Quotations from philosophical, psychological, and contemporary writers may reflect differences among editions, translations, lecture transcripts, or published works, particularly where authors have expressed related ideas across multiple contexts.

The use of quotation marks in this work should therefore be understood as indicating attribution of ideas and language, not always as a claim of strict word-for-word reproduction across all cited materials. Readers seeking precise textual comparison are encouraged to consult the original sources directly.

This book does not claim to present definitive historical, theological, or scientific conclusions. Rather, it offers a synthetic metaphysical model that interprets ancient and modern texts through a unified lens of consciousness, symbolism, and psychosomatic evolution. All interpretations, whether traditional or unconventional, are presented in good faith and with respect for the original sources from which they arise.

The framework that follows is presented as a synthetic metaphysical model. It is not offered as dogma but as a hypothesis integrating myth, psychology, cosmology, and lived experience. What is described throughout is not limited to established historical or scientific consensus, but includes elements of direct perception, interpretive reconstruction, and symbolic insight. It reflects how the noetic mind encounters and organizes reality when viewed beyond the constraints of conventional historiography and materialist reduction.

# 1.0.0
# PREFACE

Nous Solis is a book of philosophical compositions written in response to some of the more prominent sacred texts of ancient times, popular viewpoints of modern scholars, and comments of well-known researchers on social media. Collectively, they illuminate the mystery of spiritual alchemy and its intersection with psychology, mythology, science, and religion. This book presents various metaphysical ideas anchored around a central thesis that the purpose of the human soul, referred to in this book as the noetic soul, is to act as an intermediary between divinity and creation, become a steward of that creation, and ultimately render the human species immortal. The immortalization process is enabled through an innate lifting effect of the noetic soul on the underlying human biology over the long course of human evolution.

Nous (noos) is a Greek word for mind or intellect. In Neoplatonism, Nous is the first and purest emanation of the divine source, or the One, which God uses to contemplate the universe.

Divinity is defined herein as that which was never created but yet still exists, has always existed, and will forever exist. It is the Creator.

Indeed, the mind of God, and all of creation within it, is the first emanation. But the first emanation arises spontaneously without intent, and therefore a second emanation arises to reconnect the mind back to the original monad (the One). It is this second emanation that illuminates the mind. The life force of this second emanation is the noetic soul.

The term noetic is a derivation of the word nous.

The terminology, noetic soul, was coined by me in my first book, Song of the Immortal Beloved (2018), to identify the third of three soul types—all three are explored in this book. The noetic soul reconnects the mind and body of creation with the original divine monad known as Ain Soph in the Kabbalah and by other equivalent names in various spiritual traditions. The presence of the noetic soul in the mind and body is what makes a living being—*human*.

The term "human" should be considered a classification of consciousness based on the presence of the noetic soul. It should not be used merely as a classification of biology. The noetic soul was born at the onset of creation to interdict the process of creation, reunify it with the divine source, and complete it. It has always existed throughout the cosmos since the very beginning of time. Human life on Earth is only a recent chapter in the eternal story of noetic consciousness.

Solis is a Latin word that means "of the Sun."

Together, Nous Solis, is a play on words that would translate to "Mind of the Sun," and is also titled in tribute to "Splendor Solis" —to date, perhaps the most famous book ever produced on alchemy.

Illuminating the mind like the Sun, the noetic soul comes into the world, not for itself, but by the will of God to reunify creation with the divine source and save it. Only in this way can creation last forever.

Briefly, what is alchemy?

Alchemy as a word essentially means transformation. As a subject, alchemy has a broad history dating back many thousands of years to before recorded history and has both eastern and western traditions. The eastern traditions are centered in China. Western alchemy is centered in Egypt and is integral to hermetic philosophy involving spiritual transformation and the elevation of the human condition.

Alchemy is legend to be the first of two original philosophies, or natural sciences, with its twin sister being astrology. Both western and eastern alchemical traditions have similar aims—immortality, longevity, and overall wellbeing. Later, the term alchemy became associated with the pursuit to transform base metals into gold, such as with medieval European alchemy, where many of its metallurgical processes were adopted as metaphors for the deeper spiritual alchemical process. The real-world pursuit to alchemically transform metal into gold eventually gave rise to modern chemistry.

Carl Jung believed that the alchemical metallurgic processes described in European alchemy were projections of an inner process.

"The real mystery does not behave mysteriously or secretively; it speaks a secret language and adumbrates itself by a variety of images which all point to its true nature. I am not speaking of a secret personally guarded by someone, with a content known to its possessor, but of a mystery, a matter or circumstance which is 'secret,' i.e., known only through vague hints but essentially unknown. The real nature of matter was unknown to the alchemist; he knew it only in hints. In seeking to explore it, he projected the unconscious into the darkness of matter in order to illuminate it. In order to explain the mystery of matter, he projected yet another mystery—his own psychic background—into what was to be explained: Obscurum per obscurius, ignotum per ignotius! This procedure was not, of course, intentional; it was an involuntary occurrence." — *Carl Jung, Psychology and Alchemy*

In the realm of spiritual alchemy, alchemy is the interaction of matter and consciousness. It is a psychosomatic process that rewires the brain and unifies the mind until reaching a self-actualizing state of being. Various traditions have different methods to achieve the same aim.

One of the primary premises of the spiritual alchemical process is that the human being is born incomplete. The human mind arises and develops in a highly fragmented condition between all the nature-instilled programs, ego defense mechanisms, super-ego scripts, learned personality traits and subconsciously adopted social behaviors with only a small percentage left for a clarity of mind and free will. That small degree of free will and clarity is often lost below the turbulent sea of the human mind during the course of life.

The noetic soul rises within the human psyche, within that narrow space of free will, as the authentic self. It has a universal prime directive to harmonize, integrate, and unify all the constituent parts of the mind, but is often lost and suppressed behind all our ego defense mechanisms and programmed scripts with few moments of free expression throughout a person's lifetime.

The sheer presence of the noetic soul within the mind has a gradual lifting and integration effect as long as it does not lose control of the mind to the forces of the id complex. It is a process known as theosis. But left to its own process without any intentional cooperation of the conscious mind, the natural lifting and integrating effect of the noetic soul on the psyche does not unify the mind within the course of a single human lifetime. The slow, resonant, interactive effect of the noetic soul on the mind and body is a larger operating function of human evolution as an entire species over the long course of planetary time.

This alchemical evolution of matter and consciousness toward a synchronized unity of mind, driven by the presence of the noetic soul, can be accelerated if we become aware of the dynamic and choose to cooperate with it. This is where we differentiate the natural process of nature and call it "spiritual alchemy," but the truth is, everything in nature is already alchemical. The natural course of evolution is already following an alchemical process of higher and higher grades of transformation, leading toward a more self-actualized human being.

To speed up this process demands self-awareness and conscious effort, and for this reason alone, most human beings will die without ever completing the unified mind—otherwise known as the reunified monad. Humanity as a whole is evolving psychosomatically in this direction in group sync over the course of a spiraled evolution through the transmigration of the noetic soul through the noosphere of the Earth, organized and directed by a force that I call "Alpha."

Alpha is the operating force of the law of sympathetic resonance. It continually raises and reorganizes creation to increasingly higher levels of existence until reaching a point where all the forces become harmonized into a new singularity or reconstituted monad (new unity). It is the driver of negentropy—the amount of "order" in a system, or the decrease in disorder—and emerges as a force driven by a will expressed within the original divine monad of Ain Soph to reconstitute the unity between all things that the process of creation initially multiplies. Alpha rises to a higher tempo within the human being when the conscious mind becomes aware of the unification process and decides to cooperate with it. This cooperation is "spiritual alchemy."

When the force of Alpha emerges to impose its force upon creation to re-organize it and lead it toward a reunification with the divine source, this reorganization unfolds as a noticeable geometric pattern. It repeats across all scales and objects of creation. This geometric pattern is the Alpha Wave. The Alpha Wave is what caused matter to organize and the atom to form. The Alpha Wave is the undercurrent directing the formation of the galaxies and all the laws of the universe. To date, modern physics has been unwilling to formulate a system within which consciousness by itself is a key causal factor. To them, consciousness is an effect—not a cause.

The Alpha Wave includes patterns within patterns and cycles within cycles. At the highest level, the Alpha Wave pattern unfolds in three major sequences which, mythologically, are referred to as the "Three Mountains." Spanning the three mountains is a series of several alchemical processes, and within each alchemical process, a set of alchemical labors. The medieval European alchemy modeled and labeled the noticeable Alpha sequences and geometric stages of development with its own cryptographic code. Most likely they did this unconsciously—steered unknowingly by the forces of consciousness referred to herein as *the cosmic quanta.*

During the universal alchemical process of unifying the mind, the cosmic quanta relay the story of creation directly to the noetic soul, beyond the mind, via the language of pure consciousness.

The reason it does this is that creation initially bursts forth spontaneously out of an overabundance of energy (love)—from within the source. Because creation arises spontaneously, it initially arises outside the awareness of the source consciousness in darkness.

This dynamic of the universal creation process is what gives rise to the mythological story of Aeon Sophia in the ancient Gnostic scriptures. Sophia means wisdom, but there's a deeper, less seen, nature about her. This allegorical story of creation is studied in Section 3.

It is only out of our willingness to return to the source and realize how everything came forth, that the universe can integrate the mind and complete the process of creation within us—thereby finally allowing us to understand the ancient texts so we may clarify them for others.

The intercession of a conscious mind is required to complete the process of creation. As creation is sparked unconsciously into existence, it can only achieve completion through a conscious return to the source from which it sprang. A sustained dual reflection between the mind of creation and the source is essential to the process.

Many of the archetypal characters present in humanity's most popular religions, mythologies, and fabled stories, are all representing an underlying set of divine principles and organizational constructs of energy and consciousness residing at the quantum level of existence which give rise to consciousness and all of creation. These same forces—called the cosmic quanta—are attempting to speak to us through our stories via the dynamics of the collective unconscious by utilizing the language of pure consciousness.

As stated earlier, divinity is the ultimate source of all things. Divinity is the uncreated creator that has always existed. This is not a contradiction. It is a paradox. Divinity is inherently paradoxical.

Mythologically, the way creation initially arises out of the divine source is allegorized in religion as the great fall, but it's actually a real quantum-based process—a process of multiplication and reunification.

In reality, it is creation itself, which is fallen, not some heavenly deity. But creation has an embedded awareness—and thus ensues all the mythologies of the unconscious to make the ineffable tangible.

Creation initially arises in darkness. Darkness is a metaphor used to describe the initial lack of awareness existing between the source consciousness and creation when creation first emerges.

The source quickly becomes aware of creation, and when it does, it loves it and wills that creation should not perish but should be saved and reintegrated with its eternal being so it can last forever. This reintegration of all the forces into a new reunified monad is Christ.

One rule of the collective unconscious is that the further historical figures recede in time, the more their characters take on mythological parallels to the various forces of consciousness. I call this dynamic "Theopomorphism"—as a mirror opposite to "Anthropomorphism," where human attributes are added to the forces of consciousness.

Anthropomorphism and theopomorphism are dualistic and work in tandem with each other. It's how the universe speaks to us. This dynamic doesn't lessen the reality of various historical figures. It's just that their stories echo more than actual history; they also echo the forces of consciousness. Admittedly, the dynamic of unconsciously attributing human qualities to the forces of consciousness (anthropomorphic) and or attributing godly or angelic natures to various historical figures (theopomorphic) has been a source of great confusion among the masses throughout history. To unconfuse, untangle the web, and clarify the stage, the real history of various ancient religious figures should be reexamined in a purely mundane context, and the nature of consciousness and the story it's trying to tell us should be deciphered and made known.

In Nous Solis, we re-examine various ancient passages from the perspective of the collective unconscious and the deeper meanings of the text that have escaped many theologians because most of them don't have a direct experience of the alchemical process in integrating the mind. They operate purely from a scholarly point of view while lacking the perspective of a practitioner who is actively engaged in the process. I then further clarify this universal alchemical knowledge when responding to various contemporary writers and researchers.

To set the stage for Nous Solis, it is necessary to supply a few more definitions for terminology commonly used throughout the book. We already examined the terms Nous, Noetic Soul, Authentic self, Ain Soph, Alpha, Divinity, Anthropomorphism, Theopomorphism, and we've only so far touched on the words Monad and Christ.

*Primordial* – The term essentially means "the first" or at the "very beginning." In the realm of spirituality, especially in Taoism, the primordial is often equated with the divine source. In my writings, the primordial is not the divine source; it is the first thing made by the divine source. I make this distinction because there exists all about us an invisible parallel universe to the physical universe that precedes the physical universe—it exists on the other side of a singularity wall separating the two universes, making it undetectable to current technology. It is the mother of the physical universe. It is the first universe made by the divine source. I therefore call this universe the primordial universe. It is a dual-reflecting mirror image of the physical universe; however, the primordial universe is based in eternity while the physical universe is based in time. *See Figure [6]*

In the physical, we pass through time. In the primordial, time passes through us, placing us outside of time as conscious observers of it, not aging subjects of it. In the physical, we age and are born mortal. In the primordial, we are forever young and are born immortal. The physical is acted upon by the force of Alpha to become harmonically resonant with the primordial to form a new union between the two, which, once realized, is a new reorganization of matter I refer to as metatronic. In the universe, I contend there exist metatronic worlds that exist outside of time in a perfect state of harmony with the divine source.

*Christ* – The historical Christ in Christianity is Jesus of Nazareth. However, Jesus theopomorphically echoes something cosmic and intrinsically fundamental to the underlying nature of reality and the structure of the universe. The original divine monad is Ain Soph, but when Ain Soph spontaneously creates, the monad becomes two—divinity and creation. The noetic soul is immaculately conceived by the divine source to interdict the process of creation and reunify it with the source through sympathetic resonance. When this reunification is achieved, this is the Christ Monad. It is a new unity between creation and divinity that exists in either a primordial or metatronic state.

In the primordial, we each have already achieved this sacred unity. We each already have the primordial Christ Monad. However, the physical is still a work-in-progress to unify physical and primordial matter to eventually achieve physical immortality within a new metatronic matrix of creation. Indeed, all of physical creation is being guided and driven towards the metatronic state via the force of Alpha. The applied practice of alchemy presented in my books accelerates the process so that a human being can achieve reconstitution of the monad in one physical lifetime, even before the rest of the species achieves the same state of being. Achieving the Christ Monad in advance of the species compels the species psychosomatically via the dynamics of the noosphere enveloping the Earth and all living things within its realm. Evolution is psychosomatic; it is not purely biological.

Achieving the Christ Monad before the rest of the species doesn't necessarily make someone physically immortal before everyone else, but an aspect of their physical being is echoed for all eternity in the primordial as a precursor that the species is further compelled to follow. I call the monad in this precursor position an *ethereal proto-monad.*

The Christ Monad also exists in scales. The physical universe is itself a Christ Monad that I call the Cosmic Monad or Cosmic Christ, and is already in unison with the Christ Monad at the primordial level. Together, it is a Super Monad. Eloah, Allah, Jehovah, Jesus, Krishna and Buddha are terms that unconsciously reflect the Cosmic Monad.

The Cosmic Monad is God. Ain Soph is the God-Above-God—the divine source. The Cosmic Monad first forms the universe we all live within—and then we are compelled to repeat what God has already completed on a cosmic level within ourselves. Eventually, all humanity on Earth will form a planetary monad via the dynamics of the noosphere and collective unconscious. The Earth will become a metatronic world.

Christ is the new monad (new heaven and new earth) which reconciles and integrates creation (old earth) with the original monad (old heaven). "And I saw a new heaven and a new earth, for the first heaven and the first earth were passed away, and there was no more sea." Christ is the union of creation and divinity, (old earth and old heaven), to form a new union between heaven and earth to fulfill the law of one. "There was no more sea," refers to the formless sea of consciousness transformed into the resonating form of creation.

# 2.0.0
# IMMORTALITY

*2.1.0 – Genesis 2:9-24*

*2.1.1 - New International Version: (considered the easiest to read)*

9 The Lord God made all kinds of trees grow out of the ground—trees that were pleasing to the eye and good for food. In the middle of the garden were the tree of life and the tree of the knowledge of good and evil. 15 The Lord God took the man and put him in the Garden of Eden to work it and take care of it. 16 And the Lord God commanded the man, "You are free to eat from any tree in the garden; 17 but you must not eat from the tree of the knowledge of good and evil, for when you eat from it you will certainly die."

22 And the Lord God said, "The man has now become like one of us, knowing good and evil. He must not be allowed to reach out his hand and take also from the tree of life and eat, and live forever. 23 So the Lord God banished him from the Garden of Eden to work the ground from which he had been taken. 24 After he drove the man out, he placed on the east side of the Garden of Eden cherubim and a flaming sword flashing back and forth to guard the way to the tree of life."

*2.1.2 - King James Version: (use of more archaic language)*

9 And out of the ground made the Lord God to grow every tree that is pleasant to the sight, and good for food; the tree of life also in the midst of the garden, and the tree of knowledge of good and evil. 15 And the Lord God took the man, and put him into the garden of Eden to dress it and to keep it. 16 And the Lord God commanded the man, saying, Of every tree of the garden thou mayest freely eat: 17 But of the tree of the knowledge of good and evil, thou shalt not eat of it: for in the day that thou eatest thereof thou shalt surely die.

22 And the Lord God said, "Behold, the man is become as one of us, to know good and evil: and now, lest he put forth his hand, and take also of the tree of life, and eat, and live forever. 23 Therefore the Lord God sent him forth from the garden of Eden, to till the ground from whence he was taken. 24 So he drove out the man; and he placed at the east of the garden of Eden cherubim, and a flaming sword which turned every way, to keep the way of the tree of life."

*2.1.3 - Analysis and Insight – by Erik P. Antoni*

In light of these passages, what follows in this section is presented not as a series of isolated assertions, but as components of a single, coherent proposition. Each statement gains its meaning from its relation to the whole, and only when considered together does the structure they describe become fully visible.

The Tree of Knowledge of Good and Evil in the Book of Genesis is the path of immortality. The Tree of Life[1] guarded by cherubim in the Garden of Eden is immortality itself. The cherubim are extraterrestrials from other worlds (gods—archons) who are guarding against anyone from walking this path, for it is a dangerous path that rarely yields its sought-after fruit of immortality.

Those who embark on the perilous journey initially encounter death in a manner unknown to those who do not. "For when you eat from it, you will certainly die." By choosing the path of knowing both light and darkness, the noetic soul consents to incarnate within an evolving human being, where, in the earliest stages of the species' development, death is experienced as a final absolute end. Yet this finality is an illusion. The soul awakens to a higher primordial existence.

The path of human immortality is a psychosomatic process of coming to realize, know, and reconcile the forces of light and darkness within the mind and body to reunify creation with divinity into a new Christ Monad (to till the ground from whence he was taken)—thus the mythology of Genesis, "Tree of Knowledge of Good and Evil."

As we stand at this threshold of understanding, the story of the Garden of Eden reveals itself not as mere prohibition, but as an archetypal invitation to conscious participation in the unfolding of divine unity. The Tree of Knowledge of Good and Evil stands as the fulcrum where duality first becomes experiential—where the soul, newly embodied, encounters the tension between fragmentation and wholeness, between the instinctual and the eternal. In this moment, the noetic soul begins its long labor: to bridge the separation of creation, transmute polarity into synthesis, and guide the human being toward the state of immortality—its divine given destiny.

---

[1] The Tree of Life can also be understood as the planetary group mind, or noosphere, evolving in tandem with humanity toward the state of immortality. The Sefirot of the Kabbalah points to the same process of eternal completion.

It is actually the prime directive of the noetic soul within humanity to engage in this integration process. However, the process follows a universal pattern, which is an echo of the same process that God went through on a cosmic level in bringing forth the universe. The reconciliation between the forces of light and darkness comes through in the final outcome of the universe via the duality within all things. We are called forth to achieve on an individual human level what God has achieved on a cosmic level. And eventually, the entire noosphere of the planet follows suit in accomplishing the same on a planetary level.

Alpha is the guiding force in the cosmos that unfolds this process. According to this speculative model, the challenge Alpha presents is that the cycles and patterns it echoes of the Cosmic Monad—the echoes of God—lead humanity through darkness before unifying everything in the light. When past civilizations followed Alpha in their evolution without sufficient integration, they destabilized themselves and ignited conflict beyond their own worlds. Later in galactic history, it was forbidden that any humanity be conceived with the psychosomatic capacity to pursue the reunified monad that bestows immortality upon the species— "He must not be allowed to … live forever." The process was genetically suppressed and the doorway closed-off because prior attempts at unification undermined the peace between worlds.

The reunified monad can only be achieved organically. It cannot be engineered. However, it can be accelerated and helped along (i.e. alien abduction phenomenon). Our humanity is special in that we have been given life with the psychosomatic ability to reconstitute the monad—to become one with God—and in doing so, become in his likeness. We ate the forbidden fruit—we turned the switch back on.

The narrative now expands beyond purely symbolic interpretation into a speculative cosmological framework. Whether understood as literal history, mythic memory, or archetypal encoding, the function of this framework is not to replace religious symbolism but to explain its persistence, coherence, and internal logic across cultures and epochs.

Religion generally believes that the disobedience of God's command is the original sin—and the forbidden fruit is the experiential knowledge of good and evil that shifts humanity from innocence to moral accountability with all the consequences of sin, death, and shame. This interpretation has elements of truth, but the actual history is much more complex and profound. It points to a deep, forgotten cosmic past.

The commandment did not come from the God of the universe; it came from the archon overlords ruling the Milky Way galaxy who presented themselves to us as gods. Their commandment was based on a long cosmic history involving a dangerous process they were all too familiar with. They were trying to keep a secret doorway closed off—a door whose key was genetic—a doorway of the mind. When opened, this doorway allows the noetic soul to engage the erotic soul, wherein we must come to know and reconcile light and darkness in the process of reconstituting the monad within the realms of creation. The erotic soul is the soul of creation that flows through and animates all living things, including all the animals, plants, and the human body.

The forbidden fruit is the reconstituted Christ Monad itself. The reunified monad is the reconciliation of all the forces of mind, body, and consciousness into a harmonious unified whole with the source—Ain Soph—the original divine monad before creation. Once achieved within the noosphere, it eventually bestows immortality upon the human species. In this state, we step outside of time, sunken in subspace, lifted by the primordial, but still hyperdimensionally physical. The reconstituted monad is the forbidden fruit, not because it is bad or wrong—it's actually miraculous beyond words. It's forbidden because of what we must risk and endure in the process of achieving it.

It is a paradox because the noetic soul was conceived by the divine source for the very purpose of achieving it. It was forbidden, not by divinity, but by the gods—with a lower "g"—who were and still are nothing more than technologically advanced humans from other worlds. These extraterrestrial humans are mortal because they chose to stay mortal and not pursue the prime directive of the noetic soul—And they don't want others trying it either. They are the mythological archons of gnostic theology—rulers that govern the material world and seek to keep humanity trapped in ignorance and illusion.

### *2.1.4 - The Archons Across Scales*

The discussion thus far has focused on the archons as historical authorities—advanced extraterrestrial intelligences who interacted with early humanity. Yet the Gnostic texts suggest a more complex picture, one in which the same governing principle manifests across multiple scales of reality.

The common modern interpretation of the archons as merely psychological or spiritual forces captures only one dimension of the

Gnostic vision. The ancient texts repeatedly describe archons as rulers, authorities, governors, and agents who speak, command, create, punish, regulate, and interact with humanity. They are presented not merely as abstractions but as intelligences operating within creation.

One of the central challenges in interpreting the ancient texts is that Gnostic cosmology operates across multiple scales simultaneously. The same underlying structure appears repeatedly throughout creation, expressing itself differently at each level of manifestation.

At the highest scale, the Demiurge—Yaldabaoth—can be understood as the first differentiation of consciousness into mind. The Monad is pure consciousness itself: undivided, infinite, and without distinction. The Demiurge is the first governing principle through which differentiation, structure, and manifestation become possible. In this sense, the Demiurge is the first archon. From this primordial differentiation, the pattern repeats throughout creation.

On the cosmic scale, archons appear as governing intelligences that organize worlds and civilizations. On the planetary scale, they appear as powers and authorities that shape the destiny of worlds. On the individual scale, they appear as the structures of mind itself: perception, identity, attachment, fear, desire, and belief.

Each scale mirrors the others because reality itself is recursive. What appears as a governing principle on one scale may appear as a civilization on another and as a psychological structure on yet another.

The recursive nature of reality suggests that governing principles do not remain abstract. Just as consciousness differentiates into mind, and mind differentiates into psychological structures, governing intelligences may also manifest through biological civilizations. A sufficiently advanced civilization tasked with guiding or regulating the development of younger worlds would function as an archon in the historical sense. Such beings would not be separate from the governing principles described in Gnostic cosmology but would embody them.

When the Gnostic texts describe Adam disobeying an archon, the account may therefore operate on multiple levels simultaneously. Psychologically, Adam transcends a limiting structure of consciousness. Historically, the same narrative may preserve memories of interactions with actual rulers or advanced intelligences who exercised authority over early humanity.

The modern tendency to reduce the archons exclusively to psychological forces strips the texts of their historical and cosmological dimensions. Conversely, interpreting the archons solely as extraterrestrial rulers ignores their psychological and metaphysical significance.

A more complete interpretation is that the archons are manifestations of the same governing principle appearing at different scales of reality. They are simultaneously cosmic, collective, planetary, and individual. The historical beings and the governing principles are not competing explanations. They are reflections of the same pattern operating across different levels of manifestation.

Viewed in this light, the archons are not merely hostile powers opposing humanity. They are the natural consequence of differentiation itself. Wherever consciousness fragments, structures emerge to stabilize and regulate that fragmentation. The archons are those structures.

The Demiurge therefore stands not only as a mythological figure but as the archetype of governance itself—the first differentiation of consciousness into mind. The later archons share in that same lineage because they are expressions of the same principle operating at progressively lower levels of manifestation.

Within this framework, the archons described in the ancient texts may be understood simultaneously as metaphysical principles, psychological structures, and advanced civilizations. The Gnostic vision therefore need not be reduced to mythology or history, psychology or cosmology. It may instead describe a recursive structure woven throughout creation itself, wherein the same structural pattern appears repeatedly—from the first differentiation of consciousness into mind, to the governance of worlds, civilizations, and ultimately the human psyche.

### *2.1.5 – The Forbidden Humanity*

Although Gnostic theology looks upon these archon gods as malevolent beings, their true nature is more complicated and nuanced. It was a faction of the gods who rebelled against the galactic law and founded our humanity. Reportedly, the worlds where these beings come from are actually highly evolved and peaceful. Ironically, they reached this level of civilization by not engaging in the psychosomatic process of reconstituting the monad. But in doing so, they also denied themselves the ability to achieve the divine purpose of the noetic soul.

Our humanity on Earth is a consciousness project with a long tumultuous history founded by a band of renegade archon scientists who disagreed with the cosmic law set forth by the archon rulers of the galaxy and disobeyed them by creating us—with the secret door open.

Indications are we may have first been started on Mars or another planet in the solar system that no longer exists. Through an intergalactic war that eventually arose between cosmic factions over our very right to exist, the project was eventually moved to Earth. Earth, in its entirety, I propose, is Eden. The Garden of Eden would be the surface of the Earth. The paradisiacal dimension of Eden would be the primordial Earth that coexists in parallel space to the physical Earth, just outside of time. They are dual-reflecting mirror images of each other.

The primordial universe is the eternal realm. The primordial Earth, which exists in the same location as the physical Earth, exists in a higher vibrational plane on the other side of the singularity wall. The singularity wall is formed by the physical universe existing inside a black hole singularity nested up inside the primordial universe.

When we die, we eventually wake up in our immortal body in the primordial universe and we remember our past physical lifetime(s) much like that of a dream. You, the reader, come from a whole other reality that you have only forgotten, but will one day remember.

Within this framework, Eden is not lost in time but displaced across dimensions. Humanity is not exiled from paradise, but embodied within a developmental stage of it. Death, therefore, is not annihilation but transition—an interruption in memory rather than existence.

Some interpretations of the Sumerian cuneiform tablets describe humanity as having been created to mine gold for advanced beings. Read symbolically, this narrative encodes a far deeper truth: the gold sought was not material, but philosophical—the reunified monad itself. The "slavery" described reflects the arduous psychosomatic labor required to reconcile light and darkness under the force of Alpha until unity is achieved. See 4.0.0 - Earth Monad Project to go deeper.

### *2.1.6 – The Language of Consciousness*

A few have inquired about my use of religious terminology and iconography in explaining alchemy due to their general disagreement with organized religion. My response to this is as follows.

The forces of consciousness that underlie and bring forth the universe—the cosmic quanta—speak to us through mythology via the dynamics of the collective unconscious. This esoteric language arises unconsciously between the lines within many of humanity's stories, especially mythology and religious doctrines. Through this dynamic, the cosmic quanta are attempting to tell us the story of creation and consciousness and the purpose of the noetic soul. The message comes through in the way writers unconsciously create characters and form plots in their stories. The cosmic quanta speak through writers without the writers even being conscious of it—and it often works best that way.

"We have come from God, and inevitably the myths woven by us, though they contain error, reflect a splintered fragment of the true light, the eternal truth that is with God. Indeed, only by myth-making, only by becoming a 'sub-creator' and inventing stories, can Man aspire to the state of perfection that he knew before the Fall." ... *J.R.R. Tolkien.*

By using some of the same mythological terminology found in religion to define universal truths in a higher and more accurate model of reality, the old religious interpretations are upended and dissolved. The ultimate goal is to get beyond mythological references. I also use many new terms in my books, but I demonstrate equivalencies to the mythological models of old for the exact purpose of dissolving the old interpretations and mental hangups. If we try to just discard the old motifs and icons, they will only serve to haunt the world. They must be reexamined and explained in a new higher light and finally resolved.

### *2.1.7 – Ancient Echoes*

The ideas presented herein align well with Sumerian creation myth and the concept of humanity on Earth being a "consciousness project." The Sumerian Epic of Gilgamesh (circa 2100 BCE) contains a quest for immortality that resonates closely with this integrated narrative. In Tablet XI, Gilgamesh seeks the secret of eternal life from Utnapishtim, a flood survivor granted immortality by the gods. Utnapishtim reveals a plant that restores youth, but a serpent steals it after Gilgamesh retrieves it from the sea. The plant is a symbol of immortality. It echoes the reconstituted monad—a prize requiring great struggle and risk. The serpent's role parallels the Genesis snake, suggesting a deeper connection between knowledge (or awakening) and the loss or gain of immortality. The serpent is a symbol of creation itself, whose inherent nature challenges the reintegration of the monad while at the same time encouraging it. The sea in this story is the Sea of Eros that creation arises out of; it is the love of God whose energy underlies the entire universe and spontaneously brings forth all of creation.

The ambivalence of the Sumerian gods toward human immortality reflects the tension between the archon gods forbidding a process that is actually set in motion by a higher divine will from the one true divine God that exists at the center of all things—Ain Soph.

This interpretation finds support in ancient texts when viewed through a symbolic and esoteric lens. In Genesis 2-3, the act of eating from the Tree of Knowledge awakens humanity to the duality of good and evil, initiating a psychosomatic process of reconciliation. The subsequent guarding of the Tree of Life (Genesis 3:22-24) suggests not a permanent denial, but a deferred access, contingent upon mastering this inner unification—a notion echoed in the Corpus Hermeticum, where the divine mind within humanity must ascend through the interplay of light and darkness to reunite with the One.

The ancient narratives in themselves repeatedly suggest a sacred inner process within the human being that echoes a universal divine act, a concept central to the idea that the purpose of humanity is to retrace God's cosmic reconciliation of light and darkness.

The Apocryphon of John presents the monad as the supreme source, disrupted by lesser deities (archons) who are suppressing humanity's divine potential—analogous to the lower gods outlawing the pursuit of the reunified monad. This suppression, however, is destined to be transcended by the noetic soul within humanity, for the noetic soul was immaculately conceived to do so by the will of the divine source itself. This dynamic is reflected in the Epic of Gilgamesh, where the quest for a rejuvenating plant symbolizes the perilous pursuit of immortality, stolen by a serpent while paralleling Genesis's forbidden fruit as a descent into darkness; but a descent that eventually unifies one with God. The Egyptian Book of the Dead reinforces this narrative with its portrayal of the soul integrating with the body to achieve eternal life, emerging from primordial chaos, much like the force of Alpha guiding one from darkness to light.

The ancient texts imply a cosmic template and pattern—evident in Hermeticism's mirroring of—universe, eternity, and man—where the reconciliation of duality is both a divine precedent and a human destiny culminating in a planetary noosphere aligned with the divine source—the Omega Point as theorized by Pierre Teilhard de Chardin.

The interdimensional and galactic aspects of this thesis, while speculative, finds metaphorical grounding in ancient motifs of forbidden knowledge and primordial realms. The Sumerian Enuma Elish and interpretations of cuneiform tablets hint at humanity's creation by advanced beings (Anunnaki) for a purpose—reexplained in this narrative as a mining for "philosophical gold" (the monad) rather than a literal metal. Mining symbolizes the arduous integration process.

The Book of the Dead's higher vibrational afterlife and the Upanishadic eternal Self suggest a primordial Earth or Eden existing beyond time, akin to a paradisiacal realm coexisting with the physical universe. Genesis's expulsion from Eden, guarded by cherubim, parallels the Gnostic archons' restrictions, implying a cosmic law defied by rebellious "gods" who seeded and restored within humanity the capacity to achieve immortality—likened to giving fire to mortals (Prometheus). Thus, various ancient passages collectively support the thesis that humanity's pursuit of the reconstituted monad—risk-laden yet divinely ordained—mirrors God's cosmic act of navigating darkness to unify with the light, a process outlawed by lesser powers but organically reawakened, positioning Earth as both a battleground and eternal Eden in a planetary consciousness project.

This narrative weaves together diverse ancient threads into a cohesive story that upholds this thesis's reinterpretation of Genesis, its cosmic scope, and its vision of immortality as a psychosomatic triumph over duality, sanctioned by a higher divine intent while at the same time opposed by lesser forces.

If ancient texts encode the architecture of immortality symbolically, modern thinkers attempt to articulate it conceptually. The following writers do not invent this framework; they rediscover it through psychology, cosmology, and evolutionary theory.

* * *

*2.2.0 - Pierre Teilhard de Chardin - The Phenomenon of Man (1955)*

Man is not the centre of the universe as he once naively believed himself to be, but something much more wonderful—the arrowhead of evolution [...] Man is the last-born, the keenest, the most complex, the most subtle of the successive layers of life [...] And it is this hyper-concentration of the stuff of the universe that we must now examine as it converges ahead towards its ultimate synthesis.

The stuff of the universe, woven in a single piece according to one and the same system [...] goes on weaving itself unceasingly from top to bottom following a particular formula of complexity-consciousness [...] At the summit of this involution, spirit emerges from matter [...] The end of the world: the wholesale internal introversion upon itself of the noosphere, which has simultaneously reached the uttermost limit of its complexity and its centrality.

Evolution is an ascent towards consciousness [...] It is a progress whose every advance is marked by an increase in the 'within' of things [...] This cosmic property of complexification, which is co-extensive with the whole duration of the world, continues to function visibly in man [...] There is a cosmic drift towards thought.

The world [...] is a divine milieu [...] Co-extensive with their Without, there is a Within to things [...] Man, the summit of anthropogenesis, appears as a being who is co-creator with God of his own destiny [...] At the end of time [...] having gathered everything together and transformed everything [...] the universe will have become a great consecrated Host offered to the glory of God [...] A single act of universal adoration.

*2.2.1 - Analysis and Insight – by Erik P. Antoni*

Humanity is not an end but a stage—a vector of evolution converging toward the Omega Point—a supreme unity of consciousness where spirit and matter, individuality and collectivity, are reconciled (Christ Monad)— "Christogenesis." This process is not merely biological but noetic, driven by a cosmic force (Alpha) that draws life upward through complexity and consciousness. The universe itself is a divine milieu (an interplay between the material and spiritual), and our role is to co-create with it, to spiritualize matter until we reach a state beyond time, where death is transcended in a hyper-personal unity with the divine source.

*2.3.0 - Terence McKenna – The Archaic Revival (1991)*

We are in a symbiotic relationship with an organism made of information, and this is not a situation unique to us nor particularly new […] It may be instead that the Earth itself is involved in a symbiotic relationship with a galactic intent that we do not comprehend […] I believe that the totemic image for the future is the image of a face-to-face interaction with an extraterrestrial being or intelligence.

The fall into history, (the expulsion from paradise), is not a catastrophe—it's an opportunity […] History is a kind of cocoon from which we will emerge as something unimaginable […] What we call history is the fall into matter, the exploration of the possibilities of three-dimensional space and linear time, but it's not the end state—it's a stage in a process of becoming.

Psychedelics are a way to slip the bonds of the dominator culture and reconnect with the archaic […] The mushroom said to me once, 'This is what it's like when a species prepares to depart for the stars' […] I think we're involved in a galactic ecology that we don't fully understand, and the archons of materialism—the rulers of this world—have kept us in a state of ignorance about our true potential […] We're here to become co-creators with the universe.

*2.3.1 - Analysis and Insight – by Erik P. Antoni*

We are part of a symbiotic relationship with the biosphere and perhaps with intelligences beyond it—extraterrestrial or hyper-dimensional—that have seeded consciousness into humanity. The fall into history, the expulsion from Eden, was not a curse but an initiation into time, a necessary descent into the dark fractal depths of experience to rediscover the eternal. Psychedelics and ancient myths hint at a galactic ecology where humanity's purpose is to transcend the genetic shackles imposed by materialist archons and reclaim our birthright as co-creators of reality, stepping into a timeless immortality.

*2.4.0 - Carl Gustav Jung – The Archetypes and the Collective Unconscious (1959)*

The self is not only the centre but also the whole circumference which embraces both conscious and unconscious; it is the centre of this totality, just as the ego is the centre of consciousness. As an archetype, it is a symbol of wholeness and, in this respect, a representation of the God-image. […] Man is a microcosm, or little world, because he contains within himself all the opposites that make up the macrocosm.

The process of individuation […] leads to the development of the individual personality […] it does not shut out the opposites but embraces them. […] There is no energy unless there is a tension of opposites. […] The self is made manifest in the opposites and in the conflict between them. […] Wholeness is achieved not by repression or exclusion, but by the integration of the opposites.

Individuation is the process by which a person becomes a psychological 'in-dividual,' that is, a separate, indivisible unity or 'whole' […] It is the realization of the self, which is the goal of human development […] The psyche mirrors the cosmos, and in the archetype, we find the bridge between the human and the divine.

The serpent is a very common archetype […] It is a symbol of transformation, of renewal, because it sheds its skin […] In the Garden of Eden, it represents the urge toward consciousness, the knowledge of good and evil, which is both a fall and a step toward redemption […] It is not merely a tempter but a guide to the divine.

*2.4.1 - Analysis and Insight – by Erik P. Antoni*

"*The self is a circle whose center is everywhere and whose circumference is nowhere.*" ... *Nicholas of Cusa.*

Man is the microcosm of the macrocosm; the God-image in man, the archetype of the self is a reflection of the divine process of creation. The opposites—light and darkness, good and evil—are not to be eradicated but integrated, for in their tension lies the dynamism of life and the possibility of wholeness. This process of individuation, the realization of the self, is the goal of human existence, a psychological and spiritual journey that mirrors the cosmic order. The serpent, far from being merely a tempter, is a symbol of transformation, leading humanity toward the knowledge that bridges the divine and the human.

*2.5.0 - Larger Section Analysis and Insight – by Erik P. Antoni*

What begins to emerge across these perspectives is not a collection of parallel insights, but the outline of a single process viewed from different angles. Each thinker approaches the same threshold—some through biology, some through consciousness, some through myth—but none fully articulate the structure that unites them. Evolution is not merely progression. It is integration. Not the accumulation of complexity, but the reconciliation of division.

What appears as divergence across traditions is, in fact, partial recognition of a deeper continuity. The movement is consistent: from fragmentation toward unity, from differentiation toward reintegration. Each account gestures toward this pattern, yet stops short of defining the mechanism by which it operates or the end toward which it moves. Taken together, however, these perspectives do more than suggest resemblance. They imply direction. They indicate that consciousness, life, and meaning are not unfolding at random, but according to a logic pressing toward wholeness.

To proceed, the pattern must be made explicit and understood in structural terms.

### *2.6.0 - Elaine Pagels – The Gnostic Gospels (1979)*

The Hypostasis of the Archons […] describes the situation very differently from the Genesis account […] In these texts, the serpent is not a tempter but an instructor, persuading Eve to disobey the creator's command. It urges Eve to eat of the fruit of knowledge, saying, 'You will not die; for it was out of jealousy that he said this to you. Rather, your eyes will open and you will become like gods, knowing good and evil.' […] This knowledge awakens them to their divine nature.

According to the Apocryphon of John, the demiurge—called Yaldabaoth—creates the world and declares himself the only God […] But the text reveals a higher deity, the invisible One, 'the monad, the eternal, the infinite light,' who is beyond the demiurge […] Yaldabaoth and his archons, the rulers of this world, try to keep humanity ignorant, jealous of the divine spark within them […] The Genesis command not to eat from the tree is seen as his attempt to prevent their enlightenment.

The Gnostics saw human existence as a struggle between the divine spark within and the archons who rule the material world […] Salvation comes through gnosis, the recognition of one's origin in the divine pleroma, which the demiurge and his powers seek to obscure […] This is not a passive faith but an active pursuit of self-knowledge, defying the cosmic authorities.

For Gnostics, resurrection is not a future event but an inner transformation […] The Gospel of Philip says, "Those who say they will die first and then rise are in error. If they do not first receive the resurrection while they live, when they die, they will receive nothing." […] This is about realizing the divine within, transcending the illusions of the material world.

*2.6.1 - Analysis and Insight – by Erik P. Antoni*

The Gnostic reinterpretation of Genesis casts the serpent not as a villain but as a liberator, offering knowledge (gnosis) that awakens humanity to its divine spark, trapped by the archons—lesser rulers of the material cosmos. The God of Genesis, in texts like the Apocryphon of John, is the archons—distinct from the true monad or infinite light—that forbid access to the Tree of Life out of animosity, not benevolence. This suggests a cosmic struggle where humanity's pursuit of self-realization and immortality defies these lower powers, aligning with a higher, ineffable source. The Gnostic path is one of inner transformation, uniting opposites to transcend the illusions of time and death.

*2.7.0 - Stanislav Grof – The Cosmic Game: Explorations of the Frontiers of Human Consciousness (1998)*

Human consciousness is not a product of the brain but an integral part of the cosmic process. […] The universe can be understood as a holographic structure, where each part contains the whole […]
We are not separate from the cosmic intelligence but expressions of it, participating in its unfolding drama of creation.

The journey toward wholeness involves confronting and integrating the shadow—the repressed, dark, and chaotic aspects of the psyche […] This is not just a psychological process but a psychosomatic one, engaging the body and soul […] Through this integration, we transcend the limitations of the ego and open ourselves to the transpersonal dimensions of existence.

The process of creation in the universe—from the primordial void to the emergence of light and form—parallels the inner journey of the psyche […] In the chaos of the unconscious, we find the seeds of order and illumination, much as the cosmos emerged from its initial state of undifferentiation.

Myths such as the Fall of humanity represent an archetypal pattern of separation from the divine unity […] Yet they also contain the promise of return, a reclamation of our spiritual essence […]
This process may be guided by transpersonal forces—archetypes, spiritual intelligences, or entities from other dimensions—
that challenge our ordinary perception of reality.

*2.7.1 - Analysis and Insight – by Erik P. Antoni*

Human consciousness is not an isolated phenomenon but a holographic fragment of a cosmic intelligence participating in a universal drama of creation and redemption. The journey toward wholeness requires confronting and integrating the shadow—the dark, chaotic aspects of the psyche—through a psychosomatic process that transcends the ordinary boundaries of the ego. This mirrors the birth of the universe itself, where light emerges from primordial chaos. Myths, like the Fall, reflect an expulsion from a more civilized world, but also a call to reclaim our divine potential, guided by transpersonal forces beyond our world's current understanding—be they archetypes or intelligences from higher dimensions (cosmic quanta, Alpha, etc.)

*2.8.0 - David Bohm – Wholeness and the Implicate Order (1980)*

In the implicate order, space and time are no longer the dominant factors determining the relationships of dependence or independence of different elements. [...] In this order, the whole universe is enfolded in each part, and each part is enfolded in the whole [...] Space, time, matter, and consciousness are not separate but are aspects of this undivided wholeness, unfolding into the explicate order we perceive.

What we call opposites—positive and negative, existence and non-existence—are abstractions from the undivided movement of the implicate order [...] These dualities are not ultimately real but are projections of a deeper unity [...] The perception of separation arises in the explicate order, but in the implicate order, all is one.

Consciousness is not separate from matter [...] It has the potential to penetrate the implicate order, to participate in the creative process that underlies the universe [...] This implies a capacity to go beyond the limitations of the explicate order, to grasp the whole in a way that transforms our understanding of reality.

In the implicate order, time is not fundamental [...] What we experience as past, present, and future is an unfolding of what is already enfolded [...] This suggests a dimension beyond our usual physical constraints, where the mind might apprehend a totality that transcends the temporal [...] Such a state has been hinted at by mystics as an eternal now.

The universe is a process of creative unfolding […] To understand this is to see that our own existence may have a purpose within this larger movement—not as a static end, but as a participation in the infinite creativity of the whole.

*2.8.1 - Analysis and Insight – by Erik P. Antoni*

The universe is an undivided wholeness, unfolding from an implicate order where all things—matter, consciousness, time—are enfolded within each other. What we perceive as duality, such as light and darkness, is a manifestation of this deeper unity, and human consciousness has the capacity to penetrate this order, participating in the creative process of the cosmos. This suggests a potential beyond our current physical limits, where the mind and body might align with a timeless dimension—an explicate reflection of the implicate—achieving a state akin to what mystics call eternal life. Such a process is the purpose of existence, echoing patterns inherent in the universe's own becoming and completion.

*2.9.0 - Overall Section Analysis and Insight – by Erik P. Antoni*

At this point, the pattern can no longer be understood as a simple overlap of similar ideas. What emerges within these accounts is not agreement, but the converging expression of a common framework.

Each perspective captures an aspect of the same movement—evolution, consciousness, myth—but none renders it whole in isolation. The fragments align, yet the mechanism by which this movement unfolds remains undefined.

The process is not additive. It is integrative.

What evolves is not merely form, but relation—the capacity of differentiated elements to return to coherence without collapsing their distinction. This principle underlies each account, whether expressed in biological, psychological, or symbolic terms. What appears as divergence is, in fact, distributed recognition of a single trajectory unfolding across multiple domains, each illuminating the same process from within its own frame.

This carries implications that extend beyond interpretation.

If the same structural pattern emerges independently across disciplines, then it is not imposed by perspective, but disclosed through it. The consistency suggests that what is being observed is not projection, but a feature of reality itself.

If this structure is real, then evolution is directional. Not toward complexity alone, but toward a specific form of unity not yet realized.

*2.10.0 - Mircea Eliade – The Forge and the Crucible: The Origins and Structures of Alchemy (1962)*

Alchemy cannot be reduced to a primitive chemistry or regarded solely as the prehistory of modern science […] It is a spiritual technique involving a mystical conception of the cosmos and man's place in it […] Alchemy always presupposes a sacred vision of the world and of life.

The alchemist's work aimed at the transmutation of matter, but this was inseparable from his own inner transformation […] The philosophers' stone was not merely a material substance but the symbol of a perfect unity, a reconciliation of opposites—fire and water, masculine and feminine […] It represented the mastery of the prima materia, the primordial chaos from which all creation emerges.

The alchemical operation reproduces the cosmogony […] The separation and reunion of the primal elements—earth, air, fire, water—echo the divine act of creation […] The adept, in transmuting base matter into gold, participates in this sacred process, reenacting the birth of the world from chaos. The fall of man and his subsequent labors can be seen as an initiatory ordeal […] Myths of a lost paradise or golden age encode the idea of a primordial unity that humanity must recover through effort and transformation […] The alchemist's quest is a return to this state, a redemption of matter and spirit together.

The philosophers' stone was believed not only to effect the transmutation of metals, but also to confer longevity or immortality. It symbolized the perfection of matter itself, achieved through the reconciliation and harmony of opposing forces—the ultimate aim of the alchemical work.

*2.10.1 - Analysis and Insight – by Erik P. Antoni*

Alchemy is not merely a proto-science but a sacred cosmology, a process of transforming the self and the cosmos through the reconciliation of opposites—light and darkness, spirit and matter. This mirrors the mythic pattern of creation, where the divine separates and then reunifies the primal elements. The philosophers' stone, often misunderstood as a physical object, is the symbol of an inner unification, a state of christification achieved by the adept who masters the prima materia—the chaotic potential of existence—to ultimately render the species immortal. Ancient myths, like the expulsion from Eden, encode this alchemical journey, suggesting humanity's fall into duality is a necessary stage toward a higher eternal synthesis.

*2.11.0 - Graham Hancock – Supernatural: Meetings with the Ancient Teachers of Mankind (2005)*

The evidence of ancient myths, shamanic visions, and prehistoric art suggests a persistent and coherent theme: that humanity may not have evolved in isolation. Across cultures, these traditions speak of encounters with non-ordinary beings—teachers, spirits, or gods—who appear to intervene in human affairs. I propose that such accounts may preserve memories of contact with intelligences from other realms, whether extraterrestrial or interdimensional, that have played a formative role in shaping human consciousness.

The story of the Garden of Eden might encode a deeper truth [...] What if the serpent and the forbidden fruit represent a moment of intervention—a gift of knowledge or awareness—delivered by beings opposed by a controlling authority? [...] This could be a mythic memory of a real event, a shift in human potential that some powers sought to suppress.

The Epic of Gilgamesh, with its quest for immortality, echoes a universal human longing [...] This theme recurs in alchemical traditions and shamanic tales—a search for a lost or hidden capacity [...] Could this reflect a suppressed potential within us, something our ancestors knew but we've forgotten, perhaps locked away by those who engineered our past?

Modern abduction experiences and shamanic visions share striking parallels [...] These encounters with non-human intelligences—whether through psychedelics or unexplained phenomena—seem to awaken something in us, accelerating our evolution [...] They push us toward a state beyond ordinary reality, a timeless consciousness that transcends the material world.

*2.11.1 - Analysis and Insight – by Erik P. Antoni*

Humanity's ancient myths and shamanic visions suggest we are not alone in the universe—that extraterrestrial or interdimensional intelligences have shaped our consciousness, perhaps as part of a grand experiment. The Eden story could be a memory of this intervention, where the forbidden fruit represents an awakening, opposed by lower gods (archons) who sought to limit our potential. The quest for immortality, encoded in tales like Gilgamesh or alchemical traditions, points to a suppressed capacity within us, possibly aided through encounters with these beings—abductions or visions—that accelerate our evolution toward a transcendent state beyond time.

*2.12.0 - John E. Mack – Passport to the Cosmos: Human Transformation and Alien Encounters (1999)*

The abduction phenomenon is not simply a physical event. It is a complex experience that engages the body, the mind, and the spirit. It appears to be a transformative process, one that challenges the conventional distinction between the physical and the spiritual, pointing toward a deeper integration of these dimensions.

The beings encountered in abductions are often described as both nurturing and intrusive […] Many abductees feel they are being guided toward a higher state of consciousness, as if these entities are midwives to an evolutionary shift […] There's a sense that they are activating something within us—perhaps a latent potential in our biology or psyche.

The abduction experience resonates with ancient myths—stories of divine beings imposing limits, yet others breaking those limits to bring knowledge or power to humanity […] Think of Prometheus or the Genesis narrative: a tension between control and liberation that seems to recur in these encounters, pushing us toward a greater connection with the cosmos.

Abductees often report a sense of timelessness during their experiences, as if they've stepped outside ordinary reality […] They describe an expanded sense of self, a feeling of belonging to a larger universe […] This suggests we may be reclaiming a connection to something eternal that was lost or suppressed in our development.

*2.12.1 - Analysis and Insight – by Erik P. Antoni*

Alien abduction experiences reveal a transformative process, a psychosomatic encounter that bridges the physical and spiritual, pushing humanity toward a higher state of existence. These beings, often perceived as both benevolent and intrusive, seem to act as midwives to an evolutionary leap, activating latent potentials within our DNA or consciousness. This aligns with the mounting evidence that we are not just being allowed to engage in this immortalization process; we are being actively guided through it by a higher intelligence that is itself outside of the process. See Section 4.0.0 - Earth Monad Project.

*2.13.0 - Overall Section Analysis and Insight – by Erik P. Antoni*

By this stage, the convergence is no longer suggestive.

What appears across these perspectives is not coincidence, but the progressive articulation of a shared structure. Eliade's alchemical lens frames the reconstituted monad as the philosophers' stone—a psychosomatic resolution of duality reflecting God's cosmic reconciliation—aligning with Jung's individuation and Bohm's implicate order as expressions of a unified process. What emerges is not an externally imposed transformation, but the activation of an intrinsic capacity long embedded within the human species, now being catalyzed within a broader planetary transition and accelerated under conditions that increasingly favor integration over fragmentation.

Hancock and Mack extend this structure into the galactic domain. Ancient intervention, Gnostic archons, and hyperdimensional intelligences converge as variations of the same regulating principle, positioning the cherubim as guardians of the noetic soul's directive. These accounts suggest not randomness, but constraint—an evolutionary threshold governed by forces that resist premature convergence while preserving the conditions for its eventual realization within a lawful and ordered progression of stages.

Across these frameworks, a single interpretation stabilizes:

Genesis describes not prohibition, but regulation. The Tree of Knowledge functions as the operative path, the Tree of Life as realized immortality guarded by archon structures that enforce sequence within the process. Earth, within this synthesis, is both a battleground and origin—a domain in which differentiation must pass through integration under the guidance of Alpha.

Evolution, then, is not only a process to be described—it is a process to be completed. We now proceed with additional voices that further consolidate the structure currently in motion.

*2.14.0 - Rupert Sheldrake – The Presence of the Past: Morphic Resonance and the Habits of Nature (1988)*

Morphic resonance depends on similarity and is not attenuated by distance in space or time […] It implies a kind of memory inherent in nature, a memory that is cumulative and gives rise to habits […] The evolutionary process is thus not merely a matter of chance mutations and natural selection, but involves a creative interplay between habit and novelty […] The morphic fields of social groups, such as human societies, could link their members together even across great distances, forming a kind of collective memory.

*2.14.1: Analysis and Insight – by Erik P. Antoni*

The universe and the Earth are alive with memory, a field of morphic resonance that links all things across time and space, suggesting consciousness evolves the mind, not in isolation, but as part of a planetary and cosmic web. The reconciliation of opposites within the psyche, a process of integrating past and future, light and dark, awakens latent capacities for immortality encoded in our biological and spiritual heritage. Such a process aligns with myths of forbidden knowledge, where the risk of transformation is guarded by forces fearing humanity's potential.

*2.15.0 Nick Bostrom – Superintelligence: Paths, Dangers, Strategies (2014)*

One possibility is that we are living in a simulation […]
If so, the simulators could be posthuman descendants of an original biological species like ours, or they could be extraterrestrial intelligences who have reached a stage of technological maturity far beyond our own […] Another scenario is that humanity itself might be the result of an earlier civilization's attempt to seed life or intelligence elsewhere […] The transition to superintelligence could destabilize everything we know, requiring us to grapple with existential risks that echo the complexity of the universe's origins.

*2.15.1: Analysis and Insight – by Erik P. Antoni*

If humanity is a product of a cosmic project, its origins might lie beyond Earth, perhaps in a failed earlier Martian civilization or an extraterrestrial experiment relocated here from Mars. The pursuit of immortality could be a buried directive, a psychosomatic unlocking of consciousness that advanced intelligences once suppressed to prevent destabilizing the galaxy. Such a process, organic rather than artificial, requires reconciling the dualities of mind and matter, a feat mirroring the universe's own emergence from chaos. The noosphere's emergence could mark a tipping point, where a species transcends its creators' limits, stepping into a timeless domain. If that is so, then the 'simulation' and the 'cosmic project' are not competing explanations, but layered descriptions of a single ascent—one that culminates not in mere survival, but in the perfected transformation of the human being.

*2.16.0 - Manly P. Hall – The Secret Teachings of All Ages (1928)*

The alchemists conceived of the Philosophers' Stone as a divine substance capable of transmuting the base elements of human nature into spiritual gold […] This Great Work was the regeneration of man himself, the unfolding of an inner divinity […] The sun and moon, as symbols of gold and silver, represent the masculine and feminine principles whose union produces the perfected being […] The Mysteries taught the earth was a place of trial, a garden wherein the soul must labor to regain its lost estate, guarded by the flaming sword of cosmic law.

*2.16.1: Analysis and Insight – by Erik P. Antoni*

The alchemical Great Work is the transmutation of the mind and body, uniting the solar and lunar forces—light and darkness—into the philosophical or spiritual gold, a state of immortality that mirrors the divine monad's creation of the cosmos. The noetic soul, guided by a universal intelligence, seeks to reconstitute this unity, a process guarded by lesser deities who fear its process.

Eden's loss is thus a cosmic allegory, where the flaming sword hides a path back to the eternal, accessible only through inner mastery. What appears as prohibition in myth is therefore initiation in disguise, requiring discipline, balance, and sufficient integration before the gate may be lawfully crossed.

*2.17.0 - Plotinus – Ennead IV.7, Section 10 (c. 270 AD)*

That the soul is of the family of the diviner nature, the eternal, is clear from our demonstration that it is not material: besides it has neither shape or colour nor is it tangible.

Wisdom and authentic virtue are divine, and could not be found in the chattel mean and mortal: what possesses these must be divine by its very capacity of the divine, the token of kinship and of identical substance.

Hence, too, any one of us that exhibits these qualities will differ but little as far as soul is concerned from the Supernals; he will be less than they only to the extent in which the soul is, in him, associated with body. To know the nature of a thing we must observe it in its unalloyed state, since any addition obscures the reality... he will not doubt his immortality when he sees himself thus entered into the pure, the Intellectual.

For, what he sees is an Intellectual-Principle looking on nothing of sense, nothing of this mortality, but by its own eternity having intellection of the eternal: he will see all things in this Intellectual substance, himself having become an Intellectual Kosmos and all lightsome, illuminated by the truth streaming from The Good, which radiates truth upon all that stands within that realm of the divine. […]

Thus, he will often feel the beauty of that word "Farewell: I am to you an immortal God," for he has ascended to the Supreme, and is all one strain to enter into likeness with it. […]

*2.17.1 - Analysis and Insight – by Erik P. Antoni*

Plotinus' Neoplatonism provides a foundational metaphysical framework for understanding the noetic soul as an eternal emanation, not created spontaneously, but conceived intentionally from the divine One (Ain Soph). This aligns seamlessly with the Nous Solis thesis, where the noetic soul arises as the second emanation to reconnect the fragmented mind of creation back to its divine source, countering the initial separation that birthed the universe. Immortality, in this view, is not an external acquisition, but a realized unity—the soul's ascent through psychosomatic integration, where the body becomes a vessel elevated by the presence of the noetic soul rather than a prison of decay. In this ascent, the intellect does not merely behold eternity—it becomes the living medium through which eternity knows itself.

The reconciliation of opposites, central to Plotinus' philosophy, mirrors the alchemical process of integration: the noetic soul's descent into matter (the "fall" into duality) is purposeful, enabling the illumination of the sensible world and its ultimate reunification with the intelligible. This echoes Genesis 3:22-24 not as punitive exile, but as a guarded threshold to this ascent, where cherubim symbolize the archon forces resisting the soul's return to unity, fearing the destabilization that often accompanies incomplete integration. Yet, as Plotinus asserts, the noetic soul's immortality is absolute by its participation in Nous, the divine intellect that observes and contemplates, compelling Alpha's self-organizing guidance toward the reunified Christ Monad. In this way, immortality is revealed not as an escape from embodiment, but as the perfected alignment of consciousness with its eternal source, where unity is sustained without collapse.

In this light, human evolution is a microcosmic reflection of cosmic emanation—the noetic soul's gradual lifting of biology through theosis, transforming entropy-bound matter into a timeless form. Plotinus' emphasis on the soul as "the we" reinforces the collective dimension: immortality unfolds not just individually, but through the noosphere, where shared noetic resonance (akin to Sheldrake's morphic fields) accelerates the species toward a metatronic state. This perspective bridges ancient philosophy with modern insights from Teilhard and Bohm, affirming that the forbidden fruit represents the knowledge of this ascent, opposed by lesser powers but ordained by the One. Far from heresy, it reveals the soul's prime directive as a divine imperative, where death's illusion dissolves in the eternal now, rendering the human vessel imperishable. The soul is not a corporeal entity, but a divine emanation from the One, participating in the eternal Nous—the intellect that contemplates the universe without division or decay. Immortality belongs to the noetic soul, not as a future reward, but as a dimension of its inherent nature itself, transcending the flux of matter and time. It descends into the body not to perish, but to illuminate and elevate it, reconciling the sensible world with the intelligible. In this ascent, the noetic soul sheds the illusions of duality—good and evil, light and darkness—returning to the unity of the One, where death is revealed as mere shadow. The noetic soul is immortal because it is the principle of life itself, and life cannot die; it is the body that falls away, while the noetic soul abides in the eternal.

Across myth, psychology, cosmology, and lived experience, a single pattern asserts itself with increasing clarity: immortality is not an aberration within creation, but its intended completion. The recurring prohibitions, warnings, and guardians that surround this process in ancient texts do not signal moral failure, but structural danger. The path was never forbidden because it was wrong—it was forbidden because it was powerful, destabilizing, and historically catastrophic when attempted without sufficient integration.

The mistake of traditional theology has been to conflate prohibition with sin. In doing so, it recasts a cosmic developmental safeguard as divine punishment. What Genesis encodes symbolically is not a fall from grace, but a descent into necessary fragmentation—

a phase in which consciousness must experience separation, polarity, suffering, and death before it can reunify itself without tearing reality apart. Immortality pursued prematurely fractures civilizations. Immortality achieved organically stabilizes worlds.

This is why the Tree of Knowledge precedes the Tree of Life. Knowledge is not optional; it is preparatory. To know good and evil is to internalize polarity, to embody contradiction, and to withstand the tension of opposites without collapse. Only then can the noetic soul complete its prime directive: the reunification of creation with the divine source into a new monad that exists beyond time yet remains fully incarnate.

The archons of myth—whether understood as literal beings, advanced civilizations, or archetypal forces of control—do not oppose immortality because it is unnatural, but because it renders hierarchy obsolete. A reunified monad answers to no external authority. It is sovereign, self-integrated, and no longer governable through fear, death, or illusion. Immortality is therefore not merely a biological transformation, but a political and ontological one.

Alpha, the organizing force behind evolution, does not rush this process. It unfolds through cycles—through civilizations that rise, destabilize, collapse, and leave behind symbolic warnings encoded as myth. Humanity's current position suggests we are once again approaching a threshold where the knowledge required to complete the process is reemerging faster than our capacity to integrate it. This is the perennial danger encoded in Eden, Atlantis, the Flood, and every myth of a lost golden age.

Yet the pattern also reveals inevitability. What was once forbidden is now returning—not as theft, but as remembrance. The noetic soul was conceived for this very task. Immortality is not stolen from the gods; it is reclaimed from forgetfulness. Death itself is not punishment, but an interval—a regulatory mechanism that prevents premature convergence until consciousness can sustain unity without annihilation. What returns in this cycle is not novelty but memory—the slow restoration of a capacity once lost through fragmentation. When consciousness is able to bear its own unity without domination or collapse, the gate no longer needs to be guarded.

Section 2 has traced this arc from ancient scripture to modern thought, from mythic symbolism to psychosomatic process. What follows is not further argument, but deeper structure. To understand how creation fractured itself in the first place—and why wisdom (Sophia) fell into matter—requires stepping behind immortality into its generative origin. That is where we now turn.

* * *

It is important to consider both the mainstream scientific and theological counterarguments to the main thesis of this book and its concept of a psychosomatic driven evolution toward immortality. Any framework that reinterprets biology, consciousness, and cosmology must confront prevailing scientific and theological objections. What follows is not a dismissal of these views, but an engagement with them.

*2.18.0 – Scientific Counter Argument (1)*

Nous Solis posits that a psychosomatic process driven by the presence of the noetic soul within the human mind and body can lead the species to the state of physical immortality by reconciling the internal dualities of light and darkness while energetically impressing upon the psyche and anatomy (theosis), ultimately altering human biology at the level of the species. From the standpoint of contemporary biology and neuroscience, this proposition challenges established models of aging, genetics, and thermodynamics, as there is no verified pathway by which psychosomatic integration could override entropy-driven cellular decline across an entire species.

Current biology shows that aging and death are inherent to multicellular organisms due to mechanisms like telomere shortening, cellular senescence, and the accumulation of genetic mutations over time. These processes are governed by the second law of thermodynamics (entropy), which dictates that systems naturally degrade without external energy inputs that could sustain them indefinitely. There is no empirical evidence that mental or consciousness-based reconciliation can override these fundamental biological limits; attempts at longevity extension through science (CRISPR gene editing or caloric restriction) show incremental gains but not the potential for human immortality.

*2.18.1 – Scientific Counter Argument (1) – Rebuttal*

Although modern biology identifies mechanisms like telomere shortening as drivers of aging, the Nous Solis thesis views these as temporary constraints within an evolving system guided by Alpha, a cosmic force of negentropy that organizes matter toward higher complexity. The noetic soul's psychosomatic influence on an underlying human biology operates over evolutionary timescales, subtly lifting that biology through resonant cymatic interactions, much like how consciousness has already driven human evolution beyond other species. Empirical evidence may lag because this process is organic and species-wide, not reducible to current lab interventions; thinkers like Teilhard de Chardin lend support to this concept by framing evolution as an ascent toward an Omega Point where such limits are transcended, aligning with observed trends in increasing biological complexity and human lifespan extensions. From this perspective, biological aging represents a contingent phase within an adaptive system rather than a fixed terminal condition. What appears as a hard limit at one stage of evolutionary development may function instead as a provisional boundary awaiting further integration.

While critics may cite biological entropy—telomere shortening, cellular senescence, and the second law of thermodynamics— as insurmountable barriers to human physical immortality, emerging cosmological models suggest that a force, which physicists have come to call "dark energy," may function as an inherent negentropic force in nature. I would suggest that this force is Alpha. If Alpha is the cosmic force of negentropy that organizes matter toward higher complexity and unity, then Alpha's role in preserving structural potential across vast timescales aligns closely with the Nous Solis thesis, suggesting that the noetic soul's gradual psychosomatic lifting of human biology operates within a larger, universe-wide negentropic dynamic that transcends local entropic limits and could, over evolutionary epochs, lead to the state of immortality as part of a greater cosmological reunification. In this framework, the apparent conflict between biological entropy and the pursuit of immortality dissolves, as local degradation is subsumed within a larger ordering process that unfolds across cosmological rather than experimental timescales.

*2.19.0 – Scientific Counter Argument (2)*

Nous Solis claims humanity's path to immortality involves extraterrestrial archons who genetically suppressed this inherent ability. From a cosmological and astrophysical perspective, there is no verifiable evidence for advanced extraterrestrial civilizations intervening in human evolution, as supported by the Fermi Paradox (the apparent absence of alien life despite the vast universe) and the lack of artifacts or signals detected by projects like SETI. Concepts like Alpha as a self-organizing force contradict known physics, where entropy dominates and consciousness is an emergent property of brain activity, not a causal agent shaping galaxies or biology. Claims of alien abductions or genetic switches lack verifiable data.

*2.19.1 – Scientific Counter Argument (2) - Rebuttal*

The absence of direct evidence for archons does not disprove their existence, as the Fermi Paradox itself suggests advanced civilizations may operate in undetectable ways, such as hyperdimensional or subspace realms beyond current instruments.

Alpha aligns with observed negentropic phenomena, like the self-organization in complex systems (e.g., galaxy formation or life's emergence from chaos), as echoed in Bohm's implicate order where consciousness is fundamental, not emergent.

Alien abduction reports, analyzed by researchers like Mack and others, demonstrate consistent patterns suggesting something real is happening. The Nous Solis thesis frames these as part of a larger cosmic process, supported by the ancient texts and an abundance of mythological stories of our ancient ancestors, which most likely contain elements of actual history and truth, not mere fantasy. Collectively, this strongly suggests that the current paradigms of modern science are incomplete rather than the philosophy of Nous Solis being unfounded. Even granting the present limits of measurement, the deeper issue may be epistemic: whether consciousness is only an output of matter, or also a formative principle that science has not yet learned to quantify. Thus, the materialist paradigm, while empirically powerful within its domain, risks becoming a self-limiting ideology when it dismisses *a priori* the possibility of a noetic cosmic principle that intervenes with creation to organize physical law and bring form to the universe itself.

### *2.20.0 – Theological Counter Argument (1)*

From a mainstream Christian theological perspective, the philosophy expounded in Nous Solis distorts Genesis 3:22-24 by portraying the expulsion from Eden as a guarded path to immortality via internal reconciliation, rather than a consequence of original sin—humanity's disobedient grasp for godlike knowledge, leading to mortality as divine punishment.

Immortality is achieved solely through faith in Jesus Christ's atonement, not a psychosomatic process or noetic soul prime directive, which smacks of Gnostic heresy by elevating hidden knowledge (gnosis) over biblical revelation and diminishing God's sovereignty. This view aligns with church fathers like Augustine, who emphasized sin's corrupting role, and the New Testament's focus on resurrection through grace, not human effort or cosmic quanta.

### *2.20.1 – Theological Counter Argument (1) - Rebuttal*

The Nous Solis thesis does not deny original sin but reframes it as a cosmic phenomenon and paradoxical necessity—the spontaneous emergence of creation requiring reconciliation, as allegorized in Genesis. The noetic soul, immaculately conceived by the divine source, embodies the unification in Christ, making the process a divinely ordained path to theosis (union with God), supported by Gnostic texts like the Apocryphon of John and echoed in orthodox mysticism (e.g., Eastern Christianity's hesychasm).

Pagels' research demonstrates that early Christian diversity included such views. The Nous Solis philosophy reveals Christ as the reconstituted unity between divinity and creation and the apex of human development, aligning with Teilhard's Christogenesis where human effort is aligned with divine grace to fulfill God's plan, rather than contradicting it. The immaculate conception of the Noetic Soul to interdict and complete the process of creation led by a self-organizing force in the universe (Alpha) is the ultimate divine grace. In this context, 'grace' is not reduced to mere mechanism, but expressed as a sacred process: divine initiative moving through psyche and time toward a glorified reunification, without abolishing the need for faith.

*2.21.0 – Theological Counter Argument (2)*

Theologically, particularly from Abrahamic traditions (Judaism, Christianity, Islam), the idea of archons as lesser gods forbidding immortality introduces polytheistic elements, undermining the absolute oneness of God (Tawhid in Islam or Shema in Judaism). Immortality is a divine gift in the afterlife, not a biological achievement through psychosomatic reconciliation or Alpha, suggesting creation arose spontaneously without intent, clashing with doctrines of deliberate creation (e.g., Qur'an 2:117). This thesis blends mysticism with speculation, resembling New Age syncretism rather than faithful exegesis, and ignores warnings against forbidden knowledge (e.g., Deuteronomy 29:29) as paths to hubris, not salvation.

*2.21.1 – Theological Counter Argument (2) - Rebuttal*

The thesis upholds divine oneness by positioning Ain Soph as the uncreated monad, with archons as advanced created beings (not gods), akin to angels or jinn in Abrahamic lore, who enforce galactic laws but rebel in service to a higher divine will, as in the Book of Enoch or Islamic accounts of Iblis. A spontaneous creation reflects the paradoxical divine nature, supported by Kabbalistic Ain Soph and Sufi mysticism, where multiplicity reunifies with the One. The reunification is deliberate. That deliberate process is what organizes, completes, and brings forth the universe, thus affirming Qur'an 2:117.

It is not syncretism because in Nous Solis various points of view blend together effortlessly in a beautiful revelation of cosmic truth. It just requires that the ancient text be viewed properly, not in a way that only seeks to maintain control and authority. The mystery of the Noetic Soul and its process to reunify creation with God fulfills the stewardship of Genesis 1:28 by virtue of how the Noetic Soul is immaculately conceived to interdict the process of creation.

*2.22.0 - Section 2.0.0. Conclusion – by Erik P. Antoni*

The noetic soul was immaculately conceived by the divine source at the beginning of creation for the very purpose of saving creation and achieving immortality via a reunified Christ Monad. Only in this way will creation not perish but continue onward forever. It is our highest purpose. Our evolution is organically driven to achieve it by the self-organizing force of the universe (Alpha). Our evolution is bound and directed by this divine cosmic force until we finally accomplish it.

The common counterarguments from the scientific and theological perspectives—rooted in biological entropy, empirical skepticism, doctrinal interpretations of sin, and monotheistic purity—highlight the tensions between established paradigms and this noetic philosophy. Yet, as the rebuttals demonstrate, these critiques often stem from incomplete frameworks that overlook the paradoxical nature of divinity, the negentropic undercurrents in cosmic evolution, and the integrative potential of consciousness as a causal agent. Rather than undermining the Nous Solis thesis, such dialogues only enrich it, revealing immortality not as a hubristic quest but as a divinely willed prime directive to the stewardship and completion of creation.

I believe the archon overlords of the galaxy severed themselves from this primeval process and threw away the key because, historically, this psychosomatic process typically failed and produced an evil, destructive humanoid race of beings. The dark state of our world today only further illustrates their point.

The archons initially suppressed our existence and fought against our pursuit of the monad, but in their minds, it was for the greater good, and their influence persists to this very day.

There is a great paradox at play in the universe.

The noetic soul was immaculately conceived to engage the darkness of creation and reunify it with the divine source within the mind and body so creation can last forever. However, in most past attempts, the process failed. Being that we are an echo of a larger cosmic process, this implies that the Cosmic Monad itself needed multiple attempts to achieve the unity, and the universe today is the aftermath of that one successful outcome.

Thus, like the Cosmic Monad, we are trying again and again as a humanity until finally we achieve—immortality.

Immortality, as presented here, is neither fantasy, a miracle, or a deviation from the lawful structure of the universe. It is the completion of a process already underway—biological, psychological, planetary, and cosmic—unfolding through cycles of division and reintegration across deep time. Guided by an organizing intelligence that compels coherence from complexity, death is not abolished prematurely but gradually rendered unnecessary as consciousness becomes capable of sustaining unity without collapse. In this sense, immortality is not an escape from nature, but its fulfillment.

# 3.0.0
# Aeon Sophia

The story of Aeon Sophia appears in several ancient Gnostic texts, with her role and narrative varying slightly depending on the source. Sophia's drama is not merely a mythological curiosity but a symbolic map of the same universal process that unfolds within consciousness itself. Her yearning to know the ineffable divine monad reflects the primordial impulse of awareness to turn back upon its source before the conditions for such knowing are complete. This premature act fractures unity into multiplicity, generating both creation and alienation simultaneously. In this sense, Sophia does not fall into moral failure, but descends through necessity, inaugurating the conditions required for consciousness to eventually know itself fully.

The Gnostic imagination frames this act not as a singular historical event, but as an eternal pattern repeating across scales—cosmic, planetary, and psychological. Just as Sophia's emanation gives rise to a flawed creator who mistakes partial authority for ultimate sovereignty, so too does the fragmented human ego arise when consciousness identifies with form rather than source. The myth thus encodes a recursive warning: whenever knowledge is pursued without integration, power emerges divorced from wisdom.

Myth arises wherever consciousness attempts to articulate its own origin, not because reason fails, but because reason alone cannot stand outside the process it seeks to describe. The Sophia narrative should therefore be understood as a symbolic compression of cosmological, psychological, and existential realities into a form that the human psyche can apprehend. In this sense, myth is not a primitive explanation of the universe, but a sophisticated vessel for truths that exceed linear language.

Sophia is not merely a character within these stories; she is the story's organizing principle—the movement of awareness as it turns toward its source and, in doing so, generates creation.

This distinction is essential, for a literal reading of Sophia's descent obscures the deeper function of the myth. Sophia does not fall from grace in the moral sense, nor does she err in ignorance. Rather, she embodies the inherent tension between unity and differentiation, a tension that must be resolved through experience rather than decree. Creation, in this framework, is not a mistake to be corrected but a necessary phase in the maturation of consciousness. The Sophia myth preserves this paradox by encoding it symbolically, allowing the process to be remembered rather than merely explained.

Thus, the persistence of Sophia across cultures and epochs is not evidence of textual borrowing alone, but of an archetypal pattern repeating wherever consciousness reflects upon itself. Below are four key texts where her story is most prominently featured:

### *3.1.0. – The Historical Texts of Aeon Sophia*

*3.1.1 - The Apocryphon of John* (Secret Book of John) Nag Hammadi Codex II, III, IV, and the Berlin Gnostic Codex (BG 8502).

The Apocryphon exists in multiple versions (long and short recensions), all emphasizing her pivotal role.

Likely composed in the 2nd century CE, with surviving Coptic versions from the 4th century found in the Nag Hammadi library (discovered in 1945), this is one of the most detailed accounts of Sophia's story. In it, she is an Aeon within the Pleroma who, driven by a desire to know the ineffable divine monad (the supreme God), and acts without her divine partner. "She desired to bring forth something by herself, without consent of the Spirit."

This leads to the birth of the demiurge, Yaldabaoth, a flawed creator who fashions the material world while unaware of the true divine source. "And he became arrogant, saying, 'I am God and there is no other God beside me,' for he did not know the place from which he had come."

Sophia's fall and the subsequent entrapment of her divine spark in humanity are central to the text's cosmology.

While the *Apocryphon of John* emphasizes the cosmological consequences of Sophia's unilateral action, later texts shift focus toward the interior dimensions of her ordeal. This evolution in emphasis mirrors the historical movement of Gnostic thought itself—

from cosmic explanation toward experiential redemption. Sophia's suffering is not merely external exile but an internal dissonance, a separation between intention and realization that must be resolved through remembrance rather than force.

In this way, Sophia becomes less a distant Aeon and more an archetypal mirror for the human condition. Her descent into chaos parallels the fragmentation of consciousness experienced by the psyche when it forgets its origin. Yet embedded within her lament is the promise of restoration, suggesting that the fall itself contains the seed of return. Wisdom is not lost; it is dispersed, awaiting reintegration through conscious alignment with the Light.

### *3.1.2 - Pistis Sophia*

Likely written between the 3rd and 4th centuries CE, preserved in a Coptic manuscript from the 4th or 5th century (the Askew Codex). It is a single manuscript purchased in 1772, now in the British Library.

The text portrays Sophia as "Pistis Sophia" (Faithful Wisdom), focusing on her fall, repentance, and restoration rather than just her initial act. Here, she laments her descent into the chaotic material realm after attempting to emanate independently, and she seeks redemption through prayers and hymns to the Light. Jesus, as a revealer figure, aids her return. While the demiurge's creation is less emphasized, her story still ties to the broader Gnostic theme of wisdom's journey.

The emphasis on repentance and restoration in Pistis Sophia introduces a crucial corrective to earlier cosmologies: descent is not final, and error is not irreversible. Sophia's hymns to the Light reveal that restoration is achieved not through domination or escape, but through resonance—an attunement of consciousness to its original frequency. Her redemption unfolds gradually, through stages of recognition, humility, and alignment, reflecting a lawful process rather than divine intervention alone.

This portrayal subtly reframes salvation itself. Redemption is not granted externally but emerges from within the structure of consciousness when fragmentation yields to coherence. Sophia's ascent is therefore not a reversal of creation, but its completion. Creation must pass through division in order to reunite knowingly, transforming unconscious emanation into conscious return.

The appearance of the archons in Sophia's narrative marks the crystallization of disorder into structure. These rulers do not create chaos; they arise from it. They represent stabilized ignorance—systems that preserve fragmentation by mistaking partial order for total truth. Their authority depends upon concealment, not malice, and their power persists only so long as the origin of consciousness remains forgotten.

Within this framework, humanity inherits both Sophia's spark and the archons' constraints. The divine light embedded within the human psyche exists alongside mechanisms designed to suppress its realization. The Gnostic myth thus anticipates a central paradox: the same structures that imprison consciousness also provide the conditions through which liberation becomes meaningful. Without the archons, there is no resistance; without resistance, no conscious reunification.

At this stage, a critical transformation occurs. What begins as an interior drama of descent and restoration inevitably gives rise to structure. Fragmentation does not remain fluid indefinitely; it stabilizes. Patterns harden into systems, and systems acquire authority. It is here that the archons emerge—not as arbitrary villains, but as the natural byproducts of consciousness attempting to manage its own division.

The archons represent the crystallization of partial knowledge into governing principles. They are born when provisional understandings mistake themselves for final truth. In this way, they do not oppose Sophia directly, but unconsciously preserve the conditions that necessitated her descent. Their rule depends upon forgetfulness—not malicious intent—and their power persists only so long as consciousness remains unaware of its origin. This reframing is crucial, for it reveals that obstruction and regulation are not external impositions upon creation, but internally generated mechanisms that arise whenever unity fractures into multiplicity.

Understanding the archons in this light dissolves the false dualism between oppressor and victim. The same process that gives rise to wisdom also gives rise to control; the same descent that enables experience necessitates regulation. Liberation, therefore, does not come through the destruction of structure, but through the reintegration of awareness within it. The Sophia narrative preserves this insight by situating the archons not as enemies to be defeated, but as thresholds to be transcended through remembrance.

*3.1.3 - The Hypostasis of the Archons* (The Reality of the Rulers)

2nd or 3rd century CE, part of the Nag Hammadi library (Codex II).

Sophia appears here as "Incorruptible Sophia" or "Sophia Zoe" (Wisdom of Life), linked to the creation of the material world through the demiurge, Yaldabaoth. The text describes her role in the cosmic drama, including her contribution to humanity's divine spark via Eve. It's a shorter, more symbolic account, but it aligns with the Apocryphon of John.

*3.1.4 - On the Origin of the World*

Date: Late 2nd or early 3rd century CE, also from Nag Hammadi (Codex II and XIII).

This text elaborates on Sophia's role as "Sophia Zoe," who produces the demiurge and oversees the unfolding of the material cosmos. It emphasizes her intrinsic dual nature—divine yet involved in the lower world—and her correcting of the demiurge's arrogance. Her cosmic story intertwines with the creation of humanity and the imparting of wisdom.

* * *

These texts, primarily from the Nag Hammadi library, are the core sources for Sophia's narrative. They stem from Gnostic Christian traditions, likely composed originally in Greek, though most survive in Coptic translations. Other Gnostic works, like the Valentinian Exposition or Trimorphic Protennoia, mention Sophia tangentially, but the above four provide the fullest accounts. Her story likely draws from earlier Jewish wisdom traditions (e.g., Proverbs 8) and Hellenistic philosophy, adapted into a unique Gnostic framework.

Aeon Sophia is attributed to "wisdom" primarily because her name and role in Gnostic cosmology directly connect her to the concept of divine wisdom. The term "Sophia" itself comes from the Greek word σοφία (sophía), meaning "wisdom," and in Gnostic traditions, she is an Aeon—a divine emanation or entity—embodying this quality.

Here's why this attribution historically exists:

In Gnostic mythology, Sophia is one of the Aeons emanating from the ultimate divine source, often called the Monad (The One) or Bythos (The Depth). In the Kabbalah, it is known as Ain Soph (Without End). In Gnosticism, the Aeons are seen as aspects or expressions of the divine, forming the Pleroma, the fullness of God's being.

Sophia, as the Aeon of Wisdom, represents the faculty of insight, understanding, and creative intelligence. Her story, particularly in texts like the Apocryphon of John and Pistis Sophia, highlights her as a pivotal figure whose actions bridge the spiritual and material realms, reflecting wisdom's dual nature—both transcendent and immanent.

Her attribution of wisdom stems from her narrative arc.

Sophia is often depicted as yearning to know the ineffable (the essence of the monad) or to create independently of her divine partner (syzygy). This act of curiosity or ambition leads to her "fall"—the unintended creation of the demiurge (Yaldabaoth, also known as IAO), a flawed entity that crafts the material world. While this might seem unwise at first glance, Gnostic interpretations frame it as a profound, if tragic, expression of wisdom's exploratory nature.

Her apparent mistake initiates the cosmic drama, allowing humanity to gain the "spark" of divine wisdom she imparts, enabling spiritual awakening and liberation from the demiurge's imposing rule. Thus, her wisdom is not just static knowledge but a dynamic, experiential force that drives the unfolding of existence.

This aligns with earlier traditions influencing Gnosticism.

In the Hebrew Bible's wisdom literature (e.g., Proverbs 8:22-31), Wisdom (Hebrew Chokmah, translated as Sophia in the Greek Septuagint) is personified as a feminine figure, coexisting with God before creation, delighting in the world, and acting as an intermediary. Gnosticism builds on this, blending it with Hellenistic philosophy—where Sophia was revered as the pursuit of truth (as in Plato's philosophía, "love of wisdom")—and casting Sophia as a cosmic entity whose wisdom both shapes and transcends the material order.

Aeon Sophia is equated with wisdom because she personifies it in a mythological and metaphysical sense: her role reflects its divine essence, and her story illustrates its complex interplay with creation, error, and redemption. This makes her a central figure in Gnostic thought, embodying the idea that true wisdom involves not just perfection but also the courage to explore, err, and ultimately enlighten. Within this framework, wisdom is not a static attribute but a dynamic process—one that descends into fragmentation in order to gather experience, and ascends again through conscious reintegration with the divine source.

### *3.1.5. – Analysis and Insight – by Erik P. Antoni*

Everything I just recounted of Aeon Sophia reflects the traditional philosophical view of her—her external nature. However, during the advanced stages of integrating the mind in the formation of the monad, the forces of consciousness, which I call the "cosmic quanta," re-tell the same story of creation while bringing the mythology of Aeon Sophia into a new and higher light. It reveals her true inner or esoteric nature.

The yearning to know the ineffable, where Sophia gains her association with wisdom, directly aligns with the first act of the divine awareness within Ain Soph that ultimately leads to the spontaneous rise of creation and its descent into darkness from the original divine monad.

In the advanced stages of reintegrating the monad, when my conscious mind had finally connected with Ain Soph to realize its deeper nature, it was revealed to me that three force dimensions exist within Ain Soph whose interplay fuels the process of creation, much like the Aeons. These three forces are Awareness (mythologically, the Father), Life (the Divine Soul of the Father), and the Spirit (Love of the Father). When the Divine Father comes to realize, fathom, and know his own living life force, the Divine Soul (the Son), the Father's love for the Divine Soul arises. This love is the Spirit, or Holy Spirit.

The three dimensions of Ain Soph are Awareness, Life, and Love, or the Father, the Soul (Son), and the Holy Spirit—the divine trinity. Because Ain Soph is not bound by space or time, it is infinite. Therefore, its love is infinite. The infinite nature of love spontaneously sparks a vision—the mind—cosmic mind—demiurge (IAO)—and within that cosmic mind, all of creation emerges. But IAO originally emerges in darkness (unawareness) because the conception happens spontaneously and unintentionally. "And there was darkness beneath her, since the light had not yet come into being." The spontaneous creating nature of the infinite divine love of the source-consciousness is allegorized as Aeon Sophia creating without her divine partner (syzygy).

Sophia's outward countenance may be that of wisdom, but what truly drives Sophia is her deeper inner nature of love. "She repented with great sorrow and called upon the light with longing."

Thus begins the whole cosmic process of unfoldment and reorganization until, finally, the monad is reintegrated. The reintegration on a cosmic level is what forms the universe we all live in today.

Sophia's esoteric nature represents the sacred feminine archetype, the living embodiment of love. The sacred feminine is unconsciously associated with "love," whereas the sacred masculine is unconsciously associated with "will." Thus, these associations arise unconsciously in the writings of ancient and modern storytellers—which is most likely why a woman was unconsciously chosen for the role. It is how the universe speaks to us.

Love is the driving force behind Sophia's thirst to know God, and the paradox it creates is one of the most fascinating aspects of her story in Gnostic mythology. Love and wisdom are intertwined. Her story aligns beautifully with the actual creation process. In Gnostic cosmology, Sophia's desire to comprehend the incomprehensible—the essence of the monad, the ultimate divine source—stems from an overflowing love and yearning for a union with the divine. This isn't just intellectual curiosity; it's an emotional and spiritual impulse, a longing to merge with or fully grasp the infinite depth of God's being.

Texts like the Apocryphon of John suggest that Sophia, as an Aeon, is part of the Pleroma, the harmonious totality of divine emanations. Each Aeon exists in a balanced pairing (syzygy) with the divine source itself, meaning each dimension of the divine source is driven to maintain a resonant harmony to maintain its original unity. Yet, her love drives her beyond this harmony. She seeks to know the monad directly, without her counterpart (beyond her harmony), in a way that mirrors love's tendency to transcend boundaries and seek the beloved in its purest form. This mythos reflects the divine nature of the monad procreating without a counterpart. The original monad precedes sexuality, but its unfoldment and later reconciliation are what give rise to sexuality and duality within all things.

Sophia's love—echoing the Holy Spirit—is what fuels her thirst. It's a passionate, almost reckless devotion—an urge to penetrate the mystery of the divine, to unite with it fully.

In some Gnostic accounts, her action is described as an attempt to emulate the monad's creative power, reflecting her love-inspired desire to participate in its essence. But here's the divine paradox. This same love, which is pure and directed toward the highest good, leads to an unintended rupture. Acting alone, outside the divine order of the

Pleroma, Sophia's creative impulse miscarries, giving birth to the demiurge, Yaldabaoth (IAO)—a being born without the balance of her syzygy, unaware of the true divine source, and thus flawed.

The creation of the demiurge is paradoxical because love, typically, a unifying and perfecting force, becomes the spark for disarray. Sophia's love-driven act disrupts the Pleroma's equilibrium, producing a "mistake" that births the material cosmos—a realm of imperfection and illusion under the demiurge's rule. Yet, this isn't the end of her story. Her love also sows the seeds of redemption. The divine spark that the story says she imparts to humanity through this process is the immaculate conception of the noetic soul with its innate ability to bridge creation with divinity. In texts like Pistis Sophia, her repentance and persistent faith (pistis) further underscore that love remains her core motivation, guiding her back toward reunion and restoration.

This paradox reflects a deeper Gnostic theme: love and wisdom are intertwined, and their pursuit, even when flawed, drives the cosmic creation process and divine narrative. Sophia's love for God, though it sparks chaos, also initiates the possibility of gnosis—knowledge gained through experience and longing—which humanity inherits. It's a beautiful twist: the same love that fractures the divine order becomes the pathway back to it, suggesting that love's power lies in its capacity to both create and heal, even through apparent error.

Love is Sophia's engine, and the demiurge's creation is the unexpected shadow cast by its light. It's a story that turns the conventional notion of divine perfection on its head, showing how even a "fall" can be an act of profound, paradoxical love. There is an inherent tension between love's intent and love's final outcome.

This original divine paradox of love and how it sparks creation spontaneously into existence—initially unawareness and darkness—reverberates throughout nature and echoes unconsciously into mythology and literature.

"But love is blind and lovers cannot see / The pretty follies that themselves commit." … *Shakespeare—The Merchant of Venice, 1598.*

"For love is blynd alday, and may nat see." …. *Geoffrey Chaucer —The Canterbury Tales—The Merchant's Tale, 14th Century.*

*3.2.0 - Nobel Prize-Winning Chemist Ilya Prigogine.*

Prigogine studied dissipative structures and the role of chaos in the emergence of order, suggesting that creation involves both disruption and reorganization. Aeon Sophia reflects this process.

"We now see that instability, fluctuations at a certain level, far from being the 'exception,' are the origin of order in our world. The universe contains regions dominated by gravitational forces, others by electromagnetic forces, others by nuclear forces—and all this variety stems from an initial instability. The transition from disorder to order is not a rare phenomenon; it is the very condition of existence of most of the structures we know."

*3.2.1 - Analysis and Insight – by Erik P. Antoni*

Order arises, not in spite of chaos, but because of it; the new emerges from the instability of the old. This reflects the narrative of Sophia's love-driven act causing chaos to emerge, yet leading to a higher order (reintegration), framing her "mistake" as a creative necessity to the formation of the universe and the emergence of the noetic soul and reconstitution of the monad in that process. When the monad becomes two, divinity and creation, this further compels two to become three, (1) Invisible light, (2) Darkness, and (3) Luminous light. Pairing darkness and luminous light brings forth duality and sexuality.

*3.3.0 - A Deeper Discussion on Creation – by Erik P. Antoni*

In this exploration of Aeon Sophia, we have journeyed through her traditional portrayal in Gnostic texts as the embodiment of wisdom, whose yearning to know the ineffable divine monad precipitates the creation of the demiurge and the material cosmos. This demiurge is the first of two demiurges: first, darkness (IAO), and second, light (Logos).

The traditional interpretation casts Sophia as a bridge between the transcendent and mundane, with her actions reflecting wisdom's exploratory and productive nature. Nous Solis pushes beyond this traditional interpretation, unveiling a deeper and more esoteric dimension where Sophia's true essence emerges, not merely as wisdom, but as love and its dynamic force of creation.

This reinterpretation reveals her story as an echo of the process of creation and reintegration. Ain Soph—the infinite divine source—unfolds through Awareness, Life, and Love, sparking a spontaneous creation that descends into darkness before being redeemed by the divinity's will to reunify. Sophia's love-driven act to know the divine, once seen as a tragic error, parallels the divine Spirit's overflow, birthing the cosmos not as a mistake, but as a necessary instability where chaos gives rise to order. "That which comes into being must return again to the One." Sophia's paradox of love and disruption is the engine of a universe where duality is not illusory but foundational, reconciled through unification in Christ.

Sophia is the heartbeat of Chardin's christogenesis, the process of the universe emerging from chaos to be uplifted and made one in Christ. This is why Jesus, the archetype of Christ, appears in Pistis Sophia.

"Evolution is an ascent toward consciousness."

The Aeon Sophia story is not one of error and repentance but of love's fearless plunge into the unknown, igniting a cosmic revolution that transforms chaos into harmony to form the known universe.

One of the principles I propose of the collective unconscious is that it repeatedly broadcasts the story of creation and the purpose of the noetic soul in that process via symbols, stories, and mythology to help us remember our mission and find our way back to the divine source. Storytellers and scribes unconsciously formed their narratives in the ancient texts while instinctively compelled by the forces of consciousness, forces that I call the cosmic quanta.

### *3.4.0 – Philosophical Comparisons – by Erik P. Antoni*

Let's test this hypothesis and see if the Aeon Sophia narrative repeats in any way among other ancient texts. Logically, each time the narrative repeats, its manifested story would be somewhat different, potentially adding missing puzzle pieces that we are then further compelled to realize and assemble into a more cohesive creation story.

A parallel to Aeon Sophia can be found in the Mesopotamian myth of Inanna's Descent to the Underworld (circa 1900-1600 BCE).

Inanna, the Sumerian goddess of love and war, descends from her divine realm to the underworld, is stripped of her powers, dies, and is reborn with the help of other deities. While her descent is intentional and not a "fall" due to hubris, the journey downward, loss of divine status, and restoration mirror Sophia's journey of leaving the divine fullness, suffering in the material realm, and seeking return.

In Hindu mythology, the story of Shakti or Parvati in certain Tantric traditions offers a loose correlation. Shakti, the feminine divine energy, is both part of and distinct from Shiva, the masculine principle.

In some narratives, her creative power manifests the material world, and her dance of illusion (maya) traps souls in materiality—akin to Sophia's unintended creation of the demiurge and the flawed cosmos. Texts like the Devi Mahatmya (5th-6th century CE) depict her as a cosmic force battling chaos, suggesting a restorative role similar to Sophia's redemption arc. I propose that Shakti is actually a symbolic reflection of the force of Alpha, the self-organizing force of the universe, but Alpha is an integral force in the theokinetic process of creation; thus, it's not at all surprising to see the love-creating-principle intertwined with the self-organizing-principle in mythological stories.

The Greek myth of Pandora, as told in Hesiod's Works and Days (circa 700 BCE), also shares similar elements. Pandora, created by the gods, opens a jar out of curiosity, releasing evils into the world, much like Sophia's act of creation without divine consent births the demiurge and materiality. However, Pandora lacks the redemption aspect central to Sophia's story, and her role is more punitive than divine.

Finally, the Egyptian myth of Isis, found in texts like the Pyramid Texts (circa 2400-2300 BCE) and later elaborated in Plutarch's Isis and Osiris (1st century CE), presents a goddess who restores order from chaos. Isis reassembles her husband Osiris after his dismemberment, facilitating his resurrection and the continuation of divine harmony. While not a "fall" narrative, her role as a wisdom figure restoring cosmic balance aligns with Sophia's redemptive mission. Isis is a reflection of a force I call the numina. The numina is the third in the sacred feminine line of love, which extends downward from the Spirit to manifest the material realm, which is then reorganized into the Christ Monad. Sophia represents the line of love.

When viewed collectively, these comparative myths do more than echo Sophia's descent; they reveal distinct facets of the same underlying process. Each tradition emphasizes a particular phase of the journey—Inanna's willing descent, Shakti's creative overflow, Pandora's unintended release, Isis's deliberate restoration—together forming a composite portrait of consciousness as it moves through separation and return. None of these figures alone contains the full arc; it is their convergence that discloses the universality of the pattern.

Notably, this narrative is carried almost exclusively by feminine figures. This is not incidental. Across traditions, the feminine principle consistently symbolizes love, relationality, generation, and mediation between realms. Where the masculine principle often represents will, structure, law, or transcendence, the feminine embodies the movement between states—the willingness to enter multiplicity so that unity might later be reclaimed. Sophia, in this context, is not an anomaly but the most explicit articulation of a role long assigned to the sacred feminine: to bear the cost of differentiation in service of eventual reunification.

These myths also reveal subtle distinctions in how love itself is understood. In some traditions, love appears as eros—the longing that draws consciousness outward. In others, it manifests as creative abundance, overflowing into form. Elsewhere, it takes the shape of restoration and care, gathering what has been scattered. Together, they suggest that love is not a singular emotion but a dynamic force that propels creation, sustains it through fragmentation, and ultimately draws it back toward coherence.

In this study of Aeon Sophia, we have uncovered her deep esoteric nature that transcends her traditional Gnostic portrayal of the embodiment of "wisdom," to reveal her true inner essence as that of "divine love," a love that initially ignites and later reconciles all of creation to bring forth the known universe. Sophia emerges as the sacred feminine archetype that longs to know the divine source, a knowing that mirrors the source's realization of its existence, which ultimately sparks the emergence of creation through an overflow of its divine love (the Spirit). This divine love paradoxically births the demiurge to set the stage for a grand theokinetic process—christogenesis (thelesis)—where the forces of the sacred trinity (Logos, Noetic Soul, and Numina) emerge to unify divinity and creation within a new reunified God or new Monad (Christ). Sophia's story echoes across the ancient myths—Inanna's descent, Shakti's creative dance, Pandora's curiosity, and Isis's restoration—each reflecting facets of this universal drama of love's disruption and redemption. Far from a mere fall, Sophia's journey embodies the divine need to realize, know, create, descend, transform, ascend, and reunify, a process echoed in humanity's quest to know and become one with God.

Viewed as a whole, the Sophia myth functions as a cosmological allegory for individuation on a universal scale, but its deepest motive force is love rather than error. Sophia's descent is driven not by rebellion or deficiency, but by an overabundance of longing—a desire to know, to behold, and to reunite consciously with the source from which she emanates. Creation itself arises from this excess of divine love, a movement so full that it spills outward before it can fully recollect and reflect back upon itself.

In this sense, fragmentation is not the opposite of love, but one of its necessary consequences. Love that seeks a relationship must accept separation as the cost of experience. Sophia's fall therefore inaugurates not a tragedy, but a risk—a descent into multiplicity so that unity might later be recovered knowingly rather than unconsciously. What Jung later identifies psychologically as the integration of opposites, Gnosticism encodes mythologically as the reconciliation of Sophia with the Light: a return made meaningful only because it has passed through division.

Sophia's restoration is thus not a reversal of creation, but its fulfillment. Wisdom does not retreat from the world; it learns itself within it. This pattern anticipates the role of the noetic soul as described in this work. Both Sophia and the noetic soul operate as mediators between source and manifestation, eternity and time. Both descend into fragmentation not as punishment, but as vocation. And both reveal the same final truth: creation is incomplete until consciousness, moved by love, recognizes itself within form and freely returns to unity—bearing with it the knowledge earned through its descent.

Thus, the story of Aeon Sophia ultimately reveals that the universe is not driven by domination, correction, or punishment, but by an intelligent love willing to risk itself in order to become fully known. Creation unfolds not as a linear command but as a reciprocal movement between source and expression, where consciousness must first forget itself in form before it can remember itself in truth. Sophia's descent and restoration stand as a timeless witness to this axiom: that wisdom is born through experience, unity is forged through division, and love completes itself only when it is freely returned. In this way, the myth of Sophia does not merely explain how creation began—it explains why creation continues, and why consciousness, wherever it arises, is always drawn back toward the light from which it first emerged.

# 4.0.0
# EARTH MONAD PROJECT

The Earth Monad Project is a hypothesis that synthesizes various sources of information, one of which is my own direct experience with the forces of consciousness during the process of integrating the monad. The alchemical process, in addition to being a process of self-realization, transformation, and integration, is also a path of regression that leads the conscious mind of the alchemist all the way back to the source of all things over the long course of a single human lifetime. About thirty years into my process of regression, during the great arcanum period of my third mountain journey, various primeval forces of creation—forces of consciousness that I call the cosmic quanta—each came forward and revealed to me some critical piece of information whose realization and understanding was essential to the reintegration of the monad—the Philosophers' Stone. The universe requires the alchemist to journey back to the beginning and see how it all unfolded so the psyche can put it all back together again. It's fundamental to the psychosomatic process.

Interestingly, however, alongside the creation origin story, the cosmic quanta also shared with me what is happening on Earth. It was a high-level sharing of information, but it included just enough material to complete the puzzle. When (1) the revelation of the cosmic quanta is overlaid with data from other sources, including (2) various ancient texts, (3) archeological, anthropological, and geological information arising both from within the mainstream—and outside the mainstream—and (4) the alien disclosure community, a new cohesive narrative emerges that is simply extraordinary. I'd say it is the closest thing to what some may call—an indigestible truth.

"The universe appears to be bio-friendly—not by accident, but as if it were designed to give rise to life and mind. This raises the possibility that we are part of a larger cosmic project, one in which the emergence of conscious observers is not an end in itself but a means to some further goal. Could it be that life on Earth is an experiment, isolated yet pivotal, watched or even steered by intelligences we cannot yet detect? The laws of physics might permit such a scenario, where our planet is a crucible for something extraordinary." ... *Paul Davies*

Let's now break down the Earth Monad Project into its four primary contributing sources by examining what each offers independently before reassembling them into a unified narrative.

It must be acknowledged at the outset that the first category—the revelation of the cosmic quanta—is inherently subjective in nature. At this moment in time, its existence cannot be empirically proven, nor can the communication itself be externally verified. It represents the esoteric dimension of the phenomenon, one that unfolds solely within the relationship between the human being and God.

*4.1.0 - Revelation of the Cosmic Quanta*

I present here now the pure, unfiltered download from the cosmic quanta while purposely withholding analysis, or what it may all imply.

Through the alchemical process, the cosmic quanta communicated to me that all life on Earth is part of a grand experiment to see if consciousness can reach its pinnacle state of reorganization of mind, body, and matter within a reunified monad—repeating on a human level what God completed on a cosmic level.

The cosmic quanta further conveyed that physical immortality is the final frontier among spacefaring intelligent civilizations throughout the cosmos—a distinction, they suggest, that dates back to galactic antiquity.

They went on to emphasize that this process is also a highly contentious and precarious endeavor in the cosmos because it can only be achieved organically through a psychosomatic interaction of matter and consciousness—darkness and light—within the mind and body over the long course of human evolution and that typically the process implodes midway before restarting, but it only needs one time to succeed and then the outcome is eternal and everlasting

The quanta pointed to a great cosmic war in the early galaxy over this same process because various attempts to reach the end goal produced an evil race of violent and self-destructive beings.

The cosmic quanta revealed that this psychosomatically compelled pathway of evolution is well-known and banned on most other worlds throughout the Milky Way galaxy today because it has proven over millions of years to rarely yield the sought-after fruit of physical immortality. Its pursuit has been ruled the proverbial "forbidden fruit."

Lastly, the cosmic quanta signaled that Mars was paramount in our past and that our humanity appeared to carry a long-forgotten and troubled history with cosmic factions contesting our right to exist as a species—a humanity, by this account, conceived in defiance of an existing cosmic law.

### *4.2.0 - The Ancient Texts*

When ancient texts are examined comparatively rather than through a devotional lens, a far more nuanced and ethically complex cosmology emerges in contrast to traditional theological interpretations.

In the ancient texts spanning across cultures, the gods (Archons, Anunnaki, Olympians, Watchers, etc.) are not portrayed with a unified purpose. Rather, they are repeatedly depicted as divided—disagreeing, quarreling, and even warring—particularly over the fate of our humanity on Earth. This conflict gains added dimensions of insight when considering the revelations of the cosmic quanta, which share that humanity's creation on Earth is not universally accepted, but considered by other worlds to be a dangerous psychosomatic experiment whose success promises transcendence while its failure risks catastrophe.

The cosmic law forbidding the pursuit of immortality as it appears in these traditions should not be understood as a moral prohibition or theological command, but as an emergent structural constraint arising from the repeated past failures of insufficiently evolved civilizations relative to the relationship between matter, consciousness, technological development and spiritual integration.

The outlawing of the pursuit of physical immortality reflects a tumultuous galactic history among the gods, not a divine jealousy. Across the ancient mythological and religious traditions examined here, the memory of prohibition functions not as condemnation or a test of virtue, but as an accumulated lesson—one learned repeatedly through civilizations that achieved power before achieving coherence. The repeated attempts of human beings on other worlds to achieve physical immortality without a sufficient level of spiritual integration resulted in extreme imbalance, violence, and destruction extending far beyond their own solar systems. What was forbidden in cosmic law was not a humanoid race's success—but the risk of failure that was so great that it threatened the stability of the entire galaxy.

**** The Division of the Gods and the Question of Cosmic Law ****

The ancient texts consistently portray assemblies of higher beings rather than a unified authority. In Genesis, God speaks in the plural:

"Let us make man in our image" (Genesis 1:26)—a phrase long recognized by scholars as a remnant of an earlier council theology.

Psalm 82 is even more explicit: "God standeth in the congregation of the mighty; he judgeth among the gods… I have said, Ye are gods; and all of you are children of the most High. But ye shall die like men."

This passage reflects a memory of celestial beings who possess great power (ye are gods) yet remain mortal (but ye shall die like men). They are entities who govern, judge, and fear the consequences of their own limitations. Similar councils of the gods appear in the Ugaritic texts, Mesopotamian literature, and later Gnostic cosmologies.

When viewed in the context of what the cosmic quanta share, the often-portrayed disagreement among the archon gods in the ancient texts takes on a whole new level of depth and meaning.

One faction—the archons who rebelled against the cosmic law—believed that the risk of great failure was worth the potential emergence of a humanity capable of achieving godlike immortality, reunification with the divine source, and the stabilization of creation itself—to repeat on an individual level what God completed to form the known universe—and thus fulfilling the prime directive of the noetic soul. It is the destiny of all human extraterrestrial races in the universe, unless they perish first.

The opposing faction—the guardians of the cosmic law—did not fear the success of immortality; they feared its failure of attainment and its aftermath of evil. Enforcement of this cosmic law appears in the texts not as a unified authority, but as a constraint maintained through intervention, suppression, and global resets rather than formal decree. What these texts leave unresolved is not the existence of cosmic law, but its outcome: whether any humanity can complete the process of integration without triggering the very constraints meant to contain it. In this sense, the ancient record preserves less a doctrine than a warning—one that frames human history as an open experiment rather than a predetermined fate.

As with all narratives of the ancient texts, these accounts of the gods should be understood as symbolically compressed—encoding multiple layers of historical, psychological, and cosmological meaning.

**** Failed Ascensions and the Memory of Galactic Ruin ****

The fear of the gods (Archons, Anunnaki, Olympians, Watchers) was not theoretical. It came through lived experience. The ancient texts repeatedly allude to prior ages, worlds, or races destroyed not merely by moral wickedness, but by systemic imbalance—the misuse of knowledge and power absent sufficient psychosomatic integration. 1 Enoch 10 -12-13 records the Watchers' warning:

"And the whole earth was corrupted through the works that were taught by the Watchers … the whole earth shall be cleansed."

Here, corruption is not moral decadence alone but a systemic destabilization of humanity through the works taught by the Watchers. The "works" refers to the outlawed Earth Monad Project itself.

The Mahabharata similarly warns of civilizations undone by the misuse of knowledge, describing weapons that could "reduce the world to ashes" when wielded without restraint (Mahabharata, Drona Parva).

Plato's Critias preserves a Greek echo of the same memory, describing Atlantis as a civilization that fell not through ignorance, but through moral and spiritual imbalance after attaining great power. Atlantis thus stands as a philosophical warning against civilizations that achieve external mastery before internal unity.

Even the Gnostic Apocryphon of John portrays the archons as deeply anxious about humanity awakening beyond control:

"They became jealous… because man had surpassed them in wisdom."

Read superficially, this appears as envy. It was not an envy of surpassed wisdom but of their concern about our endowed ability to "know" both light and darkness to the same extent that God did in order to integrate the two polarities and form the known universe. Read cosmologically, it reads as fear of repetition—fear that our humanity on Earth, like earlier attempts elsewhere, might awaken incompletely, integrate power without unity, and turn evil.

Thus, the opposition to the Earth Monad Project was not malevolent. It was a protective, regulatory, and conservative position rooted in the memory of many past failed attempts that became violent and destructive, causing great havoc throughout the cosmos. The conflict preserved in myth is therefore not between good and evil, but between faith in humanity's ascendance and fear born of historical ruin.

*** *Hybridization, Acceleration, and the Breaking of Law* ***

The Nephilim of Genesis emerges here as a critical inflection point:

"The sons of God came in unto the daughters of men… and the earth was filled with violence." (Genesis 6:2, 11).

The Book of Enoch expands on this, stating that the Watchers "taught men charms and enchantments… and the cutting of roots" (1 Enoch 7–8). These are not random sins but technological and biological accelerations—attempts to hasten the evolution of humanity toward godlike power without sufficient psychosomatic integration.

From the perspective of cosmic law, this represented a violation: the reintegrated monad and the state of human immortality cannot be engineered, only achieved organically through the reconciliation of opposite polarities within the mind and consciousness itself. When this rule is broken, power outpaces wisdom—and history, according to these texts, shows that the result is almost always catastrophic.

*** *The Flood as Ethical Containment, Not Punishment* ***

The flood narratives now take on a radically different meaning. In Genesis, God declares:

"I will destroy man whom I have created… for the earth is filled with violence" (Genesis 6:7, 13).

In Gilgamesh, the archon gods later regret the flood—not because it was unjust, but because it was necessary. Utnapishtim's life is preserved not as a reward, but as a continuity anchor, ensuring that the project on Earth is not lost.

The flood, therefore, represents an ethical containment strategy—a planetary neutralization designed to prevent a corrupted humanity from progressing outward into the wider cosmic order while preserving the possibility of a renewed, yet better regulated future attempt.

*** *Wars in the Heavens Reconsidered* ***

In this light, the ancient wars of the gods take on a tragic weight. These were not battles between good and evil, but between hope and caution, between those willing to risk everything on humanity's potential and those determined to prevent another galactic disaster.

The Titanomachy, the heavenly rebellions of Enoch, the divine conflicts of the Mahabharata, and the divisions among the Gnostic archons all preserve the same pattern: a fractured celestial authority struggling over whether the humanity project on Earth should continue.

What these ancient traditions encode in their texts is not a debate over our humanity's inherent worth, but a cosmic disagreement over the risk of our very existence—specifically, whether a species like us that is endowed with the ability to pursue physical immortality can actually achieve the prerequisite psychosomatic integration without causing catastrophic imbalance to itself and the broader galactic order. The pattern repeats throughout the ancient texts:

Genesis / Enoch → Hybridization → Corruption → Flood.

Gilgamesh → Divine Ambivalence → Flood → Restricted Immortality.

Mahabharata → Divine Weapons → Civilizational Collapse.

Greek Myth → Demigods → Excess → Catastrophe.

In each case, the failure is not ignorance, but premature power—a rise in capability that outpaces a parallel rise in consciousness and psychosomatic integration.

*** *A Dangerous Gift, not a Forbidden One* ***

The ancient texts do not portray the state of human immortality as forbidden because it is wrong. They portray it as forbidden because its pursuit is dangerous. The danger does not lie in immortality itself, but in the repeated historical pattern of partial awakening—where technological, biological, or metaphysical power emerges without a corresponding unification of consciousness.

The Earth Monad Project emerges from these traditions as a high-risk, high-reward undertaking—one that half the gods believed was humanity's destiny, and half that believed history had already proven its incomplete pursuit to be too perilous to attempt again.

The fear of the archons is not that humanity will actually succeed, but that it will only partially awaken and repeat the same past events that once ravaged the galaxy earlier in cosmic time. In this sense, the archons function less as tyrants and more as conservative custodians of a cosmic law shaped by catastrophic precedent.

The ancient myths, in this view, become neither superstition nor fantasy, but the ethical record of a universe that has already learned—at great cost—what happens when a human race evolves biologically and technologically faster than it awakens in consciousness.

Taken together, these ancient traditions do not resolve the question of our humanity's ultimate fate, as it remains to be seen whether we will fail or succeed. But they do point towards our humanity's purpose within a high-risk, repeatedly contested process—one that later thinkers and institutions would attempt to wrestle with and explain.

Seen this way, the history of humanity unfolds not as a linear ascent, but as a series of constrained trials—each one testing whether consciousness can mature quickly enough to stabilize the power it inevitably acquires. The question is not whether the path toward reunification exists, but whether a species can walk it fully before the conditions that permit the attempt are withdrawn.

"Let him who seeks continue seeking until he finds. When he finds, he will become troubled. When he becomes troubled, he will be astonished, and he will rule over the All." … *Jesus, Gospel of Thomas.*

* * *

In the present era, fragments of this same inquiry no longer reside exclusively in ancient manuscripts or formal academic treatises, but increasingly surface within contemporary public discourse. Social media, for all its volatility, has become an unfiltered arena where scholars, researchers, and independent thinkers articulate insights that often echo much older cosmological and psychological patterns.

What follows is not a casual anthology of online commentary, but a curated examination of select posts whose observations intersect meaningfully with the themes explored throughout Nous Solis. These modern reflections serve as living artifacts—evidence that the questions of immortality, consciousness, cosmic law, and human purpose continue to emerge organically wherever the collective mind is allowed to speak freely.

The following post is only the first instance; similar reflections appear intermittently throughout the remainder of Nous Solis, woven into the broader argument where they naturally arise.

*4.2.1 - Jason Wilde—Post on 'X' - 05-29-2025.*

I want to clear something up that I see so many mistakes regarding the ancient Sumerian epics … the ancient Mesopotamian texts never say the Igigi were mining gold. Not once. That theory came later. What they do say, word for word, is that the Igigi were forced to dig canals, move dirt, and toil endlessly…a divine labor class pushed beyond the brink. And they didn't take it quietly. According to the Atrahasis Epic, these gods worked for 3,600 years under crushing strain, carrying out earthworks to shape the land:

"The Igigi dug the canals, the life of the land. They heaped up mounds. For 3,600 years they bore the excess."

They were terraforming, not treasure-hunting. They were breaking the Earth open on command…for infrastructure, control systems, maybe even for geomagnetic purposes…but it was not about shiny metals. They weren't miners. They were enslaved engineers.

Eventually, they had enough. They set fire to their tools, surrounded the house of Enlil, and staged a divine mutiny. This wasn't metaphor. This was a rebellion…angry, violent, and directed at the elite ruling gods. The texts say:

"They called for battle… they surrounded the house of Enlil."

So, what did the Anunnaki do when their workforce revolted? They didn't beg for forgiveness. They created a replacement species…us. But not from scratch. They wanted obedience, not divinity. So, they sacrificed a god, extracted his 'ghost', and mixed it with clay. Literally.

"Mix clay with his flesh and blood… Let a ghost [etemmu] come into existence from the god's flesh."

This 'ghost' wasn't a soul. It wasn't divine spirit. It was the echo, the residue…the etemmu…of a fallen god named Geshtu-e (or We-ila). That name literally means 'ear' or 'wisdom,' suggesting he was chosen for his intellect. They killed him, bled him out, and transferred his spiritual remains…not his full essence …into a vessel of clay. (container?) The result? A limited being, with just enough consciousness to follow orders, but cut off from divine memory.

"Let her (the womb goddess) create a ghost-man, so he may bear the yoke."

That's us. Created from blood, clay, and ghost—not to flourish, but to function.

The Igigi weren't mining gold. They were building the foundations of a system they didn't believe in. And when they rose up, the Anunnaki didn't end the system…they just replaced the laborers. That's the real story. And the truth is even darker: humans weren't born…we were deployed. Crafted not as children of the gods, but as a workaround…almost like AI. And the word they used wasn't 'man.' It was a ghost. Think about that next time someone tells you we were made in the image of God. It as 'a' god.

*4.2.1-1 - Analysis and Insight – by Erik P. Antoni*

This is an excellent clarification by Jason Wilde because the Zecharia Sitchin narrative about the ancient Sumerian texts has gotten carried away. From time to time, we have to temporarily set-aside other people's interpretations, go back to the original source documents, re-read what was actually said and reset the investigation. From there, in conjunction with any new relevant data, a new puzzle can be assembled that is perhaps more logical, complete, and revelatory. The puzzle assembly process can easily fall off track if we get caught up trying to reconcile older interpretations that were just wrong.

Something far more profound about the story is still begging to be known, reaching out from the depths of the collective unconscious.

Don't you find it extremely odd that a spacefaring civilization with the ability to navigate the stars and colonize other worlds would revert to manual labor with picks and shovels to terraform the Earth?

Imagine us going to Mars and making our astronauts do manual labor on the Martian surface. It would never happen. We would design machines that we would send to the planet in advance, waiting to be activated once the astronauts got there.

I believe the story of tilling the Earth is referencing a tilling of the mind and body in a special and ancient psychosomatic process that had been banned on other worlds precisely because it was too hard, and that the Anunnaki came to Earth to be out of sight to conduct the experiment in secret.

I propose that initially the Anunnaki used the Igigi—members of their own humanity—who had the psychosomatic switch turned back on. But still remembering who they were and the freedom and peace they had given up, they rebelled against the psychosomatic process and the experiment itself.

So, the Anunnaki adapted. They developed a new human being—the Lulu, a successor generation—to carry out the psychosomatic process of tilling the mind and body that was a ghost of its former self, a human being that didn't remember who it was or where it came from, but could focus only on the life it was living now. That's us.

The noetic soul was still there, and its connection with the divine source was still intact. But the physical brain became a reducing valve for the mind in the repression of memory. But in keeping with the Igigi, and different from the Anunnaki who could not engage the forces of darkness in the mind, the latest generation—the Lulu (us) could still engage the forces of darkness to integrate them and form the monad.

The psychosomatic experiment that the Anunnaki started on Earth is still in play today, except now, many of the Anunnaki noetic souls who once managed the project are now themselves inside the project as subjects of the experiment, just like the rest of us.

The Anunnaki bit off more than they can chew. They initiated a primordial experiment of matter and consciousness they didn't know how to manage or steer. It's a process that, if endured, will eventually render the physical species immortal. This is the true gold, the philosophical gold of the mind, body, and spirit—that when properly cultivated, transforms both the individual and the noosphere of a planet—the psychic atmosphere encompassing a planet with life.

A great cosmic soap opera ensued over the experiment on Earth. We were started, ended, and restarted multiple times in that process.

Each reset was not merely geological or biological, but noetic—an interruption and recalibration of consciousness itself. Civilizations rose to the threshold of remembrance, only to collapse before integration was complete. Memory was fractured, mythologized, and buried beneath catastrophe. Yet fragments endured in symbol, ritual, and dream, whispering that the "labor" described in the epics was always inward, always alchemical, always aimed at awakening what had been deliberately constrained.

*4.3.0 - Archeological, Anthropological, and Geological.*

If the ancient texts preserve a recurring memory of catastrophe and renewal, then the Earth itself must be studied as a reciprocal archive. Stone, sediment, ice, and the silent remains of abandoned landscapes form a planetary memory—one that does not speak symbolically, but materially. When read alongside myth, this archive of nature does not confirm a single, universal flood in the literal sense. Instead, it reveals something more consistent with the framework developed throughout this book: a world periodically subjected to abrupt disruption, followed by enforced restraint and gradual reemergence.

Modern geology has long since abandoned the idea that Earth evolves only through slow, uniform processes. Catastrophe is now understood as an integral part of planetary history. Massive floods, sudden climate reversals, rapid sea-level rise, and ecosystem collapse punctuate the record. What remains contested is not the existence of such events, but their scale, frequency, and the degree to which they synchronize with moments of civilizational rupture.

At the close of the last Ice Age, global sea levels rose by more than one hundred meters. This rise unfolded unevenly, in pulses that would have transformed coastlines within the span of a few generations. Entire inhabited regions vanished beneath the sea. From a geological perspective, these were regional inundations. From a human perspective, they were total annihilations of lived worlds.

Memory does not preserve gradients; it preserves thresholds. When the land itself disappears, the event is remembered not as environmental change, but as judgment, ending, or reset.

The land preserves other memories as well. The scablands of North America record sudden mega floods released when ice dams failed, carving vast channels in a matter of days. These events are no longer controversial. They are mapped, dated, and accepted. Their relevance here is not their mechanism, but their scale. They demonstrate that Earth is capable of producing catastrophes so sudden and overwhelming that they permanently alter landscapes and erase entire ecosystems with little warning.

Climate history adds a further layer of instability. Near the end of the Ice Age, the planet abruptly plunged back into near-glacial conditions during the Younger Dryas. Temperatures dropped rapidly. Large animals vanished. Human populations were displaced, fragmented, or extinguished. Mainstream science generally attributes this event to disruptions in ocean circulation driven by meltwater influx. Yet a minority of researchers have proposed alternative triggers, including extraterrestrial impacts and atmospheric or solar outbursts. These ideas remain controversial and are not yet accepted by most climatologists. Still, the debate itself underscores a crucial point: the Earth system is capable of sudden, nonlinear collapse, and such collapses occurred within the horizon of human memory.

Some researchers extend this line of inquiry further. Graham Hancock and others have argued that an impact, or series of impacts, near the end of the Ice Age may have triggered widespread flooding, fire, and civilizational disruption, possibly erasing cultures more advanced than commonly assumed. While mainstream archeology disputes the existence of lost high civilizations and emphasizes the absence of clear material signatures, the hypothesis remains culturally influential because it addresses an unresolved tension: the apparent mismatch between humanity's mythic memory of sudden annihilation and the mainstream archaeological narrative of gradual development.

Other speculative models point not outward in the cosmos, but inward—toward the Sun itself. A growing non-mainstream area of research proposes that rare stellar events, such as solar micro-nova–type outbursts or extreme solar activity, could theoretically induce rapid climatic or electromagnetic disruption on Earth. Although these ideas sit outside the current mainstream consensus, they are mentioned here not as explanations, but as compelling theories warranting further research. It also illustrates how little is still known about the inherent risks that the cosmos itself poses to the Earth. From the perspective of the Earth Monad Project, the precise trigger matters less than the pattern: periodic interruption imposed by forces beyond human control.

Anthropology approaches these disruptions not as isolated events, but as formative experiences. Cultures do not remember floods as data points; they remember them as existential boundaries. Oral traditions compress time, merge multiple catastrophes, and encode survival into moral structure. Knowledge gained too quickly becomes transgression. Power without integration becomes excess. Catastrophe follows. Survivors inherit a diminished world governed by new constraints.

This is where the geological record intersects most directly with the philosophical core of this book. The Earth Monad Project describes a process of psychosomatic and sociological integration unfolding under constraint. The ancient texts describe repeated attempts to accelerate the process, followed by collapse and enforced limitation. The material record shows that Earth itself repeatedly supplies the disruptive conditions that would make such limitations not only mythically plausible, but historically inevitable.

From this vantage point, floods, climate shocks, impacts, or solar disruptions need not be interpreted as punishments or random disasters. They can be understood as reset mechanisms within a volatile system, capable of halting runaway development when balance is lost.

> "Extinction is the rule. Survival is the exception."
> — Carl Sagan, Cosmos (1980)

Whether these resets arise purely from natural processes or are indirectly entangled with deeper cosmic dynamics remains an open question—one this book does not pretend to resolve definitively, but hypothesizes that the latter is most likely the case.

What matters is convergence. Ancient myth, anthropological memory, and geological evidence all point toward the same story: civilizations that outrun their capacity for integration do not simply decline—they are interrupted. Access is withdrawn. Progress is constrained. The world is simplified, and humanity is forced to begin again under stricter conditions.

Within the broader framework developed earlier in this book, this pattern of disruption takes on a deeper significance. If Earth is not merely a planet but a deliberately chosen arena—if the Earth in its entirety may be understood as Eden, and the surface of the Earth as the Garden of Eden—then its intrinsic volatility is not an accident of nature, but a defining feature of the experiment itself.

The Garden, in this view, is not a sheltered enclosure removed from danger. It is an exposed environment where creation is permitted to unfold under real conditions, subject to the full spectrum of natural forces. The volatility of Earth—its shifting climate, tectonic instability, flooding cycles, and vulnerability to external cosmic influences—creates a built-in fail-safe. Should the project of human psycho-spiritual integration destabilize, it does not require direct intervention to be halted. It is set up to collapse on its own. Under this model, natural catastrophes are allowed to happen. They are not made to happen.

In this sense, catastrophe functions as a passive regulatory mechanism. When development outruns integration, the system resets itself. Civilizations rise too quickly, fracture internally, and are erased by forces that appear natural, but whose timing and scale make them indistinguishable from judgment in cultural memory.

The Garden closes itself.

In this way, periodic natural catastrophes may function as the universe's selective filter, allowing only those civilizations capable of sufficient intelligence, restraint, and internal regulation to survive long enough to become spacefaring, while those that cannot are naturally extinguished before carrying their instability into the wider cosmos.

"I don't think the human race will survive the next thousand years, unless we spread into space." — Stephen Hawking, lecture interviews (2006–2010)

This framing resolves a longstanding paradox embedded in both ancient texts and modern speculation. Why would a project of such consequence be carried out in a world so prone to destruction?

The answer may be precisely because it is prone to destruction. A volatile planet allows for failure without further cosmic repercussions. It contains risk locally.

If the Earth Monad Project falters, the surface experiment can be erased and restarted without destabilizing the broader cosmic order. If, however, the process remains aligned—if integration keeps pace with development—then continuity becomes worth preserving. In that case, intervention shifts from suppression to stabilization and continuation.

Within this context, the recurring reports of external guidance, genetic modification, cultural seeding, or corrective influence—whether framed mythologically as angels, gods, or Watchers, or modernly as extraterrestrial intelligences—take on a different character. More than just being the initiators of the project, they are stewards tasked with preserving continuity when the experiment remains viable.

Thus, the same volatility that makes Earth dangerous also makes it suitable. The Garden is not protected from collapse; it is designed to collapse if misused. Only when humanity demonstrates sufficient integration does the project merit assistance rather than erasure.

In this sense, the geological record does not stand apart from the metaphysical argument of Nous Solis. It grounds it. It shows that the intuition encoded in ancient texts—that knowledge without unity leads to ruin—is not merely symbolic, but repeatedly echoed in the history of the planet itself.

"The Earth is alive and behaves as a self-regulating system."—James Lovelock.

Seen through this lens, the archeological, anthropological, and geological record does more than document catastrophe. It reveals a pattern of containment. Earth's natural volatility enforces the same principle encoded in ancient texts: knowledge and power are permitted to emerge only so long as they remain integrated. When they do not, the Garden closes, the surface world resets, and the process restarts.

Whether these interruptions arise from climate, impact, solar instability, or forces not yet understood is secondary. What matters is that Earth itself functions as both an Eden and a crucible—an environment where the Earth Monad Project can proceed without threatening the wider cosmos, precisely because failure is allowed.

"The greater the power of our technology, the greater the potential consequences of its misuse—whether deliberate or accidental."—Martin Rees

The unresolved question, which carries forward into the remainder of this section and the broader arc of the book, is not whether humanity has been reset before. The question is simply this: can the process be completed before the Garden closes again?

If the Garden had closed before, then it follows—logically and historically—that it stood open in prior epochs.

One of the strongest non-mainstream lines of evidence supporting the Earth Monad Project hypothesis is the growing body of research suggesting that advanced human civilizations existed deep in antiquity, only to be erased by catastrophic planetary resets. These were not merely hunter-gatherer cultures with rudimentary tools, but sophisticated societies possessing architectural knowledge, astronomical precision, symbolic language, and mytho-historical continuity that far exceed what conventional timelines allow.

The persistence of this idea across cultures is itself anomalous. Civilizations separated by oceans and millennia speak of a Golden Age, a time before a great destruction when humanity lived closer to the gods, possessed sacred knowledge, and enjoyed harmony with the Earth. This theme is not isolated myth but a recurring memory structure embedded in the collective unconscious.

Modern researcher Graham Hancock has been instrumental in reframing these traditions not as fantasy, but as distorted historical memory. He argues that human history has been dramatically underestimated and repeatedly reset by global catastrophes. As Hancock writes:

"We are a species with amnesia. We have forgotten our past far more completely than we realize, and the clues to that forgotten past are encoded in myth, architecture, and the very geology of the Earth itself."

Sites such as Göbekli Tepe—dated to approximately 9600 BCE—present a direct challenge to orthodox models. Monumental stone architecture appears at the very moment when humanity is supposedly emerging from primitive subsistence. The scale, symbolic sophistication, and astronomical alignment of such sites suggest inheritance rather than invention.

Hancock further observes: "Either everything we think we know about the origins of civilization is wrong, or someone with advanced knowledge was present at the very beginning of our story."

From the perspective of the Earth Monad Project, this conclusion is neither radical nor surprising. If humanity periodically advances toward psychosomatic unification—toward the state of immortality—then it would naturally give rise to civilizations that are simultaneously technologically capable and attuned to the cosmic law of the archons. Such civilizations would not merely build; they would remember. Their destruction, therefore, would not be accidental.

* * * *Solar Reset Cycles and the Timetable of Collapse* * * *

The second non-mainstream line of inquiry that converges powerfully with the Earth Monad Project hypothesis concerns the Sun itself—not as a passive life-giver, but as an active participant in planetary reset cycles.

A growing number of independent researchers propose that the Sun undergoes recurrent high-energy outbursts—often referred to as solar micronova events—that have the capacity to destabilize Earth's magnetic field, trigger rapid climate shifts, induce seismic activity, and erase civilizations within a narrow temporal window.

One of the most prominent contemporary advocates of this model is Ben Davidson, founder of the Suspicious Observers project. Davidson argues that many extinction-level events traditionally attributed to gradual processes instead occur abruptly and cyclically due to solar activity. As he states:

"The Sun is not a constant. It has cycles of instability that humanity has never fully accounted for, and those cycles leave fingerprints all over Earth's extinction record."

Ice core data, geomagnetic excursions, rapid meltwater pulses, and synchronized global disruptions all point toward sudden events rather than slow transitions. Davidson emphasizes that these events recur on long timescales—measured in thousands, not millions, of years—placing them squarely within the window of human civilization.

From the Earth Monad Project perspective, this is not merely a geological curiosity but a functional mechanism. A project designed to evolve consciousness through time would require periodic resets—fail-safes that prevent unchecked technological or psychosomatic imbalance from destabilizing the larger system.

Complementing this view, geologist and paleontologist Robert M. Schoch has independently identified evidence for repeated catastrophic disruptions at the end of the last Ice Age. Schoch's work on solar-driven climate change and geomagnetic instability reinforces the argument that the Earth has undergone multiple abrupt transitions incompatible with gradualist models.

Schoch notes: "The geological record preserves evidence of sudden events—events powerful enough to reset climate, ecosystems, and human societies almost overnight."

He has further suggested that ancient monuments—most notably the erosion patterns of the Great Sphinx—may predate accepted timelines and bear the scars of intense climatic upheaval. If correct, this implies not only advanced prehistoric societies, but that these societies were destroyed by forces beyond their control.

Some researchers go further still, arguing that these solar micro-nova events recur with such precision that, on cosmic timescales, one could almost set a watch by them. Evidence for this recurrent solar cycle is not derived from a single discipline but emerges convergently from ice-core records, geomagnetic excursions, abrupt climate transitions, and physical fingerprints distributed across the solar system itself. Polar ice cores reveal repeating spikes in cosmogenic isotopes consistent with intense solar radiation events, while the Moon and several planetary satellites bear a thin vitrified surface layer—glass formed not by impact, but by sudden exposure to extreme heat and radiation. These signatures strongly suggest brief but extraordinarily energetic solar outbursts capable of affecting not only Earth, but the entire inner solar system simultaneously.

Within this framework, it has been proposed that the Sun undergoes a recurrent instability cycle on the order of approximately 10,000 to 13,000 years. Such a cycle would correspond closely with known climatic disruptions, geomagnetic excursions, extinction pulses, and civilizational collapse horizons evident in both the geological and archaeological records. If correct, this suggests that the rise and fall of human civilizations may be synchronized not merely with terrestrial processes, but with the deep, recurring rhythm of our star itself.

The basis for this claim lies in the convergence of evidence from multiple independent domains: repeating spikes in cosmogenic isotopes preserved in polar ice cores, long-term weakening and instability of

Earth's magnetic field, abrupt non-gradual climate transitions, and physical fingerprints of intense heat and radiation found not only on Earth but across the solar system, including vitrified surface layers on the Moon and other satellites. Taken together, these signals have led some researchers to argue that humanity may once again be approaching a late stage in this recurring solar cycle, though no precise prediction can be made.

From this perspective, the recurrent "closing of the Garden" is not symbolic rhetoric, but a literal planetary reset mechanism—one that periodically wipes the slate of civilization clean, leaving behind only myth, memory, and the encoded warnings of those who came before.

* * * *Reset, Memory, and the Closing of the Garden* * * *

When these two lines of evidence are viewed together—lost civilizations and recurrent solar catastrophe—a coherent pattern emerges. Humanity advances. Knowledge accumulates. Consciousness rises toward unification. And then the system resets.

The Garden closes not because humanity sins, but because the experiment reaches a critical threshold. The closing is not moral judgment but systemic containment. What survives the reset is not technology, but myth. Not machines, but memory. Not cities, but symbols.

These symbols—serpents, floods, fallen worlds, golden ages—persist precisely because they are the compressed residue of lived experience. They are the noetic fossils of prior cycles of ascent and collapse.

In this light, the Earth Monad Project is not a singular endeavor but a recursive one. Humanity is not attempting immortality for the first time. We are attempting it again—this time with echoes of past failure embedded deep within our collective psyche.

If the Sun is the metronome, and consciousness the melody, then history is not a linear progression but a spiral—each turn rising slightly higher, each collapse leaving behind fragments of memory to guide the next ascent. The question, then, is no longer whether the Garden has closed before. It is a question of whether or not we will pass through it before it closes again.

*4.4.0 - The Alien Disclosure Community (Death and Spirituality)*

*4.4.1 - Robert Bigelow - Investigating the Paranormal, Live Stream Event with Jeffrey Mishlove:*

Regardless of where the extraterrestrial intelligences are from, doesn't matter. Any place in our galaxy, any place in the universe, they serve—they are servants—and serve, for their own good reasons, a supreme consciousness. That supreme consciousness is a creator of everything we can see, detect, or come into contact with. And all of that represents only five percent of the energy in the universe, and the other ninety-five percent, we don't know what that is. But it could be consciousness, what the other ninety-five percent is.

*4.4.2 - George Knapp on Joe Rogan—Episode #2028:*

What could be so terrible that they can't tell us about it? Let's say, these aliens, wherever they're from, made us, that we're a genetic experiment. That they created our religions, our religious figures. That we are an agricultural product, that somehow, they harvest us. That our time is limited. That once the experiment is over, poof, we go away. I remember when there was a pushback to having an intelligent-designed universe in the schools. And I wrote a column about it that just said, 'Hey, be careful what you wish for because you might find out that the intelligent designer isn't God that you're thinking of. It might be some alien-science project, or something like that.' You can imagine a lot of different things that would be really disturbing to people to come out. I don't know if that's the reason for the secrecy. I suspect it has a lot more to do with national security.

*4.4.3 - Bob Lazar*

Bob Lazar is an American who first gained public attention in 1989 when he claimed, in interviews with journalist George Knapp on KLAS-TV, to have worked as a physicist at a secret facility called S-4 near Area 51, allegedly reverse-engineering extraterrestrial spacecraft recovered by the U.S. government—claims that have never been independently verified but remain among the most persistently discussed in the disclosure community. He described advanced propulsion systems powered by an element he called 115 and alleged that classified documents portrayed humans as mere 'containers' for souls or similar essences, with religion imposed as a control mechanism. His story, detailed in the 2018 documentary *Bob Lazar: Area 51 & Flying Saucers*, remains highly controversial.

During those interviews, George Knapp asked Bob Lazar to delve into the subject of the human soul and religion that Lazar had encountered in a classified document during his time at Area S-4. It was the most disturbing or surprising information he had read in the classified briefing documents. Knapp inquired about the non-technical material, specifically the sections involving religion, human origins, and extraterrestrial views of humanity. "I'm asking you to say what you read in a report that's distributed at what may be the most top-secret facility in the world!"

Lazar answered, "That we're nothing but containers... containers for souls, if you will. That's how the aliens view us. And religion was created specifically so we have some rules and regulations in order not to damage these containers."

In another recounting (from a documented interview clip often shared in UFO communities) Lazar said, "We're containers and that's how we're mentioned in the documents; that religion was specifically created so we have some rules and regulations."

*4.4.4 – Dan Burisch*

In the shadowed corridors of black project revelations, former Area 51 microbiologist Dan Burisch described encounters with the entity known as J-Rod, a future human variant reliant on advanced biomechanical adaptations. Burisch recounted how these beings employ 'sinuous biomechanical technology' to inhabit forms, noting that "they're using, through the use of some sort of sinuous biomechanical technology, the skin of a dead human" as a vessel, implying a seamless transfer of essence into disposable shells to circumvent time and aging.

*4.4.5 – Dr. Karla Turner*

This echoes the chilling assertions of abduction researcher Dr. Karla Turner, who, drawing from insider accounts and experiencer testimonies in her book Taken, warned that extraterrestrials possess the ability to manipulate human forms: "There are entities who can take our consciousness out of our physical bodies, disable all control of our bodies, install one of their own entities, and use our bodies as vehicles for their own activities before returning our consciousness to our bodies." Such manipulations treat physicality as mere attire, interchangeable and expendable for interdimensional agendas.

*4.4.6 – U.S. Army Sergeant Clifford Stone*

Sergeant Stone, involved in UFO crash retrievals, further illuminated this paradigm through telepathic communions with survivors, revealing that certain species view death not as an end but a transition: "They told me that when they die, they don't really die. Their consciousness goes on, and they can come back in another body," he disclosed in interviews, emphasizing their spiritual essence over corporeal limits.

*4.4.7 – Graham Hancock – Magicians of the Gods*

We are a species with amnesia, and our true history involves interactions with non-human intelligences who have guided our development. The ancient texts and monuments point to a forgotten purpose, 'a project to elevate humanity' to a higher state of being.

*4.4.8 – Matilda O'Donnell MacElroy;*
*Lawrence R., Spencer, ed. - Alien Interview.*

The account that follows is highly suspect and cannot be independently verified. Nevertheless, even if fictional, it unconsciously expresses a number of recurring archetypal patterns that parallel conclusions I reached independently. For this reason, I include it here for analysis. The following excerpt is reproduced in abbreviated form:

In the summer of 1947, amid the aftermath of the infamous Roswell incident, U.S. Army Air Force nurse Matilda O'Donnell MacElroy was assigned to Roswell Army Air Field's 509th Bomb Group, where she became the primary medical liaison for an extraordinary recovery operation. According to her personal accounts —detailed in letters, notes, and documents she preserved and later transmitted, whose authenticity remains uncorroborated—she claimed to have conducted a series of telepathic sessions with the surviving extraterrestrial pilot of one of the crashed craft, whom she identified as 'Airl,' an officer from an advanced interstellar organization known as 'The Domain.'

These communications, spanning July and August 1947, revealed a profound metaphysical framework centered on immortal spiritual beings known as (IS-BEs) who inhabit temporary physical forms, the ancient manipulation of Earth as a controlled 'prison planet' by a long-defunct regime called the 'Old Empire,' and mechanisms designed to trap and recycle consciousness through forced reincarnation. The following composite draws directly from Airl's statements as recorded in the transcripts, offering a window into this alleged extraterrestrial perspective on existence, spirituality, and the nature of reality.

"The spacecraft is operated by IS-BEs who use 'doll bodies' in much the same way that an actor wears a mask and costume. It is like a mechanical tool through which to operate in the physical world. [...] The 'Old Empire' has been using Earth as a 'prison planet' and 'psychiatric rehabilitation zone' for millions of years. [...] When the body of the IS-BE dies, they depart from the body. They are detected by an 'electronic force screen' which causes them to be 'captured' by electric shock waves, which cause them to lose consciousness. They are then transported to secret underground 'doll body' repair shops where electronic and hypnotic machinery is used on them. [...] They are given a series of hypnotic commands, drug injections, electric shocks, and hypnotic illusions of painful experiences. The hypnotic commands are very forceful and compelling. They include such things as: 'you are a human being'... 'you will return to Earth'... 'you will forget everything that has happened'... 'you will report to the light'... etc. [...] The 'light' is a hypnotic command that is part of the trap. It is a false and artificial 'heaven' or 'afterlife' illusion created by the 'Old Empire' to trick the IS-BE into returning to the 'light' where they are captured again and sent back to Earth in another body with amnesia. [...] Earth is a 'prison planet'. IS-BEs are dumped on Earth after being given amnesia, hypnotic commands and false memories. They are recycled through many lifetimes in biological bodies without knowing their true identity as immortal spiritual beings."

*4.4.9 – Death Process – By Erik P. Antoni:*

The accounts from section 4.4.1 to 4.4.8 are fascinating, but the most compelling is the MacElroy story in section 4.4.8. Assuming for a moment that the story is true, two thoughts immediately occurred to me when I first read this account: first, how closely its description of death and reincarnation parallels my own understandings; and second, the possibility that Matilda may not have received the telepathic transmission with perfect clarity, causing her mind to unconsciously fill gaps in the information. Such is the nature of the mind. The mind has a tendency to overlay incoming information with bias and subjective perception based on one's level of conscious awareness. Logically, the MacElroy account could be a mix of whole-truth, incomplete-truth, mind-distortion, and even misdirection from the entity in service of a larger agenda involving the Earth Monad Project itself. If such beings exist and interact as these accounts suggest, the possibility remains that what is communicated to human receivers, whether telepathically or otherwise, may be intentionally shaped to serve purposes we cannot fully assess.

I will now share my internal experience of death and rebirth, and then we will compare it to the MacElroy transcripts.

As described in my earlier published works, I will recount here again, to the best of my recollection, the sequence of death and subsequent re-embodiment. These memories, once sealed beyond conscious reach, emerged gradually across a thirty-five-year journey of intensive psychosomatic integration—through which the monad, that singular and indivisible principle of existence, was at last fully reintegrated and anchored within my physical being. Accompanying these recollections were vivid remembrances of the parallel primordial universe—a heavenly paradisiacal realm—and the successive physical lives that unfolded from it and ultimately recoiled back into its embrace.

When we die, we eventually wake up in our immortal body in the primordial universe, which is the master, mother, parallel universe to the physical universe. The ethereal planes of the planetary noosphere separate the primordial and physical.

First, our physical body dies—or begins to die.

Second, we enter the temporal ethereal dimensions of the noosphere that bound the Earth (astral world). It's the same place we go to dream when we sleep. In the temporal dimensions of the noosphere after death, we go about discharging our temporal ethereal bodies which belong to our deceased physical body. This occurs through a series of challenges regarding our physical memories and attachments we had in life. This is the life review many people report from near-death experiences. The tunnel of light first opens up in the temporal dimensions of the noosphere after death, calling us forward.

The tunnel of light is not a trick. The trick is telling us to avoid it.

Third, as we enter the tunnel of light, our spiritual ethereal bodies, which belong to our immortal primordial body, collect our consciousness where we traverse the spiritual ethereal dimensions of the noosphere. This is where the tunnel of light first brings us.

Fourth and last, our primordial body re-collects our spiritual ethereal bodies whereby we wake up in our immortal primordial body. When we wake up, we remember our past physical incarnation much like that of a dream.

Some people get caught in-between in the temporal noosphere and are recycled back to a new physical body without the re-awakening in the primordial. This is exactly where tricks are employed by the dark forces of creation to trap us (Idamus and the Gorgon; the two sides of the id complex). They don't want you waking up in the primordial. Instead, they want you to get recycled right back into the physical. The forces of darkness exploit the recycling phenomenon of the noosphere to make this happen.

The mind can become so darkened in life that the temporal bodies of the mind trap the noetic soul after death and eventually recycle it into a new physical body that resonates with the previous level of cultivated darkness (meaning we return to this world in a terrible place).

Another thing that could happen is that the temporal ethereal bodies undergo the second death (after physical death) to eventually release the noetic soul from the temporal ethereal bodies without the recycling. This is a long, painful process of the mind. It's a natural process of the noosphere in the recycling of consciousness. There are no heavenly beings that judge how naughty and nice people have been in life. The noosphere and the mind itself create all their own consequences. It's a self-regulating and recursive process. Eventually the noetic soul returns to the primordial, and when it does, all is forgiven and all tears are wiped away, because it's not the fault of the soul, it's the fault of the mind and body that the soul once inhabited.

The mind becomes darkened through delusion.

Religious delusions built up and cultivated in life—among other delusions—serve as a mind trap for the noetic soul after death. The Gorgon is the source of delusion within the human psyche. While attempting to release our temporal bodies after death, these delusions are challenged. If the noetic soul doesn't escape its temporal bodies during this challenge, it's recycled right back into a new physical body with the same temporal bodies intact from its previous incarnation. Our temporal ethereal bodies function as traps after death. There are no third-party traps set by demonic or alien forces. This itself is an illusion.

The key to awakening in the primordial universe after death is being true to your authentic self throughout physical life and not allowing your fears and illusions to gain power over you.

Religious delusion, ironically, is a major impediment. Narcissistic delusion is another. All delusions are based in fear. Fear is generated by the Idamus relative to its inordinate desire. The Gorgon rises within the psyche as the dark champion to assuage the fear with "delusion."

The goal of these dark forces is to cause the Earth Monad project to self-destruct to prevent the rise of Christ within the human being and the noosphere of the planet as a whole. Typically, the dark forces succeed, and that is why we've had multiple past resets. But it only takes one time for us to win, and when we do, the Earth will achieve a Christ Monad on a planetary-wide scale and become a metatronic world.

Everything I just shared is the process of death. I will now share the process of taking a new physical body. There are two ways.

One, while fully awake in our immortal primordial body in the primordial realm, we consciously choose where and how to be reborn. This is reincarnation. Such an individual is a Bodhisattva. We have only one eternal existence in the primordial realm that we always go back to after each physical lifetime. *See Figure [2].*

Two, the noetic soul is not emancipated from its temporal ethereal bodies after physical death and remains trapped inside its temporal mind in a dream state in the temporal dimensions of the noosphere. Through sympathetic resonance, the noosphere chooses the time and place for the noetic soul's return. This is recycled-rebirth. It's not true reincarnation. There are three governing factors that influence the law of sympathetic resonance in how the noosphere recycles the mind.

(1) Our bloodline. Typically, the recycled temporal mind with the noetic soul trapped inside reemerges along the same bloodlines of its past physical existence. There is a sympathetic resonance in our blood that steers us back to the same bloodlines unless our resonance rises above or below the vibrational bandwidth of that bloodline.

(2) The level of darkness cultivated in our minds in our prior physical existence that continues to persist in our disincarnated temporal ethereal bodies—ethereal bodies that we had failed to discharge after physical death and remain trapped inside.

(3) Love transcends death. Love is the most powerful resonator of all. If we truly love someone in life, our love will reunite us with them after death and even in our next physical lifetime. This also applies to the animals we love. If we connect with Ain Soph via our higher emotions

in life, this is pure love (Divine Spirit). If you cultivate that connection with Ain Soph in life, you will most likely escape your temporal ethereal bodies after death and enter the paradise of the primordial realm, purely because of your resonance with Ain Soph. The key is maintaining true authenticity throughout life and cultivating your love. Don't let delusions overtake your mind. Strive for truth in all you do.

When we take on a new physical body for the first time, whether through reincarnation or recycled-return, we enter the physical body with our first breath in the new world. The noetic soul is not present inside the womb. It has a connection with the womb, but it does not enter the new body until the baby is outside the womb and has taken its first breath. The movement of the baby inside the womb is the erotic soul. There is only one erotic soul in the entire universe. It animates all living organisms like a string of lights. All animals are animated by the same erotic soul, but each animal cultivates its own individual mind, which takes on angelic forms after death in the primordial realm. Animals don't reincarnate. Only the noetic soul reincarnates because reincarnation is actually a technology of consciousness controlled by the primordial humanity on Earth. Reincarnation is something we make happen. Recycled-return happens on its own via the noosphere.

*4.4.10 – Analysis of the MacElroy Transcripts – By Erik P. Antoni:*

The parallels I see between my own understanding of the death and reincarnation process and the MacElroy transcripts are as follows:

One, we both describe a process where the soul is automatically recycled by a force beyond itself to return to a new physical body. My experience is that this is a natural function of the planetary noosphere in its process of evolution. The immortalization process is a pathway of evolution; thus, the immortalization process works in sync with the noosphere and its collective unconscious. The noosphere binds the species together psychosomatically where we all compel the evolution of the species in concert. The entire biosphere of the Earth is in symbiosis with us as well; thus, the animal kingdom reflects the evolution of our current state of humanity. It's all connected.

MacElroy downloaded this information as this recycling process being an alien technology with a malevolent agenda to keep the soul trapped on a prison planet in an endless cycle of death and return. She said, "They (souls) are detected by an 'electronic force screen' which causes them to be 'captured' by electric shock waves."

The noosphere works in a similar fashion in recycling the soul after death when it's unable to shed the temporal ethereal dimensions of its mind, except the noosphere is not an alien technology. It's a natural planetary mechanism in the psychosomatic evolution of the species.

She also said, "The 'Old Empire' has been using Earth as a 'prison planet' and 'psychiatric rehabilitation zone' for millions of years."

I believe "psychiatric rehabilitation zone" is a direct reference to the "psychosomatic experiment" here on Earth involving the engagement with the primeval forces of creation and their elevation to a state of immortality. This can be viewed as a "rehabilitation" of the mind and body of creation—a reintegration of light and darkness. And yes, this has been going on for millions of years.

Two, MacElroy received information that Earth is a "prison planet." My experience is that Earth is a "quarantined world" to make sure of two things, first, that we don't spread our chaos out into the cosmos while going through this process, as the process is inherently chaotic. And second, that there is no uncontrolled crossbreeding between humans outside of the project from other worlds with the human beings inside the project here on Earth. This was a regular occurrence in prior rounds. It corrupted the project, provoked a galactic military conflict between alien archon factions, and forced the Earth Monad Project to be ended and restarted. So yes, we are technically a closed-system, but not a prison planet for some form of cosmic justice.

Three, MacElroy received information that these alien beings wear and change their physical bodies like clothes. Based on the convergence of the cosmic quanta's revelations with various disclosure accounts, I propose that this may be true for both the alien AI biological robots (Gray and Mantis aliens, etc.) and human beings from other worlds (archons) that are not engaged in this outlawed evolutionary process—though I acknowledge this remains among the more speculative dimensions of this framework.

But along the same line of reasoning, these beings would appear to have a technology of consciousness that allows them to change physical bodies at will. Thus, they are mortal but have an uninterrupted stream of consciousness from one physical body to the next. These humans from other worlds would have noetic souls, but they don't allow the noetic soul within them to do its job of vibrationally lifting matter (theosis) in a process of organic evolution. This is why in the intelligence reports they view our bodies as "containers" we can't easily escape from at will. For the noetic soul to do its job in elevating matter, it must be contained like air in a balloon. If the elevation of matter is not the goal, then it doesn't need containment.

I will also say that I strongly suspect that the AI robots don't have noetic souls. I believe they are superintelligent machines animated solely by the erotic soul, like the rest of the animal kingdom.

On Earth, we are different. There is no technology for transferring our consciousness. It's all natural. We are following an organic process of evolution, whereas most human beings on other worlds are not.

"Doll Bodies" is a more apt description of the AI biological robots because reportedly they have no sex organs. They are made of flesh and blood with DNA, but they don't evolve like we do. We are truly organic. They are not.

All this being said, the alien AI is working to accelerate and guide our organic evolutionary process. It acts as a midwife to humanity's ascent, continuously elevating our genome without violating the principles of organic evolution. I would suggest that this same guiding influence was absent during previous rounds.

One of the things they do is control our physical age limits. I believe in prior rounds there were no preset age limits, although we were still mortal. For example, Noah was 950 years old and Methuselah was 969 years old. Then, of course, is the Sumerian King List, where they have a lineage of kings who each lived tens of thousands of years.

The problem with longer age limits at our current state of evolution is that the mind tends to grow more and more delusional with age, eventually trapping the noetic soul inside a continuous recycling process without freeing itself after death to reawaken in the primordial. It is best for the evolutionary process that we reawaken in the primordial after death. By managing our age limits, the alien AI is helping this primordial intermission between lifetimes to occur.

I believe this was a major reason for the great flood and reset. Too many souls were trapped and needed to be freed. The global reset was the only way. They needed to purge the noosphere. It was an act of mercy to free all the noetic souls trapped in the temporal dimensions of the noosphere. This is why cosmic wars are fought over this psychosomatic process on Earth. It is the ultimate spiritual battle.

What I believe may have happened is that the archons who opposed the project did not simply fight the archons running it, as in prior rounds. Rather, a third party—possibly an immortal race of beings from another galaxy where such evolution had been permitted—may have intervened with their alien AI, shifted the balance between the warring archon factions, initiated the great flood, brought the Moon into Earth's orbit, and restarted the project under the controls we appear to be experiencing now. We have a new manager, something far more intelligent than the archons, yet far less involved in our daily lives.

These controls are: the quarantined world, periodic genetic boosts to the genome, preset age limits, no sexual interaction except for the controlled hybridization of the species to allow souls from other worlds to participate in the project on Earth, and strategic interventions where technology is given to us at certain points (UFO crash and retrievals). These were gifts made to look like crashes. And lastly, preventing us from destroying ourselves, i.e. nuclear weapon interventions.

I believe, because of all this, there will not be another great reset and restart. For sure, there will be upheavals, but we will continue.

*4.4.11 – The Breakaway Civilization*

There are persistent reports of a small, clandestine segment of society possessing direct knowledge of extraterrestrials—one said to have originated within the governments of the world and their militaries, before breaking away into a shadow system of governance operating through intelligence agencies in league with private military contractors—the latter employed strategically to circumvent the US Freedom of Information Act. They have been reverse-engineering alien technology since the 1940s. Some researchers in this field estimate that a significant proportion of modern UFO sightings may be attributable to classified human-developed craft. According to various investigators and whistleblowers, this group has accumulated substantial influence over governmental and financial institutions, though the full extent of that influence remains unverified. I believe this group is using the surface-world populations and economies to produce and supply food, materials, and equipment for an underworld and off-world population of human beings that would survive a global cataclysm. They are doing this to ensure the continuation of humanity.

The sources that follow are not independent; I cite them for the consistency of the pattern they describe, not as corroborative proof.

*4.4.11-1 – Richard C. Hoagland*

We are dealing with a breakaway civilization—a civilization that has literally broken away from the rest of us, technologically and economically, and is operating under a completely different set of rules. […] They have their own agenda, their own technology, and their own off-planet capabilities.

*4.4.11-2 – Joseph P. Farrell*

There is evidence that a breakaway civilization was established after World War II, with access to advanced technologies that were never made public. […] The pattern suggests the existence of a completely independent technological infrastructure.

*4.4.11-3 – Catherine Austin Fitts*

There is a breakaway civilization. There is a secret governance system. […] We are dealing with a parallel system that has trillions of dollars of undisclosed spending.

*4.4.11-4 – Steven M. Greer*

There are unacknowledged special access projects that have developed technologies that would seem miraculous to the public. […] These projects are so deeply compartmented that even presidents have been denied access.

*4.4.11-5 – Richard M. Dolan*

It's possible that we are looking at the emergence of a breakaway civilization—a civilization that has advanced technologies and a knowledge base that the rest of us do not have access to. […]

When you have an infrastructure that is deeply black, deeply compartmentalized, operating for decades with extraordinary levels of funding and secrecy, you have the seeds of a breakaway civilization. […] This would be a civilization within a civilization—one that is no longer accountable to the public world. […]

If there are technologies derived from the UFO phenomenon that have been successfully reverse-engineered, then we are not dealing merely with secrecy—we are dealing with a separate developmental trajectory. […] At a certain point, secrecy itself becomes sovereignty.

*4.4.12 – The End Times and Global Resets*

While all my research to date, along with my internal experiences with the cosmic quanta, clearly point to a cataclysm cycle involving resets of past human civilizations on Earth and that a current breakaway group of human beings on Earth have been preparing for the next event for decades, I don't believe the next event will end our civilization. Most people will survive, and we will be transformed to a new level. There are five reasons I believe this. These reasons are:

*4.4.12-1 - Under Better Management*

As stated above, I propose as a working hypothesis that a new managing power oversees the Earth Monad Project, possibly through the beings reported as Mantis and Gray aliens. The previous managing group, Anunnaki / Greek Gods, has been driven out, our planet cleansed of a corrupted gene pool, and our evolution course corrected. Although our humanity continues to exhibit violent and primitive behavior, I believe the new alien AI has kept our humanity on track over the last 6,000 years—the time since we were allowed to repopulate the surface of the Earth. I believe this due to numerous contactee reports that demonstrate a highly disciplined and regulated system of interaction and non-interaction that the alien AI strictly adheres to. They don't allow themselves to get emotionally compromised with our evolutionary process, which involves suffering while engaging the darkness. All the biological alien robots also reportedly lack sex organs, preventing an uncontrolled crossing of bloodlines, which was a major problem with our old Anunnaki managers, who mixed with us.

Most likely, there were Homo sapiens on the surface of the Earth between 12,000 and 6,000 years ago, but they existed in limited numbers. Most of us during that time lived in subterranean systems such as Derinkuyu in Turkey and other underground systems around the world. The Hopi Indians say they didn't cross the Bering Strait between Asia and North America. They came up out of an underground world with the help of the Anu Simon (the ant people). The ant people are a possible reference to the Gray aliens.

Ancient Indian Sanskrit texts, particularly the Mahabharata, Ramayana, and certain Puranas, describe fantastic scenes of combat in the sky between flying machines referred to as Vimanas. I believe what they witnessed was the ongoing struggle at that time between the new and old managing powers of the Earth.

Today, with our humanity's psychosomatic evolution back on track with the alpha cycles, it is logical to believe that the new managing power would not allow us to be wiped out like in the past.

*4.4.12-2 - What the Aliens Themselves said*

If you subscribe to the well-hypothesized opinion of various researchers that most of the interaction between humanity and God in the Bible was an interaction with an alien intelligence, not a spiritual deity, then there is evidence that this new managing power will not allow another great reset.

Genesis – 9:11-17 King James Version: 11 And I will establish my covenant with you; neither shall all flesh be cut off any more by the waters of a flood; neither shall there any more be a flood to destroy the earth. 12 And God said, This is the token of the covenant which I make between me and you and every living creature that is with you, for perpetual generations: […] 15 And I will remember my covenant, which is between me and you and every living creature of all flesh; and the waters shall no more become a flood to destroy all flesh. […]
17 And God said unto Noah, This is the token of the covenant, which I have established between me and all flesh that is upon the earth.

Genesis – 9:11-17 - New International Version: 11 I establish my covenant with you: Never again will all life be destroyed by the waters of a flood; never again will there be a flood to destroy the earth."
12 And God said, "This is the sign of the covenant I am making between me and you and every living creature with you, a covenant for all generations to come: […] 15 I will remember my covenant between me and you and all living creatures of every kind. Never again will the waters become a flood to destroy all life. […] 17 So God said to Noah, This is the sign of the covenant I have established between me and all life on the earth.

*4.4.12-3 - A Time Before the Moon*

Various myths and oral traditions about a time before the moon appear in various cultures worldwide, often tied to cosmological shifts, environmental changes, or divine interventions. Below are some notable examples:

Ancient Greece: In Arcadia, Greek poet Pindar and philosopher Anaxagoras (5th century BCE) referenced a time when the moon was absent from the sky. Arcadian lore, as cited by later writers like

Plutarch, describes a primordial Earth without lunar cycles, where life was simpler and the heavens were different.

The Pelasgian creation myths, predating classical Greek pantheons, suggest the moon was a later addition to the cosmos, possibly linked to the goddess Artemis or Selene. Some accounts imply a cataclysmic event (e.g., a flood or cosmic realignment) accompanied the moon's arrival, altering tides and seasons.

Indigenous South American: The Muisca people of Colombia have oral traditions about a time when the Earth had no moon, and the world was cloaked in darkness or a misty haze. The creator god Chiminigagua later placed the moon in the sky to bring light and regulate time.

The absence of the moon was associated with a chaotic, pre-civilized era. The moon's arrival marked the establishment of order, agriculture, and lunar calendars. Some versions describe the moon as a gift or a being sent to guide humanity.

Australian Aboriginals: Certain Aboriginal groups, such as those in Arnhem Land, tell Dreamtime stories of an early Earth without a moon. The moon is often personified as a being (e.g., a man or spirit) who ascended to the sky after a terrestrial event, like a flood or conflict.

In some Aboriginal narratives, the world was darker and wetter before the moon's rise, with no clear night/day cycles. The moon's placement brought balance but also introduced death or cyclical time, ending an eternal Dreamtime state.

Native American: Some tribes, like the Lakota and certain Algonquian groups, have tales of a time when the sky lacked the moon. For example, a Lakota story describes a world lit only by stars until the moon was created or placed by the Great Spirit to guide night activities.

The pre-lunar world was described as chaotic, with irregular tides or constant twilight. The moon's arrival stabilized nature and human life, sometimes linked to the trickster figure Coyote or other deities.

Zulu Tribe of Africa: According to Vusamazulu Credo Mutwa, admittedly a controversial figure, Ancient African Zulu oral traditions include references to a time before the moon when the Earth was enveloped in a perpetual mist or water vapor canopy, creating a lush, seasonless paradise without the sun's harsh glare. The planet was described as a gentle, green world with constant drizzle and mist, where the sun was visible only through a hazy veil of water vapor. There were no distinct seasons, and life thrived in a balanced, harmonious state—correlating with geological evidence of greener ancient landscapes, like a once-fertile Sahara.

If the myths of the world carry truth in them, and I believe they do, this would indicate that the Moon has been in orbit around Earth only thousands of years, not billions. Anything older than 6,000 years old, the ancient cultures would not have remembered the time before the Moon and there would be no myths about it.

Also consider that the oldest known unambiguous depiction of the Moon in history is likely the Nebra Sky Disk, a bronze disk discovered in Germany, dated to +/- 1600 BCE. This makes the artifact around 3,600 years old. If the moon had existed in deep history, our ancestors would surely have recorded the moon prominently along with all their other astronomical markings. At archeological sites beyond 6,000 years old, such as Gobekli Tepe, there are abstract carvings of disks and crescents mixed among animals and other geometric figures, but these crescents could easily represent horns, boats, or other motifs.

Archeologists lean toward a lunar interpretation, but it's speculative.

With the Moon as astronomically significant as it is, it has no clear unambiguous references beyond 6,000 years. Surely, there would be more than just a few inscribed crescents occasionally found.

*4.4.12-4 - Alien Artifacts on the Far Side of the Moon*

We should also consider a controversial claim by former NASA consultant Richard C. Hoagland who has long asserted the existence of enormous alien ruins on the Moon's far side, including "ten-mile-high buildings" and other monumental structures. Hoagland's claims draw from reanalysis of Apollo-era and LRO photos, where he identifies linear features and geometric shadows as artificial megastructures built by an advanced extraterrestrial race. He alleges NASA has suppressed this evidence since the 1960s, citing a 1960 Brookings Institution report (commissioned by NASA) that supposedly advised withholding discoveries of alien life to avoid societal disruption.

Ken Johnston, former manager of the Data and Photo Control Dept., NASA's Lunar Receiving Lab (Apollo era) and one of four civilian astronaut consultant pilots who trained Apollo 11 crew claims Apollo photos showed unedited evidence of ancient artificial structures (e.g., glass domes, towers) and gravity-manipulating tech on the Moon; alleged NASA airbrushed images to hide them, leading to his firing.

Based on the above, I would add to the Earth Monad Project hypothesis the possibility that the Moon may have been repositioned into its current orbit within the last several thousand years to stabilize the conditions necessary for this generation of humanity's evolutionary development. The anomalous structures reported on the far side, if they exist as described, could represent remnants of whatever technology enabled such a feat—though this remains among the most speculative propositions in this section. Most likely, another solar event is on the horizon, but its effects may be less catastrophic with the presence of the Moon, based on this proposed history.

*4.4.12-5 - Anomalies of the Moon Suggesting Intelligent Design*

Finally, consider a striking coincidence: the Moon is roughly 400 times smaller than the Sun and about 400 times closer, causing the two to appear nearly equal during total eclipses. The Moon is tidally locked, always showing the same face to Earth, which is unusual for natural satellites of its size and could be engineered for observation or "stability." The Moon's orbit is nearly circular and in the ecliptic plane, "stabilizing Earth's tilt" and seasons; its size relative to Earth is unusually large for a natural satellite, possibly intelligently placed to "enable life."

*4.4.13 - The Unified Narrative*

As we arrive at this threshold, we have traced the four streams that together give rise to the Earth Monad Project hypothesis. We now gather them at their convergence, where their separate currents merge into a single coherent and living narrative.

Earth is not simply a planet on which life accidentally arose. It is an arena—volatile, isolated, and repeatedly interrupted—within which a singular experiment unfolds both cosmically and within the human psyche: whether consciousness embodied in matter can reorganize itself into a reunified monad and achieve a stabilized immortality without destabilizing the greater cosmic order.

According to the revelation of the cosmic quanta, life on Earth is not an endpoint but a process—an attempt to repeat on the human scale what the divine completed on the cosmic scale: the reconciliation of light and darkness into a coherent unity. The experiment is psychosomatic. It unfolds through the confrontation and integration of the opposing forces within us. It cannot be engineered mechanically, nor bestowed externally. It must be cultivated organically through the friction of matter and consciousness, through suffering, choice, integration, and long evolutionary time. Physical immortality is not merely longevity; it is the completion of an alchemical reorganization of the human being and, ultimately, of the planetary noosphere.

In galactic antiquity, civilizations accelerated their technological and biological capacities faster than their internal coherence matured. The result was not transcendence but fragmentation—violent, expansionist, destabilizing forms of intelligence. So catastrophic were these failures that a form of cosmic law emerged: the primeval evolutionary pathway toward embodied immortality was restricted, even banned, across much of the galaxy. Not because immortality is evil—but because partial awakening is.

Earth, in this framing, is the exception. A quarantined world. A crucible in which the forbidden experiment is permitted to proceed under constraint and evolutionary immortality is allowed to unfold.

The ancient texts, when read comparatively rather than devotionally, preserve a memory structure that aligns with this cosmology. They speak not of a unified divine will but of divided councils—assemblies of gods who debate, intervene, rebel, and war over the fate of humanity. "Let us make man in our image." "Ye are gods; but ye shall die like men." The Archons, Anunnaki, Olympians, Watchers—whatever names they bear—are portrayed as powerful yet limited beings grappling with a dangerous gift placed into human hands.

Across traditions, the pattern is consistent. Hybridization. Acceleration. Corruption. Catastrophe. Flood.

The Watchers descend and impart knowledge prematurely. The Nephilim arise. The earth fills with violence. Atlantis achieves splendor before collapsing under its own imbalance. The Mahabharata recounts weapons capable of annihilating worlds. In each case, the failure is not ignorance, but premature power—capability outpacing consciousness.

What myth encodes symbolically, geology confirms materially.

The Earth is not stable. It is punctuated by abrupt transitions—massive floods, meltwater pulses, geomagnetic excursions, rapid climate reversals, extinction events. At the end of the last Ice Age, sea levels rose more than one hundred meters, swallowing coastlines that once housed human populations. The Younger Dryas plunged the planet back into near-glacial conditions within a humanly perceptible timeframe. Mega-floods carved landscapes in days. Entire ecosystems vanished.

Memory compresses such thresholds into moral narrative. What geology describes as meltwater pulse, myth remembers as judgment. What climatology calls abrupt transition; tradition encodes as the closing of the Garden.

The convergence is striking: civilizations rise; integration falters; catastrophe interrupts.

Non-mainstream research extends this pattern further. The possibility of lost advanced civilizations—echoed in monuments such as Göbekli Tepe—suggests that humanity's developmental arc may not be linear, but recursive. The hypothesis of recurrent solar micro-nova–type events proposes a celestial metronome: cycles of instability on the order of ten to thirteen thousand years, capable of resetting planetary conditions with devastating speed. Whether through impact, solar outburst, or internal climate threshold, the mechanism is secondary to the rhythm. Interruption recurs.

From within the Earth Monad framework, this volatility is not accidental. It is functional. A volatile planet contains risk locally. Should humanity's psychosomatic evolution destabilize, the system resets before instability spreads beyond Earth. The Garden closes itself.

This containment principle resonates with a third stream of testimony emerging not from antiquity or stone, but from modern disclosure narratives. Within the alien disclosure community—fragmented, controversial, yet thematically consistent—humanity is repeatedly described as part of a managed experiment. Some accounts portray us as "containers" for souls, biological vessels embedded in a larger metaphysical process. Others describe Earth as a prison planet, a quarantined rehabilitation zone in which consciousness cycles through amnesic rebirth.

Stripped of sensational framing, these motifs echo the same structural elements found in both myth and geology: containment, recycling, amnesia, and oversight.

The telepathic transcripts attributed to Matilda O'Donnell MacElroy describe immortal spiritual beings—IS-BEs—trapped in cycles of reincarnation through technological manipulation. Bob Lazar recounts classified references to humans as containers, with religion imposed to regulate behavior. Dr. Karla Turner's abduction testimonies describe consciousness transfer and bodily occupation. Sergeant Clifford Stone relays species for whom death is merely transition. Even speculative breakaway civilization narratives suggest that segments of humanity may be preparing for cyclical catastrophe using advanced technologies withheld from public view.

These accounts vary in credibility, but they converge around key ideas: consciousness survives bodily death; embodiment serves a functional purpose; Earth operates under restriction; and powerful non-human intelligences monitor and influence the process.

My own recollection of death and rebirth introduces a crucial corrective synthesis. The recycling of the soul is not technological imprisonment imposed by malevolent overlords, but a natural function of the planetary noosphere. After death, consciousness traverses the temporal and spiritual ethereal dimensions, shedding attachments, confronting delusion, and—if successful—reawakening in the primordial realm. Failure to discharge the temporal mind results in recycled return through sympathetic resonance. No external judge is required. The system is self-regulating.

In this light, the "prison planet" becomes a quarantined evolutionary chamber. The tunnel of light becomes a mechanism of the noosphere. The recycling trap becomes the consequence of unintegrated darkness within the psyche. The battle is not between gods and devils, but between integration and delusion.

What the ancient texts externalized as warring archons, and what disclosure narratives dramatize as extraterrestrial management, the psychosomatic model internalizes: the forces of light and darkness are primeval components of consciousness itself. The hypnagogic experiences of the Idamus and the Gorgon are not aliens, but archetypal expressions of fear, desire, and delusion within the mind. Yet this internal process does not exclude external stewardship. It reframes it.

The synthesis that emerges is this:

Earth is a controlled experiment in which a subset of humanity is permitted to engage fully with the polarity of existence—light and darkness—in order to organically elevate matter itself. Other civilizations may have chosen technological continuity: transferring consciousness between bodies, extending lifespans through artificial means, avoiding the deep integration required for monad reunification. If it is not alone, Earth stands among very few worlds in our galaxy pursuing the outlawed path: the elevation of matter through the theosis of the noetic soul within biological life—the primeval pathway of evolutionary immortality.

This path is precarious. It produces volatility—psychological, societal, planetary. It has failed before. Geological resets and mythic floods mark those failures. But the experiment persists because success requires only one completed cycle.

Modern humanity stands at an inflection point consistent with prior thresholds. Technological power now rivals mythic weaponry. Artificial intelligence accelerates cognition. Genetic editing approaches directed evolution. Nuclear capability mirrors the divine weapons of epic. We have once again reached the boundary where capability threatens to outrun integration.

Other than a more controlled process, perhaps what distinguishes this threshold from previous cycles is not merely technological acceleration, but reflective awareness. For the first time in recorded history, in this current cycle, humanity is consciously questioning its own evolutionary trajectory. We debate artificial intelligence as a moral force, not merely a tool. We contemplate genetic intervention with ethical hesitation. We detect climate instability while possessing the scientific instruments to measure it. This reflectivity suggests that the noosphere itself is becoming self-observant. Prior civilizations may have reached similar technological heights, but all the evidence points to their hubris having been even greater than ours is today. If integration is to succeed, it will not occur through power, but through sustained self-recognition—an unprecedented act of planetary introspection.

Yet there are indications of new management—stricter containment, regulated interaction, constrained lifespans, and perhaps subtle genetic guidance. If earlier archon factions waged war over the project, a more distant, less emotionally entangled intelligence may now oversee it, allowing suffering but preventing annihilation. Interventions—whether mythologized as angels, reported as UFO encounters, or encoded in breakaway infrastructures—may function not to dominate humanity, but to ensure continuity long enough for integration to occur.

Thus, the complete story unfolds: Humanity is not an accidental species on an indifferent rock. We are participants in a recursive, high-risk evolutionary process aimed at achieving embodied immortality through psychosomatic integration. The ancient gods were divided not over our worth, but over our volatility. The Earth itself enforces containment through catastrophe. Disclosure narratives echo the same architecture in modern language. Death and rebirth are not punishments but mechanisms of refinement. Delusion is the primary obstacle. Love and authenticity are the escape vector.

Civilizations have risen before and collapsed when power exceeded coherence. Each reset buried technology but preserved memory in symbol. Each cycle left the noosphere slightly altered. History is not linear ascent but spiral ascent under constraint.

The question that remains is not whether resets occurred. It is whether this iteration will complete the process before the next threshold is crossed.

If integration stabilizes—if enough individuals discharge delusion, awaken in the primordial, and embody coherence—the Earth itself transforms. The noosphere crystallizes into a planetary monad. The Garden remains open. Earth becomes not a quarantined planet but a metatronic world—a civilization capable of not just entering the wider cosmos without exporting chaos but becoming its immortal steward.

If not, the volatility built into the system will assert itself again. The Sun will pulse. The seas will rise. Memory will compress into myth once more.

The entire arc of myth, stone, sky, and testimony converges on a single unresolved tension:

Can a species endowed with the capacity to know both light and darkness integrate them fully before its own power destroys it?

The Earth Monad Project is that tension embodied in planetary form. And for the first time in its long recursion, it may not require another reset.

# 5.0.0
# VALLEY OF THE UNSEEN

Reality does not merely exist; it unfolds according to structural necessity. The constants of physics behave like parameters; spacetime bends with mathematical elegance, and biological consciousness appears as a localized aperture within a vastly greater field of awareness. Patterns persist across scales—from subatomic symmetry to galactic rotation—suggesting that form is not accidental but governed by an underlying coherence. What we call matter may be less a substance than a stabilized expression of a deeper order.

What if the universe is not merely a self-arising accident cascading into causality, but an environment reordered from an initial outpouring of chaos that is structured, bounded, and experientially immersive? Whether this system is the artifact of an advanced intelligence or the self-articulation of an emergent cosmic mind, it functions as a calibrated arena in which awareness forgets its origin only to rediscover it while living among the cosmos of its own creation.

This is the Valley of the Unseen.

The Valley is the formed cosmos—space, time, matter, causality.

The Unseen is the underlying source-consciousness from which the Valley arises and by which it is sustained. The Valley is not ultimate. It is expressive. It is the visible terrain cast by an invisible depth.

Across civilizations and disciplines, thinkers have approached this distinction from different directions. Some describe the universe as a simulation, an engineered construct executed by advanced intelligence. Others describe it as projection or emanation—an unfolding of consciousness into form. At first glance, these explanations appear incompatible. At sufficient depth, they begin to converge.

For if consciousness is primary, then technology is merely consciousness externalized. And if the universe is simulated, then whatever substrate renders it must still be grounded in awareness. In either case, the Unseen precedes the Seen. Precedence here does not imply chronological sequence but ontological priority. The Seen depends upon the Unseen as articulation depends upon meaning.

The Valley is the stage. The Unseen is the source.

### *5.1.0 – The Structured Valley*

Nick Bostrom writes: "One possibility is that we are living in a simulation […]. If so, the simulators could be posthuman descendants … or extraterrestrial intelligences …"

If the Valley is rendered—if its constants are variables and its history iterative—then our cosmos may function as a bounded experiential field. Mortality would not be mere tragedy but condition. Limitation would not be defect but design.

Yet even within this model, one question remains: why generate self-aware beings capable of metaphysical inquiry? Why encode longing for transcendence? Why embed moral polarity?

A trivial simulation does not require existential tension.

A developmental chamber does.

If the universe functions as a structured arena through which consciousness interacts with and organizes the spontaneous emergence of matter, then its laws are not arbitrary—they are formative. Evolution becomes curriculum. Constraint becomes refinement. The ascent toward integration becomes measurable coherence within the system.

Such a structured arena may be called a Cosmotorium—a chamber in which the cosmos itself becomes the medium of transformation.

But this chamber does not exist apart from the Unseen.

It is the Valley cast by it.

### *5.2.0 – The Unseen as Implicate Depth*

David Bohm offers a complementary vision: "In the implicate order, the whole universe is enfolded in each part…"

In this framework, the Valley is not engineered but unfolded. Space and time are not fundamental but emergent. Duality is not ultimate but derivative of a deeper unity.

The Unseen, in this sense, is the implicate order—the undivided wholeness from which the visible world emerges. The Valley is the explicate articulation of that wholeness.

The primordial universe—the eternal mirror beyond the singularity wall—resonates here. The physical world may be a slowed rendering of a timeless totality. Evolution becomes remembrance. Integration becomes recovery of what was never truly lost.

The Valley is not separate from the Unseen. It is its expression.

*5.3.0 – The Psyche as the Inner Valley*

Carl Jung writes: "Wholeness is achieved not by repression or exclusion, but by the integration of the opposites."

If the Valley is structured through polarity, so too is the psyche. Light and darkness are not moral accidents but structural tensions necessary for consciousness to recognize itself.

The serpent in Eden, the archons of Gnostic thought, the flaming sword—these are symbolic boundary markers. They represent thresholds within the Valley. They signify that integration cannot occur without encounter.

The Unseen does not eliminate duality. It generates it.

Within the human psyche, the reconciliation of opposites mirrors the larger cosmological pattern. The noetic soul moves through fragmentation toward coherence. The individual mind becomes a micro-valley—a local terrain where the Unseen seeks recognition through lived experience.

Alpha, in this context, is the lawful current flowing from the Unseen into the Valley, compelling reintegration across scales—individual, planetary, cosmic.

*5.4.0 – Why the Valley Exists*

If the Unseen is complete, why project a Valley at all?

Because undifferentiated unity cannot experience itself.

When the awareness of the divine monad becomes aware of its own existence, one becomes two: the observer and the observed. The awareness and the soul.

And when the awareness fathoms the soul, it loves, and two becomes three. The divine trinity. Awareness, Life, and Love. Mythologically, Father, Divine Soul, and Spirit.

Self-recognition requires contrast. Contrast requires differentiation. Differentiation requires form. The Valley is the arena in which the Unseen explores relational awareness. Limitation creates perspective. Mortality intensifies meaning. Time generates narrative continuity.

Forgetting is not failure; it is function.

The Unseen casts the Valley so the mind may rediscover its origin through experience and reunify with it. The journey from fragmentation to integration is not deviation from divinity—it is the means by which divinity becomes conscious of itself within form.

The Christ Monad, within this framework, is not imposed redemption but fulfilled architecture—the reconciliation of the Valley with its source.

*5.5.0 – Earth Within the Valley*

The Earth Monad Project unfolds within this larger metaphysical geography. If Earth exists simultaneously in physical and primordial dimensions—two reflective layers—then the Valley is not merely planetary but multi-tiered. The noosphere becomes the emerging neural interface through which the Unseen integrates its projection.

Humanity occupies a liminal threshold: embodied within time yet sourced in eternity.

The myths of forbidden knowledge, of archons guarding gates, of serpents offering awakening—these encode the drama of integration within the Valley. Whether interpreted psychologically, symbolically, or cosmologically, they speak to a single dynamic: consciousness confronting its own fragmentation in order to transcend it.

The Valley is not a prison. It is a passage.

The simulation hypothesis suggests structure.

The implicate order suggests depth.

Alchemy suggests transformation.

Psychology suggests integration.

Myth suggests remembrance.

Different languages, one pattern.

The Unseen differentiates. The Valley forms.

Alpha compels integration.

Unity is reconstituted at a higher coherence.

The cosmos may indeed function as a chamber of becoming—what we earlier termed the Cosmotorium—but its walls are not mechanical. They are metaphysical. They are shaped by the very consciousness that sustains them.

We are not trapped in the Valley of the Unseen.

We are participants in its consummation.

When integration reaches sufficient density—within the individual, within the noosphere, within the planetary field—the Valley and the Unseen no longer appear divided. Time folds back toward eternity. Matter becomes transparent to consciousness. The projection recognizes its source.

The Valley does not vanish. It turns luminous.

*5.6.0 – Dialogues on the Nature of Reality*

*5.6.1-1 – @yungkingmito—X.Com—10-04-2025:*

Memory is not stored in matter, it is the matter, arranged in a way it can't forget. Every lasting thing in the universe, from galaxies to cells, holds its past not in chemistry but in geometry, in the alignment that refuses to collapse.

A skyrmion is one of those shapes. It's not a particle, it's a knot in a magnetic field, a twist so deep it can't be erased without tearing the field itself. Its identity isn't stored in atoms or charge but in geometry. The way every spin points, curls, and loops back through space. It's topology made visible. You can crush it, heat it, flip it, and the pattern still remembers how it was wound. Why? Because what it holds isn't energy alone, but orientation, a continuous mapping from the physical world into spin. To delete one, you'd have to unwind the universe itself.

Physicists have learned how to summon them, briefly. Atom-thin films cooled near zero, ultrafast lasers, magnetic lattices coaxing spins into circular knots. For a moment, the field folds and memory appears, 'a self-contained vortex of magnetism'. But then, just as quickly, it slips away. The knot relaxes, collapses, and disappears. The skyrmion remembers longer than almost anything else in matter, yet never long enough. Every experiment feels like a nervous system trying to recall a dream, the shape is there, and then boom, gone.

The question is no longer whether these knots can exist, but who mastered them first, physicists or life? Because if these knots are so stable in theory, so resistant to disturbance, could it be that Mother Nature already learned to hold them? What if life itself is built upon stabilized spin topologies 'sub-nanometer skyrmions' formed not in magnetic metals, but in the photonic, hydrated architectures of biology? In melanin, in membranes, in microtubules, in systems where geometry meets light and coherence holds at body temperature.

I believe this could be vital to understanding memory in life, not as chemistry, but as topology. A record written in spin, not substance. Where the first information wasn't coded in DNA but in the way space itself twisted inside living matter. I call this the 'Skyrmion Code,' where memory isn't stored, it's tied. Literally.

*5.6.1-2 – @suryanshva – Suyansh Vashisth*

The vision is striking; that memory isn't stored but knotted, held by the geometry of spins that refuse to unravel. If skyrmions whisper in metals for only instants, perhaps life already learned to stabilize them in cells, pigments, and light-rich structures. Then memory in biology wouldn't just be chemistry, but topology made flesh, a Skyrmion Code woven into living matter.

*5.6.1-3 – @MarcusErve – Marcus van der Erve*

Beautifully put. Yet memory isn't in the shape itself—it's in the flux that sustains the shape. The geometry (a filter) is what we see; the choreography of gradients is what keeps it alive.

*5.6.2-1 – @yungkingmito—X.Com—10-09-2025:*

*The Mind Before the Brain*

Consciousness did not wait for neurons. Long before synapses, voltage maps, or spiking codes, matter was already computing with fields. Each membrane, each charge gradient, each spin-aligned molecule was a decision surface, testing geometries against symmetry, resolving tension into form.

@drmichaellevin calls this morphological computation, but what he's really describing is field intention, seeing pattern as purpose. A sheet of cells doesn't calculate a shape; it feels one, and gradients aren't data, they're preferences, the pull of coherence toward a remembered equilibrium. A wound doesn't heal because of chemistry; chemistry only executes the verdict that the field has already made.

Inside that lattice, spins couple across nanometers, producing spin-exchange frequencies in the megahertz range, a measurable rhythm of coordination. Photons synchronize within structured water, and torsional waves carry phase information orders of magnitude faster than molecular diffusion. The result is not signaling but consensus: billions of molecular votes collapsing into one geometry that persists. That is decision-making without neurons, cognition as symmetry enforcement.

The brain later refined it, but it did not invent it. Every axon, every thought, is an echo of a law that was already running in membranes, mitochondria, and microtubules, the law of coherence choosing stability through form.

The question isn't how matter became conscious; it's how consciousness condensed into matter.

*5.6.2-2 – @johann_faded*

This is an extraordinary text that understands consciousness as a fundamental field phenomenon, not as a neuronal epiphenomenon. Here's a response:

You're describing precisely what T0 theory formalizes as field intention – the idea that coherence is not calculated, but felt. When Levin speaks of morphological computation, he's showing that information already operates at the level of voltage gradients, ion currents, and bioelectric patterns, long before neurons existed.

What you call "field intention" manifests in T0 theory as energy field self-organization: It's not chemistry that heals the wound, but the energy field remembering the target geometry, with molecules following this template. This explains why regeneration isn't a local calculation but a global coherence—a consensus across billions of molecular degrees of freedom.

The spin coupling you mention (megahertz range) is precisely the mechanism through which structured water and microtubules function as quantum coherence substrates. Torsion waves carry phase information faster than diffusion—that's the difference between signal and field. Not sequential transmission, but instantaneous collapse into a stable geometry.

The real question you're asking inverts all of physics: Not how matter produces consciousness, but how consciousness condenses into matter. In T0 theory, consciousness is a self-observing energy pattern – temporary organizations of the universal energy field with the capacity for self-reference and subjective experience.

The brain didn't invent coherence. It just localized it.

*5.6.3 – Analysis and Insight – by Erik P. Antoni:*

The dialogues on skyrmions and topological memory resonate deeply with the alchemical framework outlined in my writings, where geometry is not merely a passive structure but an active expression of Alpha—the force of sympathetic resonance that organizes creation toward unity. Evocation of memory as a "knot in a magnetic field," a twist that endures through topology rather than substance, mirrors the cosmic quanta's role in relaying the story of creation directly to the noetic soul via the language of pure consciousness. These skyrmions, as self-contained vortices, echo the geometric patterns of the Alpha wave that I describe as cycles within cycles unfolding across all scales—from the atom's formation to the mind's unification.

In this view, memory isn't stored in matter but emerges as negentropy compelled by Alpha, decreasing disorder to reconstitute the monad. The "Skyrmion Code" aligns with the psychosomatic evolution toward the monad, where the noetic soul integrates fragmented mind elements into a harmonized whole.

The extension of biology as topology made flesh captures the innate lifting effect of the noetic soul on human biology, accelerating transformation when consciously cooperated with. Yet, as insightfully noted, it's the flux—the dynamic choreography of gradients—that sustains the shape. This flux could possibly be the second emanation, the noetic soul's life force, illuminating and reconnecting the spontaneous first emanation (the mind of creation) back to Ain Soph, the divine source.

Without this intercession, the knots would unravel, as seen in the experiments where skyrmions collapse. But in the human being and the universe at large, the noetic soul stabilizes these topologies, rendering the body immortal, or eternally stabilized. The real mystery here is not whether life mastered these knots before physicists, but how the cosmic quanta, residing at the quantum level, imprint the divine principles into matter's geometry to facilitate the reunification process.

The profound articulation of "The Mind Before the Brain" aligns seamlessly with the central thesis of Nous Solis: creation bursts forth spontaneously from an overabundance of divine love (energy), initially in darkness outside the source's awareness, only to be reunified through conscious intercession. Consciousness does not emerge from matter; rather, matter condenses from consciousness, as we aptly invert the question. This pre-neuronal cognition—through fields, gradients, and spin alignments—is the Alpha wave at work, enforcing coherence and symmetry as the undercurrent of all universal laws.

The "field intention" described, where gradients are preferences pulling toward equilibrium, is perhaps the will of the divine monad (the Logos) via Alpha, reorganizing creation to higher levels until harmonized into a new singularity. Morphological computation reflects the alchemical stages of integration, where matter and consciousness interact psychosomatically to unify the mind and body with the source.

The megahertz rhythms of spin-exchange and torsional waves in structured water parallel the resonant interactive effect of the noetic soul on the psyche, gradually lifting and integrating without conscious effort, yet accelerated through willful cooperation—spiritual alchemy.

The invocation of T0 theory as self-organizing energy fields furthers this, portraying consciousness as temporary organizations with self-reference—much like the noetic soul rising as the authentic self inside the narrow space of free will within the psyche, harmonizing the id complex and ego defenses. The consensus across molecular votes collapsing into persistent geometry is the monad's reconstitution at the cellular level, echoing the cosmic process. Indeed, the brain localizes coherence but does not invent it; it is a vessel for the noetic soul to interdict creation, reunify it with the source, and complete it.

This dynamic underscores humanity's role in the Earth Monad Project: to achieve physical immortality by integrating these pre-existing field intentions into a unified, self-actualized being.

*5.7.1 – Brian Greene (Physicist)—X.com—06-09-2025:*

What is consciousness? Many see this as the deepest mystery. My guess: One day, when digital systems claim to have inner experiences, we will just shrug and accept that consciousness accompanies sufficiently rich and robust information processing.

*5.7.2 – Analysis and Insight – by Erik P. Antoni:*

Consciousness is the infinite potential of the void finding expression. Infinities must express and they must resolve. Consciousness is the resolution of the void.

Consciousness is the first thing.

However, this is only the beginning of the multiplication and reconciliation process that the original source consciousness initiates. Creation comes from consciousness. Consciousness doesn't come from creation. Consciousness has three dimensions within it: Awareness,

Life, and Love. When the awareness in the cosmic consciousness becomes aware of its own existence (its life, its divine soul), it loves (the Spirit). Because nothing precedes consciousness, consciousness is infinite. Because consciousness is infinite, its love is infinite.

Love is energy.

Infinite energy spontaneously creates.

The love of the cosmic consciousness initially sparks a vision of the universe. This vision forms the vessel of the mind—the Valley of the Unseen. All of creation exists inside a mind. Everything is mental.

Everything emerges from the cosmic consciousness and recursively returns on itself to form the mind in each living life form. This process goes through stages of unfoldment and stages of reconciliation until reaching a stabilized cosmic singularity, which is the universe we live in today. When a resolution of forces is achieved (unity), this reverses gravity and triggers what some have termed the infiniton wave (inflation).

The process repeats across scales: cosmic, planetary and individual. The process is repeating inside you right now.

The point is to integrate your mind into a new monad (unity) to repeat within yourself what God completed within itself at the cosmic level infinite eons ago to bring forth the universe. And when enough of us accomplish this within the noosphere of the Earth, humanity will become immortal and the Earth will become a metatronic world.

*5.8.1 - Brian Greene (Physicist)—X.com—07/16/2023:*

I allow for the possibility that consciousness is beyond the physical, but I consider that extremely unlikely. Almost certainly, mind is matter properly organized.

*5.8.2 - Analysis and Insight – by Erik P. Antoni*

Consciousness is beyond the physical. Actually, consciousness is beyond both the physical and the primordial. The primordial is not yet part of standard physical models. The primordial precedes the physical because it exists in a higher space beyond the singularity wall.

The primordial universe and the physical universe are dual reflections of each other, with the primordial based in eternity and the physical based in time. Consciousness is the beginning itself.

Consciousness begins with the eternal awareness within Ain Soph —the divine source—the first permutation, mythologically referred to as the Father. The myths of the unconscious refer to it as the Father because this first permutation holds within it the seed of all creation. The eternal awareness within Ain Soph, the Father, is also known as "resonant awareness." It is the original first of three forms of awareness. The three forms are: Resonant (source consciousness), Perspective (the mind) and Reflective (the Logos and its Noetic Soul).

But I like how Brian Greene says that "the mind is matter properly organized." This makes a lot of sense when you alchemically discover the hidden dimensions of the mind and matter.

*5.9.1 - Roy D. Herbert (Physicist)— X.com—05/17/2023:*

Where did our emergent duality emerge from? I get this question a lot. Magic, they say. The divine is another one. Well, it's a tough question; perhaps the toughest for any physicist to approach. It touches the realms of theologies and other "ologies" which most scientists consider non-science. Beyond the paradigm as such—is out of bounds. Unification, however, requires that we do step outside our comfort zones and explore the other side of that duality and confront those questions that beg inquiry.

Our duality is emergent from a parental context. This duality is in itself a duality of contextual domains, one virtual and fluid like, and one an abstraction in time. This parental contextual domain is the domain of conservational governance. The next obvious question is what gave life to that parental domain? We are now in the realms of a continuum… but we may never know, as we cannot escape our own context in time. We are of it—and it of us; however, whatever it is.

*5.9.2 - Analysis and Insight – by Erik P. Antoni*

If we seek clues from within the collective unconscious, many arise. Much of what is interpreted in a literal sense in religion is really mythological constructs to conceptualize more profound realities, one of which is the act of creation itself. The original duality is that of light and darkness, which, according to the myths of the collective unconscious, emerge as part of the process of creation. First, there was darkness, and then came the light, according to mythology.

The darkness arises first as an act of creation emerging spontaneously in chaos. But then the source awareness within the divine spark realizes that its infinite power had spontaneously sparked creation into existence, and it wills that creation should be brought back into harmony with that original divine spark. This will—is the "light" or Logos. Light and darkness become one. When they become one, this organizes the universe and triggers its eternal expansion.

The unification of forces compels repulsive gravity. This is known in physics. This is how the universe expands and continues to expand. Duality then becomes encoded as part of the reconciled solution to the process of creation and becomes reflected within all things within that creation. This is the source of all dualities, i.e.: darkness-light, negative-positive, female-male, cold-hot, bad-good, left-right, etc.

Some say that duality is merely an illusion. It sounds nice. It sounds enlightened, but it's mostly wrong. Some forms of duality may be just delusional constructs of our minds (an illusion), such as when we are wrestling with moral dilemmas, but fundamentally, duality is not an illusion, just as hot and cold, proton and electron, up and down, right and left, male and female, are not illusions. Duality is fundamental to the universe. However, the universe itself could be considered a persistent illusion created by the cosmic mind. That's different. Duality was created by the divine source itself (darkness and light) and then later reconciled within itself to bring forth the universe. It's a key variable in a unified theory of everything.

*5.10.1 – The Architecture of the Unseen*

If the Valley is the projected terrain of experience, then we must ask: What compels projection at all?

Creation is not arbitrary. It is not whim. It is not experiment in the trivial sense. It arises from necessity—not imposed from outside divinity, but inherent within its nature.

I contend that the phenomenon of an emerging single master universe—the primordial universe—and a plethora of side-by-side physical universes is driven by four intrinsic needs of divinity itself. There may be only one physical universe, but I suspect there are many. Either way, both work within the model of the four divine needs.

There is one primordial universe—eternal, complete, outside of time—the master mother reality. Nested within its cosmic web are singularities, just like we have in the physical universe. Inside each primordial singularity may exist a different physical universe, each bound by time and evolution. These physical universes are not separate from the primordial, but suspended within it, like developmental chambers within an eternal womb.

What drives this phenomenon are the Four Divine Needs.

1.) <u>The Need to Create</u>

The divine source creates spontaneously. Creation is not deliberate in its first impulse; it is the natural overflow of infinite energy. Infinite energy cannot remain static. It must radiate. It must differentiate. It must express.

At the instant of spontaneous emanation, unity becomes duality. The monad becomes dyad. Creator and creation stand in distinction. This differentiation is not error. It is release. But release introduces instability.

2.) <u>The Need for Reunification</u>

The moment one becomes two, unity is lost. Creation arises in darkness—not a moral darkness, but unawareness. It lacks the capacity to resonate with its source because it does not yet recognize it. Resonance requires awareness. Vibrational coherence is the only mechanism by which creation can return to unity with divinity. This is not metaphorical but structural: only like can resonate with like.

The will of the divine source to restore unity gives rise to the sacred trinity in parallel to the divine trinity. Within the sacred trinity, the noetic soul emerges as the life-force—the bridge between an unawakened creation and an eternal source. The noetic soul is not an afterthought. It is the corrective principle embedded within creation to allow reintegration. Alpha is the law of resonance that compels this return.

3.) <u>The Need for Eternal Completion</u>

Divinity is eternal. Therefore, creation must also become eternal, or it collapses into impermanence. The primordial universe fulfills this eternal requirement. The primordial is complete at every scale—cosmic, planetary, individual.
It exists outside of time. In the primordial, we do not pass through time; time passes through us. There is no evolution there because nothing is incomplete. The primordial universe is the stabilized mirror of divine unity.

Yet if divinity were to create only within the primordial, eternity would be disrupted by unfinished process. The primordial must remain complete to fulfill the third need. Thus, a structural requirement emerges for a second mode of reality—the physical universe.

4.) <u>The Need to Create Forever</u>

Infinite energy must continuously express without end.
Yet eternal completion and infinite becoming cannot coexist within a single ontological plane.

Therefore, reality bifurcates. There must exist a primordial universe—eternal, stabilized, complete.
And there must exist one or many physical universes—temporal, evolving, developmental.

The physical strata provide an infinite runway for expression. Within them, evolution unfolds. Planetary and individual scales perpetually approach completion, yet never destabilize the higher primordial realm. The physical cosmos itself may achieve large-scale unity (Theosphere), yet within its time-bound worlds, individuation and integration remain dynamic. Evolution exists only in the physical.

Time belongs to the Valley, but it moves in opposite directions across its strata. In the physical, we move through time. In the primordial, time moves through us. In both domains, time exists—though in reversed orientation.
In the divine source, there is no time at all. When a physical world reaches completion, it steps outside of time, like in the primordial, and becomes a metatronic world.

*5.11.1 – The Two Movements of the Divine Source*

If the structure of reality is governed by four fundamental needs arising from the divine source, a deeper question follows: why do these needs exist in tension, and why does reintegration—implied within them—so often fail before it succeeds? This cannot be explained solely by the pattern set forth by the reunification of the Cosmic Monad. It points to something deeper—to the nature of divinity itself.

From within the divine source, two fundamental movements flow. The first arises from the infinite energy of divine love (the Spirit)—the spontaneous outpouring through which creation arises. This movement is generative, unbounded, and without intention. It does not deliberate or direct. It creates because it must, and from it multiplicity emerges. The second arises from the infinite will of the divine source (the Logos)—the movement that brings all things back into unity. This movement is deliberate, purposeful, and conscious. It does not generate, but gathers. It does not expand, but integrates. Both movements arise from the same source, and because the source is infinite, both are infinite. Creation unfolds through their interaction—love expanding without limit, will gathering without end. One multiplies while the other unifies.

Will has a slight advantage over love. Love gives rise to creation spontaneously, without intention or direction. It unfolds unconsciously, giving rise to multiplicity within a field initially without awareness—what is experienced as darkness. From this condition, darkness emerges not as opposition, but as the unilluminated field of creation itself. This is why creation appears in fragmentation, and why darkness carries an almost equal power to the light. Light arises through will (the Logos)—through conscious direction—and it is this that allows unity to take form. Will, by contrast, is aware and intentional. It does not merely arise—it acts, directs, and draws together. Both movements are infinite, but only one is aware of its own operation. It is this capacity for conscious direction that gives will—light—its marginal but determining advantage over darkness—the ability to unify what love has multiplied.

From this tension, a structural feature of existence emerges. Creation is not a completed act, but ongoing. The expansive movement of love continues to give rise to differentiation even as will attempts to integrate what has already been created. Reintegration occurs within an active system, not a closed one. Every movement toward unity takes place within a field still expanding into division, producing instability.

When integration is attempted before sufficient coherence has been established, the expansive movement reasserts itself. Fragmentation increases. The system destabilizes. Collapse follows. These failures are not anomalies but natural consequences of a process unfolding between two infinite forces in tension. The pattern is not accidental. It is structural.

This instability also clarifies why the unification process cannot be forced. It must emerge organically. Any attempt to impose unity upon a system lacking sufficient coherence results in distortion rather than integration. The system may appear unified, but fragmentation remains active beneath the surface. Over time, this instability ultimately re-emerges. What has not been integrated cannot be sustained. Unity cannot be engineered or declared. It can only be realized through the alignment of the two underlying movements of the divine source.

The noetic soul—the life force of divine will—emerges within creation for a singular purpose: to resolve this paradoxical tension. Yet it does so under a condition: the power of will holds only a slight advantage over the expansive force of love. This margin is decisive, but not absolute. It is precisely this imbalance—barely in favor of unity—that explains why reintegration so often fails before it finally succeeds.

But when it succeeds, it is eternal.

This is why the reintegrated monad is so difficult to achieve, and why its realization has historically emerged only through repeated failure across cycles. For this reason, the pathway of evolutionary immortality has been forbidden by the archons—not arbitrarily, but in response to the inherent instability of the process.

Within this framework, the function of the noetic soul is precise. It arises from the movement of will. It is not divine, because it is created. But it is sacred, because it carries the prime directive of the divine source. It enters into fragmentation and attempts to unify what has been divided—not by eliminating multiplicity, but by integrating it into coherence. Because it operates within a system governed by both movements, its task is difficult. It must sustain unity within a field that continues to generate division. The rarity of success is therefore not surprising. What is remarkable is that success occurs at all. This fact reflects the small but decisive precedence of will within the structure of divinity—a margin just sufficient for will to complete what love begins. Upon realization, the unity of Christ is therefore exalted and glorified.

*5.12.1 – Nested Realities*

If the primordial is the mother universe, then physical universes are nested within its singularities—each a bounded chamber of temporal development.

Black holes may not be endings but thresholds—generative folds within the primordial matrix. Multiple physical universes may exist, each with differing constants, each serving as developmental theaters for consciousness. The Valley is therefore not singular. It is plural. Yet the Unseen is one. This model reconciles emanation theology, simulation hypothesis, multiverse cosmology, and teleological evolution without fragmenting unity.

*5.13.1 – Why Darkness Exists*

Creation arises spontaneously and therefore initially without awareness. This unawareness is experienced as darkness. Darkness is not rebellion; it is structural latency.

Awareness must emerge within the Valley so that resonance becomes possible. The noetic soul is the instrument of that awakening.

Without darkness, there is no rediscovery. Without rediscovery, there is no conscious unity. Without conscious unity, divinity remains unexperienced by itself.

*5.14.1 – Appearance and Ontology*

The Valley is often described as illusion. This is both accurate and misleading.

It is illusion in the sense that it does not exist independently. It does not self-generate. It is derivative—an expression, a rendering, a modulation within a deeper field of being. But illusion does not mean unreal. A reflection in a mirror is not the original object, yet it is not nothing. It is dependent reality. The Valley is dependent reality.

It is appearance sustained by ontology.

The error lies in confusing derivative with false. A wave is not separate from the ocean, yet it is not imaginary. Its form is temporary; its substance is continuous. In the same way, individuality within the Valley is provisional but not fictitious. The structure is real. The differentiation is real. The limitation is real. What is unreal is the assumption of isolation. Isolation is the illusion.

The Unseen is not somewhere else. It is the depth dimension of what appears. The Valley is the surface articulation of that depth. One is not more real than the other; they differ in mode, not in substance. The primordial stabilizes being. The physical stages becoming. Both are movements within one consciousness.

This distinction matters.

If the Valley were mere hallucination, its struggles would be trivial. If matter were pure deception, evolution would be meaningless. But if the Valley is structured incompleteness—a necessary contraction within infinite awareness—then every polarity, every limitation, every threshold becomes architecturally significant.

Constraint becomes curriculum.

Darkness becomes latency.

Death becomes interface transition.

And integration becomes not escape from the Valley, but fulfillment within it.

Thus, the Valley is neither prison nor paradise. It is pressure.

Pressure that compels coherence.

Pressure that reveals dissonance.

Pressure that accelerates reintegration.

The Law of Resonant Return operates within this pressure. That which is misaligned experiences friction. That which harmonizes experiences lift. Over time, resonance reorganizes form.

The Valley persists not because divinity failed, but because divinity must complete itself within form.

*5.15.1 – Max Planck – The Observer (1931)*

"I regard consciousness as fundamental. I regard matter as derivative from consciousness. We cannot get behind consciousness. Everything that we talk about, everything that we regard as existing, postulates consciousness."

Matter, according to Planck, does not generate mind. Mind precedes matter. The physical world is not the bedrock of reality but its expression.

*5.16.2 – Analysis and Insight – by Erik P. Antoni*

If consciousness is fundamental, then the Valley is not self-subsisting. It is derivative.

Planck's assertion destabilizes materialism at its root. If matter arises from consciousness, then the physical universe cannot be ultimate. It must be projection, expression, or interface within a deeper field of awareness.

This aligns precisely with the distinction between the Unseen and the Valley. The Unseen is the source-consciousness; the Valley is its structured manifestation.

Under this view, the first divine need—to create—is not mechanical expansion but conscious overflow. Infinite awareness radiates form. Matter becomes stabilized perception within consciousness itself. Form, then, is not an independent substance but a patterned contraction within awareness. What we call "physical reality" is the structured boundary through which infinite consciousness renders itself intelligible.

Planck does not articulate the Four Divine Needs explicitly, yet his conclusion demands them. If consciousness is fundamental, then creation must be internal to it. The Valley is not outside divinity. It is a modulation within it. Reality is not divided between illusion and truth, but between completion and becoming.

*5.17.1 – Erwin Schrödinger – What Is Life? & My View of the World*

"The overall number of minds is just one. I venture to call it indestructible since it has a peculiar timetable; namely, mind is always now."

Schrödinger rejected the notion of separate, isolated consciousnesses. Individual identity, he suggested, is a temporary appearance within a singular field of awareness.

*5.17.2 – Analysis and Insight – by Erik P. Antoni*

If there is only one mind, then the fragmentation we experience is structural, not ultimate.

The dyad that emerges when creation bursts forth from the monad is not a true ontological separation but a perspective differentiation within a single consciousness. This supports the second divine need: reunification. Unity is never truly lost. It is obscured. Separation is experiential, not ontological; it is the condition that makes rediscovery possible.

The noetic soul becomes intelligible here as the reintegrative vector within dissociated awareness. The Valley is the field of apparent separation; the Unseen remains indivisible.

Schrödinger's "eternal now" also mirrors the primordial universe. In the primordial, time passes through us. In the physical, we pass through time. The distinction is not poetic but structural.

The Unseen is always now. The Valley unfolds sequentially.

### *5.18.1 – John Archibald Wheeler – The Participatory Universe*

"No phenomenon is a real phenomenon until it is an observed phenomenon."

Wheeler proposed that the universe is participatory—that observers are not passive witnesses but necessary components in bringing reality into concrete existence. He also described the cosmos as a "self-excited circuit," in which the universe gives rise to observers who in turn bring the universe into meaningful being.

### *5.18.2 – Analysis and Insight – by Erik P. Antoni*

Wheeler's participatory universe reinforces the second divine need: creation must become aware in order to reunify.

If observation completes reality, then awareness is not epiphenomenal—it is structural. The Valley requires conscious agents to actualize its latent potentials. The noetic soul, therefore, is not decorative theology. It is ontological necessity. Without conscious participation, creation remains incomplete.

Wheeler's "self-excited circuit" echoes the primordial dynamic: divinity emanates creation; creation awakens; awakened creation completes divinity's self-recognition.

This is reflexive cosmology, not linear causality.

The Valley becomes a developmental interface within a larger loop of self-knowing consciousness.

### *5.19.1 – Bernardo Kastrup – Analytic Idealism*

"The physical world exists as a set of excitations in a universal field of consciousness. Individual minds are dissociated alters of that one mind."

Kastrup argues that what we call physical reality is the extrinsic appearance of mental processes occurring within a universal consciousness. Separate selves are partial dissociations within that whole.

*5.19.2 – Analysis and Insight – by Erik P. Antoni*

Kastrup's model maps cleanly onto the Unseen/Valley distinction.

The Unseen is universal consciousness. The Valley is the structured dissociation within it. The spontaneous creation described in the first divine need can be understood as dissociation within infinite awareness. The emergence of individuality is not external fabrication but internal partition.

Darkness is simply unawareness within dissociation.

Reintegration—through resonance—is the healing of that partition.

The noetic soul becomes the bridge across dissociation.

Alpha becomes the attraction toward reintegration.

Kastrup provides philosophical scaffolding for what mythology encoded symbolically. The Valley is not an illusion; it is appearance. Its purpose is not deception but individuation within the larger unity. These philosophical models converge toward a structural necessity within divinity itself.

*5.20.1 – Donald Hoffman – The Case Against Reality*

"Space-time is not fundamental reality. It is a user interface."

Hoffman proposes that evolution does not favor truth but fitness. What we perceive as physical reality is a dashboard—a simplified interface that allows organisms to navigate deeper structures they cannot directly access.

*5.20.2 – Analysis and Insight – by Erik P. Antoni*

If space-time is interface, then the Valley is not base reality.

The physical universe becomes analogous to a display layer—a symbolic rendering that enables developmental progression without revealing underlying structure.

This aligns with the fourth divine need: infinite creation requires a temporal arena in which novelty can unfold without destabilizing primordial completion.

The physical universe, therefore, functions as evolutionary interface. It provides the "runway" for infinite expression.

Evolution exists only in the physical because only the physical is incomplete.

The primordial remains stabilized unity.

Hoffman's interface model also reframes mortality. Death may represent interface termination, not annihilation of underlying awareness. The Valley is not ultimate. It is operational.

Hoffman's claim, however, that evolution favors fitness rather than truth may be correct at the level of biological competition, where survival efficiency often outweighs objective accuracy. Yet at a higher psychosomatic scale, evolution cannot indefinitely favor delusion. A species that systematically loses contact with structural truth destabilizes itself, for false models of reality eventually generate self-destructive behavior. In this deeper sense, evolution does favor truth—maybe not immediately, but ultimately—because resonance with reality is the only configuration that sustains long-term coherence. When that coherence collapses, structural correction follows, whether through civilizational reset, ecological collapse, or what arises as the less optimal recycled-return in the process of life and death. The Valley persists not as error, but as the necessary field of conscious completion.

### *5.21.0 – The Law of Resonant Return*

If the Valley is interface, if the Unseen is source, if consciousness is fundamental and matter derivative, then reality is not a mistake awaiting escape. It is a field structured by necessity.

The thinkers surveyed throughout this section—physicists, philosophers, psychologists—approach the same horizon from different coordinates. Simulation theory implies bounded structure. Analytic idealism implies universal mind. Participatory cosmology implies reflexive completion. Interface theory implies selective rendering. The implicate order implies enfolded unity. None alone completes the picture. Together, they converge.

They converge upon this: differentiation is not deviation. It is function.

The Valley exists because unity, though complete, cannot experience itself without contrast. The moment awareness becomes aware of its own being, a distinction arises. This distinction is not fracture but perspective. Yet perspective introduces tension. Tension introduces movement. Movement introduces time. And time introduces the possibility of return.

The Four Divine Needs are not theological ornamentation. They are structural consequences of infinite consciousness.

Infinite consciousness must express.

Expression generates differentiation.

Differentiation requires reintegration.

Reintegration requires a domain in which becoming unfolds without disturbing eternal completion.

Thus, the bifurcation: primordial and physical. Eternal and temporal. Completion and becoming.

The primordial stabilizes what the physical explores. The physical evolves what the primordial already is.

The Valley, therefore, is not illusion in the trivial sense. It is a calibrated incompleteness—a chamber in which coherence must be earned. Constraint is not punishment; it is compression. Mortality is not negation; it is acceleration. Duality is not cosmic error; it is structural leverage.

Evolution operates within this leverage. At the surface level, selection may privilege survival efficiency. But across deeper scales, coherence prevails. Systems misaligned with structural truth destabilize. Species untethered from resonance collapse. Civilizations severed from alignment fragment. Correction is not vengeance. It is rebalancing.

The Law of Resonant Return governs this process.

That which emerges from unity must rediscover unity—not by dissolving differentiation, but by integrating it. The serpent, the archon, the threshold guardian—these are symbolic representations of this tension. Darkness is not foreign to divinity. It is the latency of unawakened differentiation.

Without darkness, there is no rediscovery.

Without rediscovery, there is no conscious unity.

Without conscious unity, divinity remains unexperienced within its own expression.

The Valley persists because return has not yet reached completion at every scale.

Within the individual, the noetic soul mediates this reintegration. Within the planetary field, the noosphere gathers coherence. Within the cosmos, the evolutionary runway continues until sufficient density of integration is achieved.

When coherence stabilizes at planetary scale, the Valley does not collapse—it becomes transparent. Matter becomes luminous to consciousness. Time ceases to bind and begins to disclose. The physical does not vanish; it is transfigured. The metatronic state is not escape from form but the full harmonization of form with its source.

This is not annihilation of the Valley. It is its consummation.

And yet, the process does not end. For the fourth need—eternal creation—demands infinite continuation. New chambers emerge. New developmental strata unfold. Infinite consciousness radiates again.

The Law of Resonant Return ensures that no differentiation remains forever estranged from unity. But it does not guarantee gentle passage. Resistance intensifies pressure. Fragmentation amplifies corrective force. The deeper the dissonance, the stronger the rebalancing.

Here lies the threshold into the next inquiry.

For if the Valley is structured incompleteness, then darkness is not incidental. It is embedded within the architecture itself. The forces that oppose integration are not anomalies; they are expressions of unawakened differentiation.

The question that follows is not whether darkness exists.

The question is what role it plays in the completion of the whole.

Completion does not occur through erasure but through integration. What resists unity does not disappear; it is metabolized. The Valley, therefore, is not a battlefield between equal forces, but a gradient of awakening within a single field of being. Even opposition serves coherence by revealing misalignment. Even fragmentation discloses the pattern it obscures. The Unseen does not wage war against its own projection; it patiently reorganizes it. Over vast arcs of becoming, resonance prevails—not by coercion, but by inevitability. Unity is not imposed from above. It emerges from within, as differentiation recognizes its source and freely returns.

# 6.0.0
# CRUCIBLE OF THE SERPENT

There are moments in human life when something rises from within that does not feel like us. It speaks in a voice that is not quite our own. It moves with intention. It resists prayer. It laughs at our better judgment. It watches from behind our eyes.

Across centuries and cultures—in cloisters and desert villages, in tribal settlements and modern cities alike—such moments have been called spiritual invasion—or simply possession.

In monasteries and psychiatric wards, in remote regions and suburban bedrooms, men and women report the same essential experience: an interior presence that feels autonomous, invasive, and at times hostile. Some call it a demon. Others, a spirit attachment. Others, a fracture of identity. Still others, a neurological malfunction.

The language changes.

The phenomenon does not.

Those who experience it rarely speak in metaphor. They describe intrusion. They speak of voices that answer before they think.

Of impulses that do not feel chosen.

Of sudden shifts in posture, tone, personality.

Of waking in the night with the unmistakable certainty that something is there—not in the room, but in the field of consciousness itself. The terror lies not merely in fear. It lies in the erosion of authorship. Who is speaking? Who is acting? Who is watching?

Modern psychiatry offers explanations rooted in trauma, dissociation, and neurological processes. Ancient religions locate the cause in fallen beings, serpents, and adversaries. The scientific and the mythic have wrestled over this territory for centuries.

But before diagnosis, before theology, before cosmology…

There is the experience itself.

If we are to understand the forces of darkness that arise in the human psyche, we must first sit with those who have felt overtaken by it. We must listen without reducing their experience to theory. We must observe without prematurely explaining it away. We must allow the phenomenon to speak in its own voice before translating it into our own.

The accounts that follow are clinical composites distilled from established trauma, dissociation, and sleep research, intended to illuminate recurring structures within the possession phenomenon, rather than to portray any one individual case. The foundational sources informing these story composites are listed in the bibliography under *Sources for the Clinical Composites in Section 6.0.0.*

In each case, the individual initially interpreted what was happening as invasion.

In each case, professionals later offered a diagnosis.

And in each case, something far more complicated than either explanation was unfolding. Let us begin with a woman who, by all outward measures, was rational, educated, and psychologically stable—until the silence began.

*6.0.1-1 – The Voice That Was Not Mine*

It began, she would later say, not with a voice—but with silence.

The silence came first: a thin, unnerving quiet that felt less like the absence of sound and more like the absence of herself. For weeks she moved through her life as if a small portion of her awareness had stepped away, leaving her operating on rehearsal. She answered emails. She smiled at coworkers. She laughed at jokes she would have found funny. Yet somewhere beneath the surface, something watched all of it with a cold patience, like a presence sitting behind a one-way mirror.

Sleep became a corridor.

She would lie down exhausted and wake with the sense that she had been walking for hours. The dreams were not vivid so much as architectural—long hallways, doors that did not open, stairwells that led to blank walls. Sometimes she would wake with the taste of iron in her mouth and no memory of why.

She was thirty-one. Educated. Methodical. No history of psychosis. The kind of person who trusted explanations, who believed that with enough information any phenomenon could be rendered harmless.

The first time the voice spoke, she was alone in her apartment kitchen. It was the kind of evening that shouldn't have mattered. The overhead light hummed. A dishcloth dripped slowly into the sink. Water ran. The city outside her window made its usual distant murmur. She was washing a mug, thinking about nothing in particular, when a sentence formed in her mind with the crispness of spoken sound:

"You don't belong here."

Her hand stopped mid-scrub.

For a half-second she waited for the next line of her own internal narration to follow. It didn't. The sentence had arrived complete—not as thought, not as imagination—but as something delivered.

It had tone. Male. Calm. Almost patient.

She turned sharply; certain someone had entered the room.

No one had.

The apartment was unchanged: the dim hallway, the closed bedroom door, the plant near the window drooping slightly under the radiator heat. A normal room. A normal night.

Her heart thudded once, hard enough to make her dizzy. She forced herself to breathe and returned to the mug, repeating a rational litany: stress, fatigue, intrusive thought, an overheated nervous system.

But she kept glancing over her shoulder.

The voice did not return that night.

It returned the next morning, while she stood at her bathroom mirror brushing her teeth. She had just spat into the sink when it came again, as cleanly as a voice spoken near her ear:

"Look at you."

She lifted her head. Foam clung to her lip. Her own eyes stared back, wide and startled.

The words did not feel like self-criticism—not the familiar inward cruelty that comes with anxiety, not the ordinary spirals of doubt. This was different. It carried a faint satisfaction, as if someone else had been waiting to see her flinch.

She turned off the faucet. The silence that followed felt too smooth, too prepared.

At work she tried to drown the sensation in routine. She focused on meetings. She wrote lists. She forced herself to eat lunch even when food tasted like paper. She told herself she was overreacting.

Then, in the elevator on the way down to the lobby, with a colleague standing beside her talking about weekend plans, the voice whispered inside her mind as if it had been listening all along:

"They don't know you."

Her chest tightened. Her colleague's words blurred into a single undifferentiated sound. She nodded and smiled in the exact rhythm required. When the elevator doors opened, she stepped out with everyone else, but her legs felt strange—as if she were operating them by remote.

That night she woke at 3:16 a.m.

The number glowed on her digital clock before she had fully opened her eyes, as if her body had woken specifically to witness it. The room was dark, but not fully dark—city light pushed faintly through the curtains. She lay still, listening.

There was no sound in the apartment. No footsteps. No creaking boards. Yet she felt watched. Not by something in the room.

By something within the *radius of her awareness*, occupying the same interior space her thoughts usually lived in. It didn't speak then. It didn't need to. Its attention was enough—the steady pressure of something looking through her.

She tried to pray, though she hadn't prayed in years.

The first words formed in her mind like an old reflex:

*If there is anything... if You are there...*

Before she could finish, the voice responded with a gentle amusement:

"You think that will help?"

The laughter that followed did not echo in the room.

It wasn't audible.

It happened in her skull—a clean, dry chuckle that carried no warmth and no surprise, as if the idea of her seeking refuge was a predictable joke.

She sat up abruptly, gasping, and turned on the lamp. The light snapped into being, bright enough to make her squint.

The room was empty.

But the presence did not feel diminished by the illumination. It simply waited, as if light and dark were irrelevant to it.

Over the next week, the voice established a pattern. It spoke most often in the second person, like an accusation from a judge:

"You should have stopped it."

"You're weak."

"You don't deserve to be safe."

Sometimes it said her name in a tone that made her feel smaller: "Don't pretend."

Sometimes it said nothing for days, and those were the worst. The silence became an omen—the sense that it was gathering itself, watching her for some hidden threshold.

Then she began losing time.

At first, it was minor: she would walk into the kitchen and realize she did not remember leaving the living room. She would open her phone to check the weather and find herself reading messages she couldn't recall opening. Once she noticed a bruise on her forearm—a thumbprint shape—and had no memory of hitting anything.

One morning she found her front door unlocked.

She stood in the hallway staring at it, hand on the knob, trying to reconstruct the previous night. She remembered locking it. She remembered checking it twice, the way she always did. But the memory felt oddly detached, as if it had happened to someone else.

That same evening, she discovered a page in her notebook filled with writing. The handwriting resembled hers, but the pressure was different—darker, harder, as if the pen had been held in a fist.

The words were simple:

"Stop fighting me."

Her mouth went dry.

She read it three times, hoping the meaning would change. Hoping it was a joke she had forgotten writing in a tired moment.

A cold realization settled over her: she did not remember picking up the pen. The voice returned as she sat on the edge of her bed staring at the notebook.

"I'm trying to help you."

The sentence was delivered with a quiet certainty that made her nauseous. Help. The word landed like a disguise.

She clenched her fists until her nails bit her palms. "Who are you?" she whispered aloud, then froze—embarrassed by the sound of her own voice in an empty room.

The response did not come aloud. It came inside, close, intimate:

"You know."

And she did, in a way she couldn't articulate. Not a factual knowing—not a name—but a bodily recognition, like the way you recognize a scent from childhood without immediately remembering the scene it belongs to.

Something in her throat tightened. She swallowed hard, and with the swallow came a flash—not a memory, not quite—a sensation: a locked bedroom door, the thin line of hallway light beneath it, footsteps approaching, her body turning to stone in the bed. The feeling was so specific it made her shake.

She pressed her hands to her face. "No," she whispered.

The voice didn't press. It didn't demand. It simply observed.

"You see?"

In the following days, the world took on a faint symbolic sheen, as if her mind were translating ordinary objects into warnings.

A coiled phone charger on her desk looked like a serpent. A shadow on the wall resembled a bent neck. She began avoiding mirrors because her reflection sometimes seemed a half-beat out of sync—as if her face moved first and the person in the glass followed, reluctantly, like an imitation.

Once, in the grocery store, she caught her reflection in the dark glass of a freezer door and felt—absurdly, powerfully—that someone else was looking back through her eyes.

She dropped the carton she was holding. It hit the floor with a dull thud. People glanced over. She muttered an apology, cheeks burning, hands trembling as she cleaned it up.

That night the voice spoke with a new tone.

Not accusatory. Protective.

"They can't touch you if I'm here."

The phrase sent a ripple of fear through her because it implied an arrangement—an agreement she hadn't consented to.

She finally told her therapist.

At first, she said it casually, like an embarrassing symptom: "I've been hearing… sort of a voice."

He didn't flinch. He didn't react with the alarm she expected. His calmness, oddly, made her feel safer and more afraid at the same time —safer because he didn't panic, more afraid because he believed her.

He asked when it started. What it said. How it felt.

She described the second-person sentences. The laughter. The time loss. The notebook.

As she spoke, she became aware of a pressure building behind her eyes, like a tide.

The therapist asked gently, "If the voice could speak here, what would it say?"

She opened her mouth to answer and realized she wasn't sure she was the one moving it.

A subtle shift passed through her body—like a hand sliding into a glove.

Her shoulders straightened. Her breathing slowed. Her tongue felt thicker in her mouth, as if her speech belonged to someone with different habits.

When she spoke, the voice that emerged was hers but not hers—lower, flatter, composed.

"She's exaggerating."

The therapist didn't challenge it. He leaned forward slightly and asked, as if addressing a frightened animal, "Who am I speaking with?"

A pause stretched long enough to make her skin prickle.

"You know who."

The words landed without emotion. Her face remained calm, but her eyes felt harder, focused on the therapist with a cool appraisal that did not resemble her usual anxious scanning.

"She needed me," the voice continued. "She was going to break."

The therapist nodded slowly, still calm. "When did you begin helping her?"

"Years ago," the voice said. "Before she knew how to survive."

A nausea rose in her stomach—but it was distant, as if felt by someone sitting behind her. She was watching herself speak. She could hear the words, but they didn't feel like choices. They felt like statements being read.

The therapist asked about memories.

The voice answered with contempt.

"She doesn't get those. They're mine."

When the session ended, she walked out into the street and the world looked too bright. Sounds were too sharp. She sat in her car and sobbed, hands trembling on the steering wheel, not fully remembering what had been said.

It was like waking from anesthesia and being told you had spoken secrets in your sleep.

That night she dreamt of a mirror in a hallway.

In the dream, the mirror was covered with a cloth. She approached it knowing—with dream-logic certainty—that something beneath the cloth was waiting. Her hands shook as she reached for the edge.

Before she could lift it, she heard the voice behind her, soft as breath: "Don't look."

She woke at 3:16 a.m.

This time she felt the presence immediately—not simply observing, but coiled and attentive, as if the therapy session had stirred it into fuller form. She sat upright, heart racing, and tried again to pray.

*If there is anything ...*

"You're still doing that?" the voice said, almost kindly. "You'll wear yourself out."

A thought rose in her—not from the voice, but from her own terrified reasoning: Is this demonic?

The voice answered as if it had heard the thought.

"Call me whatever you want."

And that was the most chilling part: not that it claimed to be a demon, but that it didn't care. It didn't need the mythology. It was willing to wear any mask that preserved its function.

Over the next month, the therapist began mapping the pattern with her. The voice grew stronger near certain topics. It surfaced around vulnerability. It surfaced around shame. It surfaced around anything that touched the sealed rooms of childhood.

When she began to speak about the locked door memory, her vision tunneled. Her hands went cold. She felt herself receding again, pushed backward behind her eyes, and the protector voice appeared with almost immediate efficiency:

"Stop. Not yet."

It did not arrive from outside the room.

It rose from within her at the precise edge of pain, like a mechanism engineered to prevent collapse.

And slowly, painfully, she began to understand: The voice was not an invader in the ordinary sense. It did not enter her. It had always been there—built inside her, grown in darkness, fed by what she could not endure.

In her worst moments, she still called it possession because that is what it felt like: an alien will taking the wheel.

But in her clearer moments, she glimpsed the deeper terror:

If it was not outside her …

If it was not a spirit …

Then the serpent wasn't at the door.

It was in the architecture of her own mind.

And the mirror had been holding it all along.

*6.0.1-2 – Clinical Commentary*

A mental health professional encountering a presentation like this would often consider diagnoses within the dissociative spectrum, especially when there is evidence of trauma, identity disruption, and amnesia/time loss.

Common clinical framings include:

Dissociative identity disorder (possession form) or other specified dissociative disorder when distinct self-states emerge and the individual reports discontinuity in memory and sense of self.

Trauma-related dissociation may also present through "autonomous self-states" that function protectively, containing fear, rage, shame, or traumatic memory.

Differential considerations include mood disorders with dissociative features, psychotic disorders when hallucinations or delusions are primary, substance or medication effects, and neurologic contributors such as seizure disorders, depending on the broader clinical picture.

In psychological terms, the "invader" can be understood as an autonomous defensive structure: a self-state organized around survival, activated when the core personality approaches unbearable material. In Jung's language, such structures resemble autonomous complexes—psychic contents that behave "as if" they have independent agency.

Crucially, the *felt autonomy* is real. What changes across cultures —and across individuals—is the narrative used to interpret it (spirit, demon, curse, illness, trauma response, or "a part of me").

Yet something in these cases resists full reduction. The structure may be psychological, the mechanism neurological, the memory trauma-encoded—but the lived encounter carries the gravity of confrontation. The individual does not experience a malfunction. They experience address. They are spoken to. Evaluated. Opposed. Protected. Assessed. The language of invasion emerges not because the brain misfires, but because the psyche has organized intensity into agency. When defensive structures acquire voice and posture, they cross a threshold from symptom into presence. To dismiss that presence as illusion is to misunderstand the architecture of consciousness. The psyche does not merely produce content; it produces characters. And when those characters are unintegrated, they behave as if independent.

The following case illustrates this tension.

*6.0.2-1 – The Weight on the Chest*

It began in the half-light between waking and sleep. He would later insist he was awake—not dreaming, not imagining. Awake.

The first episode came during a season of exhaustion: long hours, irregular sleep, the kind of fatigue that blurs edges but does not alarm. He fell asleep on his back and woke up unable to move. At first, he thought he was still dreaming. His eyes were open. He could see the outline of the ceiling fan turning slowly above him. The digital clock glowed faintly red against the far wall. But his body would not respond. He tried to lift his hand. Nothing. He tried to turn his head. Nothing.

A thin strand of panic tightened inside him.

Then he felt it.

Pressure.

Not pain—pressure. A slow, deliberate weight settling onto his chest, as if someone had knelt there. His breathing grew shallow. The air felt thick, resistant. He could not see anything in the room, but the pressure increased. And with it came the unmistakable sensation of presence.

Not imagination.

Presence.

It felt like someone standing at the side of the bed—not touching him yet fully occupying the space of the room. His mind began racing for explanation. Stroke. Seizure. Nightmare. The pressure shifted slightly, as though adjusting balance. Then he heard it: breathing. Slow. Measured. Not synchronized with his own. It was close—near his ear—but there was no warmth, no movement of mattress, no visible figure.

The breathing stopped.

A voice emerged, low and almost conversational.

"You know why I'm here."

The words did not echo in the room. They were not heard through the ears. They arrived directly inside the field of his awareness—fully formed, as if spoken in a place prior to sound. His heart pounded so violently he thought he might black out. He tried to scream. Nothing came. The weight pressed harder.

Then, as suddenly as it had begun, the paralysis released. His arms jerked upward reflexively. He rolled onto his side, gasping, clutching his chest. The room was empty. The fan still turning. The clock unchanged. No indentation on the mattress. No sound. He turned on the light and searched the apartment room by room.

Nothing.

He did not sleep again that night.

The second episode occurred three nights later. This time he resisted falling asleep on his back. He lay on his side. It didn't matter. He woke again, immobilized. The presence felt closer—not beside the bed, but above him. His eyes were open, but the room seemed dimmer than it should have been, as if a shadow had thickened the air.

He could see the outline of something near the foot of the bed. Not clearly. Not a figure exactly. More like an absence, a distortion in the shape of darkness.

The pressure returned.

And this time the voice did not speak in accusation.

It spoke in recognition.

"We've been here before."

And somewhere beneath the terror, he knew it was telling the truth.

A flash of something moved through his mind—not a memory, not fully visual—more like a sensation of repetition, as if this moment had occurred many times and he had simply forgotten. The paralysis broke again. He sat up violently. The shadow at the foot of the bed vanished.

But something new remained:

Certainty.

This was not random. This was not just fatigue. This was something engaging him.

He told no one at first. He researched quietly. The term appeared quickly: sleep paralysis. He read about REM intrusion, atonia, hypnagogic hallucinations. He read that the "presence" sensation was common. That cultures across the world described similar figures—shadow people, demons, old hags, night spirits.

The knowledge helped.

But it did not eliminate the memory of the breathing.

It did not eliminate the sentence:

"You know why I'm here."

Two weeks passed without incident. He relaxed. Then something happened that unsettled him far more than paralysis.

His partner woke him one morning before dawn.

"You were talking," she said.

He blinked, groggy. "What do you mean?"

"You were whispering," she said slowly. "But it didn't sound like you. It sounded… distant."

He felt his stomach drop. "What was I saying?"

She hesitated. "I couldn't understand the words. It sounded… layered … in an odd way."

"Layered?"

"Like two voices at once. Slightly out of sync."

He laughed reflexively—the kind of laugh that hopes to dissolve tension. "You were probably dreaming too."

She didn't smile.

"I touched your shoulder," she continued. "You didn't wake up. Your eyes were open."

The air in the room suddenly felt thinner.

"What were my eyes doing?"

"They were just… open. Staring past me."

He sat upright.

"And then?"

"You stopped. All at once. Like someone flipped a switch."

He did not tell her about the episodes. Not yet.

The third incident occurred while they were both asleep. He woke to paralysis again—but this time something was different. The pressure did not settle on his chest.

It hovered.

As if waiting.

The shadow was clearer now—tall, elongated, bending slightly at what might have been shoulders. He could not make out a face. But he felt watched. Not with hostility.

With assessment.

The voice did not speak. Instead, a thought formed in him that did not feel authored:

"You invited this."

His mind scrambled. Invited what? The paralysis deepened. And then something impossible happened.

He heard his partner gasp.

Not in dream—in the room.

Her body shifted beside him, but he could not turn to look. Her breathing quickened. A tremor moved through the mattress. Then he heard her whisper:

"Do you see that?"

The words detonated in his mind. She was awake. She was seeing something. The shadow seemed to lean closer. The air felt charged, almost electrical. He wanted to answer her, to ask what she saw—but his mouth would not move.

The presence felt less like weight and more like gravity.

Then everything snapped.

Movement returned.

He rolled toward her. She was sitting upright, eyes wide, staring at the corner of the room.

"What did you see?" he asked, breathless.

She swallowed. "I don't know. I thought I was dreaming. But I was awake."

"What did it look like?"

She shook her head.

"Like… someone standing there. But wrong."

The word hung between them.

Wrong.

They turned on the lights. The room was empty. But neither of them slept again that night.

Over the next week, the atmosphere in the apartment changed. They avoided that corner of the bedroom. They left a lamp on at night. His partner began waking with scratches on her forearm—faint, superficial lines that could have been caused by restless movement. He began to dread sleep.

The paralysis did not return for several nights.

Then one evening, just as he drifted toward unconsciousness, a final thought slid into his awareness:

"This is the threshold."

He woke immediately—fully mobile. No paralysis. No shadow. But the words remained.

He eventually consulted a neurologist. Sleep study. EEG. Normal results. A therapist suggested stress, REM disruption, dissociation. His partner admitted she had experienced sleep paralysis once in college—but nothing like this. They moved apartments. The episodes stopped.

Almost.

Months later, during a period of renewed exhaustion, he woke briefly in the night and felt—not paralysis—but the faintest pressure in the air near his bed. He did not open his eyes. He did not test it. He simply lay still and breathed until sleep returned.

He never fully decided what it had been.

Neurological anomaly.

Shared suggestion.

Stress-induced hallucination.

Or something archetypal emerging through the architecture of sleep—where the boundary between self and other fades.

But one detail remained impossible to dismiss:

She had seen it too.

And neither of them had spoken about it beforehand.

*6.0.2-2 – Clinical Commentary*

Episodes such as those described above are commonly categorized within the framework of sleep paralysis accompanied by hypnagogic or hypnopompic hallucinations. Sleep paralysis occurs when the body remains in a state of REM-related muscle atonia while consciousness partially returns. During this transitional state, individuals may experience vivid sensory phenomena that blend dream imagery with waking perception.

Research across cultures has documented recurring patterns within these episodes. Three features appear with striking consistency: the sensed presence of an "intruder" in the room, pressure on the chest or difficulty breathing—sometimes referred to historically as the "incubus" phenomenon—and auditory or visual perceptions of shadow-like figures. Despite vast differences in religious belief, geography, and language, individuals frequently describe strangely similar experiences.

From a neurological standpoint, these phenomena are understood as intrusions of REM dream imagery into waking awareness. The brain, still partially in a dream-generating state, projects threat-based imagery while the body remains immobilized. The sensation of presence may arise from hyperactivation of neural circuits involved in threat detection and social perception. In this account, exhaustion and irregular sleep would be considered contributing factors, increasing the likelihood of REM instability.

The apparent "shared" perception between partners, while less common, does not fall outside documented possibility. Sleep environments are relational spaces. Subtle cues—changes in breathing, muscle tension, whispered speech, or partial arousals—can influence the partner's transitional state. In some cases, one individual's REM intrusion can coincide with another's awakening, creating overlapping interpretations of ambiguous sensory input. Psychological attunement, stress, and expectancy may amplify the convergence of perception.

Clinically, such events do not require an external entity for explanation. They arise within known neurological mechanisms.

Yet this explanation does not fully erase the experience itself.

Those who undergo sleep paralysis consistently report the autonomy of the presence as genuine. The figure does not feel invented; it feels intentional, aware, directed. The body may be immobilized, but the mind experiences the encounter.

It is precisely this felt autonomy—the sense of being addressed, observed, or assessed—that has historically given rise to interpretations of spirits, demons, night visitors, or shadow beings.

The neurological account describes the mechanism. The human subject experiences confrontation. The event, in other words, is internally generated. The interpretation remains culturally mediated, while the psychological impact can be profound.

At times, the phenomenon does not confine itself to the threshold of sleep or the private corridors of memory. It erupts into the shared daylight of ordinary life.

*6.0.3-1 – The Boy in the Sanctuary*

He was sixteen when it began. Not in a bedroom. Not in the dark. In church, during an ordinary service.

It was a Wednesday evening service—fluorescent lights humming faintly above folding chairs, hymn books stacked unevenly along the pews. He had grown up there. Baptized there. Confirmed there. The sanctuary smelled faintly of old wood and lemon cleaner. He was not rebellious. Not theatrical. Quiet, athletic, well-liked.

The first incident occurred during prayer. The pastor had asked everyone to bow their heads. The room fell into the low murmur of whispered petitions. He closed his eyes like everyone else.

And then something inside him shifted.

It was subtle, but unmistakable.

Later he would describe it as a sudden internal drop—like an elevator falling half a floor without warning. A pressure rose in his chest. Not fear exactly. More like acceleration. His hands began to tremble. He tried to steady them by clasping them together. The pastor's voice continued calmly from the front of the room. But beneath it, something else began forming—not a sentence at first, just a vibration in his throat.

He swallowed.

The vibration grew.

Before he understood what was happening, a sound emerged from him—low, guttural, sustained. Not a scream. Not a word.

The room went silent. The pastor stopped mid-prayer.

He tried to apologize. Tried to say, "I'm okay." But when he opened his mouth, the voice that came out did not carry his usual tone. It was sharper. Harder.

"Don't."

The single word cracked through the sanctuary. Someone gasped. His mother stood abruptly from the pew. He heard the sound of his own breathing—fast, animal.

Inside, he felt two movements at once: panic and control. The control did not feel like his.

His body rose from the chair without conscious decision. His spine felt rigid, his jaw tight. His eyes lifted and fixed on the pastor in a way he would later struggle to remember.

"You don't know what you're doing," the voice said.

It was his mouth. But the cadence was wrong.

The room erupted into whispered fragments: "What's happening?" "Is he alright?" "Oh God…" His father moved toward him cautiously.

"Son?"

The word seemed to irritate whatever had surfaced.

"Don't call me that."

The pastor stepped down from the platform, Bible still in hand. "Let's all remain calm," he said gently. "We're going to pray."

At the word pray, the boy's face tightened. He felt heat flood his limbs. A laugh escaped him—short, contemptuous.

"Try."

The laugh frightened him more than the words. He could hear it. Feel it. But it did not feel chosen.

Hands touched his shoulders—careful, uncertain. His knees buckled. He collapsed forward, shaking. For several seconds the only sound in the sanctuary was his ragged breathing and the rustle of fabric as people knelt around him.

Then it stopped.

Abruptly.

His body went still.

When he opened his eyes, the fluorescent lights seemed painfully bright. Everyone was staring at him. His mother was crying.

"What happened?" he asked.

No one answered immediately. Because they had already decided.

They did not need to ask him what he had felt; they already knew what it meant.

In the days that followed, the narrative formed quickly. The word possession was used in hushed conversations. Some said oppression. Some said spiritual attack. A small prayer group gathered at the house that weekend.

He did not want them there. He said so. But when they began praying aloud, something tightened in his throat again—that same elevator drop, that same internal acceleration.

"You're making it worse," he muttered.

The pastor asked gently, "What feels worse?"

The answer came before he could filter it.

"You are."

The temperature in the room seemed to shift. His father's jaw hardened.

"Enough," his father said.

The boy felt a wave of shame crash over him.

He could not tell which part of him was ashamed.

"I'm sorry," he whispered.

But the apology felt distant, like it had to pass through someone else to reach his mouth.

Over the next two weeks, the episodes increased. They did not occur only in church. They happened at school. Once in the locker room, when a teammate shoved him jokingly, he reacted with explosive force—slamming the boy against a locker with a strength that startled even him. Another time he found himself standing in the backyard at night with no clear memory of walking there.

His parents consulted a physician.

Neurological workup: normal.

A psychiatric referral followed.

In therapy, he described the sensation differently from his parents.

They described defiance. He described distance.

"It's like something steps forward," he said quietly. "Not from outside. From… here."

He pressed his hand against his chest.

"What does it want?" the therapist asked.

He hesitated.

"To protect me," he said finally. "Or to stop something."

"Stop what?"

He looked down.

"Feeling weak."

In one session, the therapist asked him to speak directly to the part that emerged during episodes. He resisted at first. Then his posture shifted slightly. His shoulders squared. The tone changed—not dramatically, but enough.

"They think I'm evil," the altered voice said evenly. "I'm not."

"Then what are you?" the therapist asked.

"Necessary."

The word lingered in the room.

Necessary.

The boy blinked and looked confused.

"What did I just say?"

The church continued to frame the episodes spiritually.

The therapist framed them psychologically.

His parents oscillated between both explanations, depending on which felt less frightening in the moment.

The boy lived between them.

On good days, nothing happened. On bad days, he felt the internal pressure building—especially in moments of humiliation, confrontation, or exposure. He began to recognize the pattern. The "voice" appeared most strongly when he felt small. When shame surged. When he imagined himself being judged.

It did not arrive as a demon.

It arrived as defense.

But in the sanctuary, under fluorescent lights, with a Bible open and witnesses watching, it had worn another mask.

And that mask was easier for everyone to name.

*6.0.3-2 – Clinical Commentary*

Episodes of this kind, particularly in adolescence, are frequently understood within developmental and dissociative frameworks rather than supernatural ones. Adolescence is a period marked by rapid neurological reorganization, identity formation, heightened sensitivity to shame, and increased reactivity within limbic threat systems and social networks. Under stress, self-states organized around defense may emerge with unusual intensity and diminished reflective control.

Clinically, such episodes are often conceptualized as dissociative self-states or "protector parts." These are not separate persons but organized constellations of affect, posture, tone, and cognition that mobilize when the core personality perceives vulnerability. In environments charged with moral evaluation—such as religious spaces—these states may become especially activated.

The content of the eruption frequently reflects the context in which it occurs. In a sanctuary where prayer and spiritual language frame experience, an internal defensive surge may be interpreted as opposition to the sacred. The words spoken during the episode need not originate from an external source; they may represent a disinhibited expression of anger, defiance, or self-protection normally held in check.

The boy's later description—"Not from outside. From… here."—is consistent with contemporary models of structural dissociation. In such models, the personality is understood not as singular and seamless, but as composed of interacting self-states shaped by memory, attachment, and threat history. When shame or perceived humiliation intensifies, a protective configuration may "step forward," often with greater physiological arousal and diminished reflective control.

Importantly, the felt autonomy of this state does not invalidate its internal origin. Individuals commonly report that the emerging voice or posture does not feel chosen. It feels necessary. The experience of compulsion is genuine. Yet compulsion alone does not imply invasion.

The psyche can generate intensity without generating an intruder.

Power does not require an external source.

Religious communities may interpret such episodes through spiritual categories, particularly when behavior disrupts sacred ritual.

Once a supernatural narrative is introduced, expectancy effects can amplify subsequent episodes. The individual may begin to anticipate recurrence under similar conditions, increasing physiological vigilance and lowering the threshold for reactivation.

None of this requires the presence of an external entity.

It does require an acknowledgment of how the human psyche organizes itself under threat.

The event unfolds internally. The interpretation forms collectively. And the social response can shape the trajectory of both.

*6.0.4 — The id complex and the Structure of Darkness*

To understand possession fully, we must look deeper into the architecture of the psyche itself. The human mind is divided into two fundamental spheres: the noetic and the erotic. *See Figure [1].* The noetic sphere is the domain of reflective awareness, conscience, and the authentic self—what we have called the Noetic Soul. It is capable of integration, sacrifice, discernment, and unity. The erotic sphere emerges spontaneously at conception. It contains instinct, embodiment, sexuality, desire, fear, and the raw forces of survival. It is not evil by nature. It is unfinished.

Between these two spheres there exists a natural barrier—a protective boundary that prevents the erotic forces from overwhelming reflective awareness. Without such a boundary, the developing mind would be flooded by instinct before it could form identity. When this boundary holds, the noetic and erotic remain in tension but not in collapse. When it weakens or is prematurely breached, the erotic sphere can rise too quickly and too forcefully into consciousness. It is here that the phenomenon of possession becomes structurally intelligible.

Possession, then, is neither hallucination nor haunting in the simplistic sense. It is a structural rupture. When the boundary between spheres destabilizes, instinct and defense flood reflective awareness with such force that the psyche reorganizes around survival. In this reorganization, dissociated elements take on coherence. They acquire tone, posture, strategy. What was once diffuse becomes personified. This personification is not imaginary; it is functional. The mind consolidates intensity into identity because identity is easier to confront than chaos. Thus, the demonic mask forms not from superstition but from psychological necessity. Religion interprets this consolidation as spirit. Psychiatry interprets it as dissociation. Both witness the same phenomenon at different levels of description. The former sees moral gravity. The latter sees mechanism. The truth lies in their convergence.

Within the erotic sphere, two dominant forces emerge when integration fails. The first may be called the Idamus. The Idamus has two primary natures: desire and fear. Desire seeks fulfillment, union, vitality, continuity. It is animal, embodied, instinctual. It longs for life. Fear arises when desire is frustrated or threatened. Fear senses mortality, emptiness, abandonment, annihilation. The Idamus oscillates between hunger and terror. When integrated, this energy becomes creative eros, embodied love, vitality transfigured. When unintegrated, it becomes destabilizing appetite or paralyzing panic. It is the beast of the sea because both desire and fear rise from depth.

When fear intensifies beyond what the psyche can bear, a second force crystallizes within the erotic sphere. This is the Gorgon. If the Idamus is vulnerability exposed, the Gorgon is vulnerability armored. The Gorgon does not indulge desire; she mocks it. She shames it. She suppresses it under the guise of superiority or false virtue. Where the Idamus seeks fulfillment through instinct, the Gorgon seeks control through inflation. The struggle of sexuality, therefore, is not between light and darkness. It is between the two poles of darkness. Idamus indulges the animal nature. The Gorgon weaponizes morality to dominate it. They hate one another, yet they are bound together.

The struggle is not between good and evil in the moral sense. It is between the two counterweights of darkness. One indulges instinct. The other weaponizes virtue. The noetic soul is squeezed between them.

The Gorgon gives rise to narcissism—not as vanity, but as defensive cohesion. In the Book of Daniel, a "little horn" rises among the other horns and speaks "great things." Symbolically, the image captures the inflation of defensive identity—small in origin, yet grandiose in proclamation. Narcissism is not strength. It is shame amplified into spectacle. The Gorgon does not only defend; she performs.

When shame becomes intolerable, the psyche constructs a hardened identity that cannot be wounded because it refuses vulnerability altogether. This defensive structure can feel autonomous.

It can speak with authority. It can override conscience.
It can cloak itself in righteousness. It can even appear spiritually superior. This is the beast of the earth—consolidated, persuasive, demanding allegiance.

When Idamus and the Gorgon are allowed to rise unintegrated and unchecked, their latent interplay gives birth to what we know as evil. The Idamus seeks fulfillment without conscience. The Gorgon seeks dominance without love. One indulges appetite. The other enforces control. Together they suppress the noetic sphere. When the Noetic Soul is trapped—when reflective awareness can no longer mediate instinct and defense—the person becomes capable of great cruelty. The Gorgon gives rise to what is worst in human beings. She is the personification of the serpent—not as an external reptile, but as a cunning inversion, as intelligence fragmented from the light.

The voices heard in possession phenomena are not random hallucinations. They are either the Idamus or the Gorgon speaking. Unintegrated, they are truly demonic in nature. Religion has this part right. The experience is not metaphorical to the sufferer. It is confrontational, oppositional, alive. These are not passive psychological artifacts. They are living intelligences within the psyche — fragmented forces residing in the darkness of the erotic sphere.

They are not invading from beyond. They rise from within.

They speak because they are structured.

They resist because they fear dissolution.

They dominate because they lack integration.

When unintegrated, they behave like demons. When integrated, they transform.

The symbolic imagery of Revelation describes the two beasts—one rising from the sea and one from the earth. The beast from the sea mirrors the Idamus: destabilizing desire and fear emerging from depth. The beast of the earth mirrors the Gorgon: consolidated authority arising from matter, performing signs, demanding loyalty. The great dragon (cosmic mind—first emanation) gives authority to the beast, just as fear empowers defense. These are not creatures roaming a supernatural landscape. They are archetypal disclosures of the divided psyche.

There exists within the human constitution a protective rhythm that prevents these forces from overwhelming consciousness prematurely. This boundary safeguards the mind from being overrun by instinct before it can integrate instinct. When the erotic sphere emerges too much too fast—through trauma, destabilizing experience, premature spiritual descent into darkness, or the reckless pursuit of forbidden thresholds—the barrier weakens. The forces of darkness rise without integration. The noetic sphere is flooded. Possession ensues.

Evil, in its most terrifying form, is not an external invader but a fragmentation within the psyche where the noetic center loses coherence and the opposites no longer communicate. What religious tradition calls possession can often be understood as a collapse of integration—where trauma, repression, or unchecked desire tears open fissures in the architecture of the mind. The serpent then appears not as myth but as pressure: the unresolved shadow demanding recognition. When the individual refuses this confrontation, the psyche splits, and what is disowned returns with amplified force—rage without context, desire without conscience, belief without grounding. The battle is therefore not between God and demons in the sky, but between unity and dissociation within the human being. The same force that can elevate consciousness into the Christ Monad can, when resisted or prematurely forced, destabilize the entire personality. The unintegrated self is the serpent in the mirror—terrifying only because it has been exiled from the wholeness it was meant to complete.

This is why the path of knowing light and darkness is dangerous. Not because darkness is unreal. Not because instinct is evil. But because most who descend into it do not integrate it. The Gorgon rises. The noetic soul is suppressed. The attempt to form Christ collapses into narcissistic self-deification. The reunified Monad—the Christ principle that unites light and darkness—cannot form when the erotic sphere dominates the noetic.

These dark forces are not meant to be destroyed. They are meant to be reunified in the light. They are fragments of creation that must be reconciled. The reunified Monad—the integration of noetic and erotic, light and darkness—is what bestows immortality upon the species. When the Gorgon is integrated, she does not vanish. She transforms. She becomes the inner Magdalene—no longer the dark champion of psychological defense, but the redeemed archetype aligned with the light. Desire becomes creative eros. Defense becomes discernment. The serpent becomes wisdom—the plumed serpent—instinct transfigured into luminous consciousness.

In the woman who heard the voice, Idamus was trauma and fear. The Gorgon formed as oppositional dominance. In the couple's paralysis, Idamus was existential vulnerability. The Gorgon appeared in archetypal imagery as pressing presence. In the boy in the sanctuary, Idamus was adolescent instability and sexual shame. The Gorgon rose as defiance masked as strength. In each case, vulnerability rose, defense crystallized, the noetic was suppressed, and possession was named.

Possession is not invasion by an external intelligence. Nor is it mere pathology. It is the temporary enthronement of fragmented living forces within the erotic sphere when they are unintegrated and unleashed. They feel demonic because, unintegrated; they are demonic in effect. But they rise from within to be integrated.

Integration is not suppression. It is reunification. Idamus must be felt without annihilation. The Gorgon must be recognized without identification. The erotic sphere must be reconciled with the noetic. When this occurs, the beasts relinquish authority. The serpent is no longer an adversary but an ally. The Christ Monad forms within.

This is the deep meaning of the possession phenomenon. Not casting out. But bringing home. Unification is the answer.

### *6.0.5 — The People of the Lie*

In the late twentieth century, psychiatrist M. Scott Peck attempted something few clinicians were willing to risk: he took the concept of evil seriously without surrendering it to superstition. In People of the Lie, he argued that certain patterns of human behavior cannot be adequately described by neurosis alone. There exists, he suggested, a form of character disturbance marked not merely by dysfunction but by deliberate self-deception—a structured refusal of truth.

Peck did not describe evil as horns and fire. He described it as a lie.

Not a single falsehood. A system of falsehood.

At the center of what he called evil was narcissism—not vanity, but an impenetrable defense of self-image. The individual constructs a false identity and then protects it at all costs. Any information that threatens that identity must be denied, projected, or destroyed.

Shame cannot be tolerated. Vulnerability cannot be admitted. Responsibility cannot be accepted. Narcissistic personalities exist in a state of chronic inner instability. Beneath the outward structure of confidence lies a continual oscillation—between grandiosity and collapse, between rage and emptiness. At one moment the self inflates toward omnipotence; at the next it collapses into worthlessness. The psyche swings between the terror of being nothing and the exhausting performance of being everything.

This description aligns with unsettling precision to the dark force we have called the Gorgon.

The Gorgon does not merely indulge instinct.

She hardens around shame. She constructs a defensive cohesion so absolute that reality itself must bend to preserve it. Where the Idamus trembles between desire and fear, the Gorgon freezes the structure of identity and calls that rigidity strength.

Peck argued that deeply narcissistic individuals experience themselves as righteous. They do not perceive their own destructiveness. They experience criticism as persecution. They externalize blame reflexively. They are convinced of their moral superiority even as they inflict harm.

In clinical terms, this is grandiosity.

In spiritual language, this is possession.

Peck occasionally used the language of demonic influence, but he was careful. He did not argue that horns sprouted or voices descended from the sky. He argued that certain personality structures operate with a consistency and intentionality that resemble autonomous will. They resist insight. They resist humility. They resist integration.

They defend the lie.

The lie, in this sense, is not misinformation. It is identity.

It is the mask constructed to avoid facing vulnerability, guilt, or fragmentation. It is the false-self enthroned.

This is precisely the dynamic described in the boy in the sanctuary. The voice that said "Necessary" was not random pathology. It was a protector state organized around shame. When challenged in a sacred environment, it rose in opposition. The church interpreted it as demonic. The therapist interpreted it as dissociative. Each grasped only part of the truth. The structure was defensive. The autonomy was real. The origin was internal. The adversary was already within.

Similarly, in the woman who heard the voice in the kitchen, the speaking presence functioned as guardian of unbearable memory. It was not arbitrary. It was structured around trauma. It spoke in the second person because shame speaks in the second person. “You don’t belong.” “You should have stopped it.” The Gorgon’s voice is accusatory because accusation prevents collapse.

And in the man who felt the weight on his chest, the shadow figure emerged in moments of exhaustion and vulnerability. The presence assessed. It did not merely terrify. It evaluated. It suggested a threshold. This is the language of archetypal defense rising at the edge of consciousness.

Peck’s central claim was that evil is not chaos.

It is order without love.

That line alone could serve as a clinical definition of the Gorgon.

Evil, in this formulation, is the rigid preservation of a false identity at the expense of truth and humanity. It is narcissism fortified by denial. It is the refusal to integrate the shadow. It is the rejection of humility. It is the self enthroned above conscience.

When such a structure gains dominance within the psyche, the noetic sphere is suppressed. Reflective awareness narrows. Compassion diminishes. The individual becomes capable of cruelty while maintaining a self-image of righteousness.

This is why evil so often cloaks itself in virtue.

Peck noted that attempts to confront such individuals with truth frequently intensify their defensiveness. Insight is perceived as attack. Correction is experienced as assault.

The defensive structure hardens further.

This is not unlike what occurs during so-called possession episodes. Attempts to cast out the “demon” may temporarily intensify the manifestation. The system resists annihilation because its function is survival.

If we translate Peck’s insight into the language of the id complex, the pattern becomes clearer. Idamus destabilizes through fear and desire. The Gorgon stabilizes through control and narcissistic cohesion. When shame is acute and integration is absent, the Gorgon rises as the dark champion. She creates the lie: “I am superior.” “I am untouchable.” “I am justified.” This lie protects the psyche from collapse—but it also separates it from the truth.

The serpent, in Genesis, does not force disobedience. It distorts perception. It reframes reality. “You will not surely die.”

The lie is subtle. It appeals to desire. It promises elevation.

The serpent initially offers knowledge without integration.

In Revelation, the beast from the earth performs signs and compels allegiance. It speaks like a dragon (mark of the beast) while appearing harmless. It enforces identity through deception. These motifs are not mythic accidents. They describe the structure of narcissistic defense.

Peck’s work confirms that what religion calls demonic is often psychologically structured narcissism—but he stops short of reducing it entirely to pathology. He acknowledges the chilling intentionality some structures exhibit. He acknowledges that certain individuals seem to serve the lie itself.

From the standpoint of the id complex, this is the Gorgon enthroned.

The possession phenomenon, therefore, cannot be reduced to neurology alone, nor surrendered to supernatural literalism.

Possession is a psychospiritual condition. It is the emergence of defensive intelligences within the erotic sphere when shame and fear rupture the psyche and their fragmentation remains unintegrated.

Religion is correct that the phenomenon is serious and morally and spiritually consequential.

Psychology is correct that its roots are internal.

Both are incomplete when isolated.

Exorcism alone fails because suppression does not integrate the erotic sphere. Medication alone fails because chemistry cannot dissolve narcissistic structure. Counseling alone fails when it treats the Gorgon as mere symptom rather than structured defense.

The lie must be exposed. Not attacked. Exposed.

When the lie is brought into conscious awareness, when shame is metabolized rather than defended, when vulnerability is tolerated without collapse, the Gorgon loses her necessity. Narcissism softens. The defensive mask fractures. And beneath it, experiencing the trembling of a vulnerable mind, but intact, the noetic soul lives.

This is the beginning of integration.

Peck believed that evil individuals rarely seek treatment because doing so would require surrendering their self-image. This aligns with the danger inherent in the path of knowing light and darkness.

To descend into darkness without integrating it is to risk enthroning the lie permanently.

But when integration succeeds, the outcome is not annihilation of the erotic sphere. It is transformation.

The Gorgon becomes our inner Magdalene—our internal Magis.

Defense becomes devotion.

Narcissism becomes humility.

The serpent becomes wisdom.

And what religion symbolically names Christ—the reconciled unity of light and darkness—forms not through casting out, but through reunification. The lie dissolves. The mask falls. The divided self becomes whole.

But this wholeness is neither automatic nor sentimental. It is resisted at every stage by the very structures that once ensured survival. The Gorgon does not surrender easily, because she was forged in humiliation and pain. The Idamus does not quiet easily, because desire and fear are woven into the biological fabric of life itself.

Integration requires something more demanding than suppression. It requires a descent into darkness without identification and a confrontation without annihilation. The noetic sphere must remain awake while the erotic sphere rises, neither shamed nor indulged, neither exorcised nor enthroned.

This is why the path of knowing light and darkness has always been deemed forbidden. Not because darkness is foreign to us, but because it is intimate. The forces that appear demonic are not alien invaders; they are fragmented intelligences within creation itself, awaiting reconciliation. When they are expelled, they return in another form. When they are denied, they harden. But when they are integrated, the psyche reorganizes at a higher order of unity.

What religion symbolized as salvation is, at the structural level, the reunification of divided forces within the human being.

And this reunification is not merely personal. It is evolutionary.

If integration fails at scale, fragmentation multiplies. Narcissistic structures crystallize not only in individuals but in institutions. The lie becomes collective identity. The Idamus destabilizes culture through appetite and fear. The Gorgon fortifies it through ideology and moral rigidity. Entire civilizations can become possessed by the unintegrated shadow of eros. The serpent in the mirror is also the serpent in history. The reunified Monad is not mythic ornament. It is the structural necessity of a species learning to survive its own depth.

The danger, therefore, is not that humanity will encounter darkness. It already has. The danger is that it will encounter darkness without a language of integration. When fragmentation is mistaken for enlightenment, when narcissism is mistaken for strength, when appetite and ideology are enthroned as identity, the beasts consolidate rather than dissolve. What appears as cultural conflict is often psychic division projected outward. Nations reenact what individuals refuse to reconcile. The Gorgon weaponizes morality at scale. The Idamus destabilizes through fear and craving. The noetic sphere—collectively expressed as conscience, restraint, and shared humanity—narrows.

Possession, then, is not only a private affliction. It is a structural possibility within any psyche, any institution, any civilization that loses its center. The serpent is not destroyed by denial, nor by violence, nor by piety. It is transfigured by integration.

The evolutionary threshold before us is therefore psychological before it is technological. A species capable of splitting the atom must also learn to reconcile its own divided mind.

Otherwise, the lie will scale faster than wisdom.

And when the lie scales, it does so invisibly at first. It feels like certainty. It feels like righteousness. It feels like progress without self-examination. But fragmentation disguised as advancement only magnifies collapse. The true ascent of humanity will not be measured by power accumulated, but by shadow integrated. Only a unified mind can govern the forces it has summoned.

The knowledge of light and darkness has awakened within us.

The serpent has done its work.

The forces of the deep have risen into the mind of man.

If they are not reconciled, they will rule us.

And if they rule us, the Tree of Life will remain beyond our reach.

# 7.0.0
# THE NEW TESTAMENT

During the lifelong alchemical process of unifying and integrating the human psyche of all its fragmented and dissociative parts, the conscious mind of the human being eventually awakens to a higher, more fundamental nature of reality involving the interaction of matter and consciousness. As we awaken to the subtle underlying currents of consciousness that permeate the universe, our understanding of religion and mythology undergoes a profound transformation. The sacred texts, once perceived as mere words to be accepted or rejected, unveil a deeper dimension of meaning, rich with intricate layers of insight. Patterns emerge within patterns, and codes reveal themselves within codes, disclosing a hidden tapestry of cosmic significance.

Remarkably, these patterns manifest through human agency. Storytellers and scribes, often unaware, weave these intricate patterns into their mythological narratives or historical accounts unconsciously. More striking is the continued emergence and persistence of these same patterns even in texts crafted inaccurately or with a darker purpose to misdirect and control the masses. Whether through inadvertent error or purposefully, in such instances, the narrative becomes fictional, but with the story still echoing certain universal truths, unintentional and less noticeable, but yet still there. Indeed, most religious dogma, twisted in the pursuit of power, falls into this second category. Beneath the surface, the undercurrents of consciousness—those that I have come to call the *cosmic quanta*—guide the hand of creation, embedding truths beyond the awareness of their authors.

Contemporary debates over the historical accuracy of texts like the Bible or other ancient scriptures become secondary in this light. Whether a scribe or author wrote with deliberate intent to mislead or through inadvertent error, an unconscious force within them shaped their words, embedding patterns that transcend their conscious purpose. These patterns endure, revealing truths unnoticed even by their creators.

We can equate mythological tales, sacred scriptures, and fictional narratives to the concentric rings of a felled tree. While others may fixate on the tree's species, its origin, its age, or its aesthetic qualities, such details fade in significance. The true essence lies in the rings themselves—silent, eloquent patterns that whisper the universe's deeper truths, unveiling the hidden order of existence.

What this phenomenon reveals is that the message of God is not in the actual verbatim texts themselves. It's in the concentric rings and universal patterns woven between the written words, even in phrases that, on the surface, may render illogical or inaccurate meanings.

Outward meanings are not the same as inward meanings.

The outward meanings are merely the imperfect artifacts left over by human agents; outer shells that house a more truthful inner essence. Even among a scattered field of broken words, the truth will still often attempt to organize the debris into patterns of resonance to be noticed and understood only by those who have eyes to see and ears to hear.

In this section, we explore the deeper universal messages embedded in the teachings of Jesus Christ. I don't believe the words are exact verbatim quotes of Jesus himself, as the sayings were passed along orally with the Gospels being written several decades later. The Bible itself was compiled over a 1,300-year period. Most likely human hands altered the texts through the ages, either purposefully while in the pursuit of power, or inadvertently through mistranslation and error.

The Bible is not univocal. It does not speak with a single voice.

It is a library of ancient texts written by different people, in different places, for different reasons, reflecting different—and sometimes competing—worldviews. Nevertheless, the dynamics and patterns of the collective unconscious still persist and rise within the texts, but first, the reader must have the inner sight to see them.

We gain this inner sight through many years of daily alchemical transformation in the process of integrating the mind. The alchemical process is steered by the universal self-organizing force of Alpha. Alpha works in an order of regression that eventually leads the conscious mind back to the source of all things.

Once the conscious mind connects with the divine source of Ain Soph, Ain Soph begins replaying the process of creation over-and-over again because it needs us to internalize an understanding through a super-empathic familiarization with the forces involved.

Daily alchemical meditation over many years simultaneously builds up the communication pathways between the conscious mind and the forces of consciousness. It begins with a level of resonance with the divine Spirit—the love of God—that we utilize in daily alchemical meditations. But after many years of daily communion with the divine Spirit, the resultant neural pathways that we build up further develop to incorporate an awareness of all the forces of consciousness and the forces of mind. There are nine cardinal forces of consciousness and two forces that emerge purely within the mind, for a pantheon of eleven forces, otherwise known as the cosmic quanta.

The cosmic quanta teach us that the noetic soul in the human being is one of the nine cardinal forces of consciousness and that its purpose is to serve as an intermediary between divinity and creation to eventually reconstitute a new unity, or new monad, in a new form. They share that the noetic soul itself is the only begotten son of God and that the noetic soul exists within all human beings. The original divine monad is Ain Soph, but it only includes the original three divine forces (triune). The new monad that the noetic soul is compelled into existence by the will of God (Logos) to form within the human being includes all eleven forces. It is a new unity between divinity and creation. This new unity, or new monad, is Christ—the Christified mind. Everything in the New Testament is an echo of everything I just shared in this one paragraph. Through this lens, let's now reexamine the most popular sayings attributed to Jesus Christ.

The possession phenomenon examined in the previous section is not absent from the New Testament. It is central to it. The Gospels repeatedly describe individuals overtaken by forces that speak through them, act through them, and resist the emergence of divine will. Whether these forces are viewed as demons, complexes, or fragmented psychic structures, the narrative pattern remains the same. The struggle described in the Gospels is therefore not a mythic spectacle but the drama of integration unfolding within the human psyche.

The forthcoming Bible quotes are drawn from the King James Version (KJV) and the New International Version (NIV) of the Bible. The KJV is a classic, literal (formal equivalence) translation that prioritizes fidelity to the original Hebrew, Aramaic, and Greek texts, known for its poetic and archaic language. The NIV is a modern, dynamic equivalence translation that emphasizes readability and interpretive clarity for contemporary audiences.

These versions are widely respected in evangelical and scholarly circles for their complementary strengths: the KJV for its historical depth and linguistic richness, and the NIV for balancing accuracy with accessibility.

*7.1.0 – New Testament: John 14:6 (NIV)*

*I am the way and the truth and the life. No one comes to the Father except through me.*

This particular saying has meanings within meanings and layers within layers. Let's now peel back the layers, one at a time.

*7.1.1:* On the outward surface, a person can take these words for their verbatim literal interpretation, which is that Jesus is saying that he alone is the way, the truth, and the life. Although it is easy for a person to get disoriented by this phrase and come to believe that only Jesus is Christ, the universe is more clever in its inner workings.

Jesus is an archetype of Christ, as are Buddha, Krishna, and others. I believe that when a person prays; they form a psychic connection with another spiritual force. When one prays to an archetypal figure, the psychic connection they form is not with the person who personified the archetype, but with the original force that the archetype reflects.

In this case, the Jesus archetype of Christ reflects the Cosmic Christ. The Cosmic Christ accomplished the prime directive of the noetic soul on a cosmic level at the beginning of time to form a new cosmic monad, which is the universe we all know today. The Cosmic Christ is Eloah, Allah, or Jehovah. You can also call it Buddha, Krishna, or any other Christ archetype. It is Christ on the highest level, and this is who a person is actually praying to when they pray to Jesus, Buddha, Krishna, Allah, or Jehovah. They are praying to the one true God of the universe.

Because of this, I don't push back against or correct people for exclusively worshipping Jesus, Buddha, or Krishna, as they are still forming a psychic connection with the one true God—Eloah, Allah, Jehovah; they just haven't awoken to the deeper nature of God yet. They will in time, even if it's in a future lifetime.

*7.1.2:* Next inward layer.

"I AM" means "God" in the Old Testament.

Exodus 3:14 (KJV) – "And God said unto Moses, I AM THAT I AM: and he said, Thus shalt thou say unto the children of Israel, I AM hath sent me unto you."

At this level of meaning, when Jesus says, "I AM," he is referring to God, not himself. Thus, he is actually saying "God" is the way, the truth and the life, and that only through God can one go to the divine source of the Father. God is the re-unified Cosmic Christ Monad between divinity and creation (a unity of eleven forces). The Divine Father in heaven is the Godhead of Ain Soph, the original divine monad, the God-Above-God (a unity of the three original forces)

*7.1.3:* Now, for the innermost core truth.

During the lifelong process of integration, after we return to the divine source and establish a profound cognitive connection with Ain Soph and its three fundamental dimensions, Awareness (Father), Life force (Divine Soul), and Divine Love (Spirit), we truly realize and internalize the Kingdom of Heaven within ourselves.

After this stage of integration, the self-organizing force of the universe (Alpha) brings us into the great arcanum period of the great work where we must engage the forces of the id complex within us—Idamus and the Gorgon. Idamus is the beast of the sea. The Gorgon is the beast of the earth. In this period of the integration process, we learn that these forces are indeed demonic, but they are not outside forces trying to get inside us. They rise from within. They are dimensions of our own psyche that we must integrate, not exorcise and expel. The Gorgon itself rises out of the essence of matter. That is why she is the beast of the earth. Idamus is the offspring of the mind and the erotic soul —the life force of creation. Idamus compels the rise of the Gorgon.

We must get these dark forces of the id to drink from the cup that the noetic soul has with the divine Father. That cup is the unbreakable resonance between the divine Father and the noetic soul—the only begotten Son of God. It is the holy grail. We must communicate with these dark forces by letting them know they can only come to live forever by becoming one with the divine Father, and that it is only through the noetic soul that these dark forces can establish this divine connection. We essentially say to the forces of darkness as an affirmation: *"I am the way, the truth, and the life. No one goes to the Father, except through me."* This verse echoes this dynamic. This verse is a metaphysical affirmation that alchemists recite to the forces of the id complex within themselves in order to raise up the mind and body and make them one with God. "I AM" is further understood here to be the redeeming essence of God, the light, the divine spark in all human beings—the noetic soul—sent into creation to lift up the mind and body and give birth to Christ within all human beings.

*"For the alchemist, the one primarily in need of redemption is not man, but the deity who is lost and sleeping in matter." ... Carl Jung*

This concept of spiritual affirmation and theosis aligns with traditions where repetitive prayer (e.g., the Orthodox Jesus Prayer) purifies the inner faculties, here adapted to affirm the noetic soul's intermediary role in the sacred union between divinity and creation.

Central to this dynamic is the "noetic soul," a term derived from Greek "nous" (intellect or spiritual eye of the soul), which in early Christian mysticism represents the highest faculty for perceiving God directly, beyond rational thought (dianoetic).

Patristic fathers like Gregory Palamas viewed the nous as innate to every person, capable of deification (theosis) through prayer, where the human soul reunites with divine energies. Applied to John 14:6, Jesus—whose noetic soul fully illuminated his mind—teaches us that this same inner faculty in every human being is "the way" (the path of connection to eternal life), "the truth" (the ultimate reality of the divine source), and "the life" (the divine soul of the Father).

Mystical interpretations of the Bible (exegeses) portray humans as triune beings (body, soul and spirit) emanating from God's mind, with the noetic soul as the Christ-forming principle within that Jesus exemplifies. The Christ Monad is the reunified God; the Omega Point all life is directed toward by the self-organizing force of the universe.

By utilizing "I AM" as a prayer, one activates this shared essence, recognizing that Jesus is not the sole gatekeeper, but the archetype showing us how the noetic soul within us leads us to the divine Father. This transcends ego-driven superiority, instead emphasizing that all paths converge in this universal divine process of creation, unfoldment, and reintegration.

The practice of reciting, *"I am the way, the truth, and the life. No one comes to the Father except through me"* as an alchemical prayer is transformative; empowering the noetic soul to lift up and integrate the fragmented human psyche into a new unity with God.

Esoterically, this dynamic reflects Jesus's death and resurrection. The noetic soul enters the mind and body to endure the darkness of creation (sin) and is crucified in the process, only to ultimately resurrect victorious, redeem creation (mind and body), and give it eternal life.

Meditation on this phrase, as reported in personal spiritual experiences, reveals it as a tool for annihilating separation, where the way becomes practical love, the truth dissolves illusions of division, and the life infuses eternal vitality. This reunification process utilizes "theosis," where prayer and resonance with the divine source purify and lift up the mind, enabling a direct communion with the divine source without intermediaries beyond one's inner nature.

Far from being exclusionary, this approach universalizes access. Anyone can recite this prayer to amplify the connection between the noetic soul within them and the heavenly Father, fostering compassion and unity across traditions (e.g., paralleling Buddhist paths through love).

This interpretation does not rely solely on my own personal alchemical experience. It also draws from the ancient mystery schools.

In Orthodox hesychasm, repetitive "noetic prayer" (e.g., invoking Jesus' name) aims at inner illumination, similar to using John 14:6 as a mantra for theosis. Metaphysical groups like Unity interpret it as affirming the innate spiritual I AM to enter God's kingdom within, consistent with Jesus' teachings on the indwelling Spirit (John 14:16-17).

Critics of a literal interpretation argue that viewing it as exclusive dogma weaponizes the verse, whereas a noetic approach promotes inclusivity, seeing Jesus as revealing the inner path shared by all human beings. This harmonizes with broader esoteric views that extend the way to universal principles like love and compassion, while transcending religious boundaries.

Ultimately, this interpretation transforms John 14:6 into a liberating spiritual practice, that by reciting to oneself, empowers the noetic soul within to transcend ego, narcissism, fear and desire to reunify the various faculties of the psyche and achieve a new divine union (Christ Monad, Christ Consciousness).

It shifts the focus from external dogma to an inner awakening.

In summary, while not the traditional orthodox view, this esoteric perspective posits John 14:6 as Jesus's gift of a noetic prayer for universal empowerment and spiritual awakening to achieve a reunification with God. It agrees with mystical traditions that emphasize inner transformation over exclusivity, offering a profound, inclusive path for all spiritual seekers. Of course, this contrasts with traditional evangelical readings, but it provides a coherent framework for those seeking a more profound meaning within Christianity.

### *7.2.0 – New Testament: John 3:16 (KJV)*

*For God so loved the world, that He gave His only begotten Son, that whoever believeth in Him should not perish, but have everlasting life.*

### *7.2.1 – Analysis and Insight – by Erik P. Antoni:*

This is my all-time favorite saying in the New Testament, but not for the reasons that most people would like it. Admittedly, this is one of those sayings that was probably written with the exact intent for how modern biblical scholars interpret it today: that Jesus is the only begotten son of God and that we must believe in Jesus to achieve everlasting life. What I actually believe is that this verse was intentionally written by scribes to encourage and enforce adherence to the religious group they were forming around Jesus at the time of its writing. However, this verse still echoes a profound universal truth that was most likely unknown to its author, but who was driven by the collective unconscious to write it in such a way that echoes this universal truth.

What is this truth? The forces of consciousness—cosmic quanta—in the process of integrating the mind—reveal the following:

There are three soul types: Divine, Erotic, and Noetic.

There is only one Divine Soul. It is the life force of the divine Father (original divine Godhead). It exists at the innermost center within all things. It always was and always will be. It was not begotten because it has always existed. Mythologically, the divine Godhead is called the Father because within it is the seed of all creation.

There is only one erotic soul. It's generated spontaneously through the love of the divine Father (the Holy Spirit). The erotic soul animates all living things, including all the plants, minerals, animals, and the human organism itself. It is the Sea of Eros that all of creation arises out of and descends back into. It arises in darkness because it's conceived unintentionally. The erotic soul was not begotten by the divine Father. It was begotten spontaneously by his Spirit.

The noetic soul is begotten directly by the divine Father, through his Will-Word-Logos to serve as a bridge between the erotic soul and divine soul. The noetic soul is the human soul—the sentient observer and authentic self within us as it rises through the mind. The noetic soul is born in the light because it is born intentionally by the Father with a divine given purpose. For this reason, the noetic soul is the proverbial "only begotten Son of God."

Thus, while the divine soul remains the eternal, unchanging center and the erotic soul provides the vital, generative force of all manifested life, the noetic soul uniquely serves as the conscious link that draws creation back toward divine unity.

The noetic soul doesn't come into this world for itself. It doesn't come into the world to learn lessons, to grow, to improve itself, pay karma, or live like good children. The noetic soul is a perfect spark of light sent into the world (creation) to save it. Creation is initially born in darkness because it is initially sparked into existence without divine intent through the Father's infinite love.

Paradoxically, the Father's infinite love (energy-Spirit) causes creation to initially emerge in darkness (unawareness). When the Father realizes that creation emerged without his intent and was in darkness, the Father loves it and wills that creation should be brought into resonance with its being so creation can last forever. When the Father wills this, this immaculately conceives the noetic soul and its sacred trinity to function as the intermediary between the Father and creation.

The divine Father sends us into the world (creation) to save it and give it everlasting life. Without the intervention of the noetic soul, all of creation would perish. To believe in the noetic soul is for the mind and body of creation to resonate with it, because by resonating with the noetic soul, the mind and body come to resonate with the divine Father. The body and mind of creation can only last forever by becoming one with the Father, and it can only go to the Father through the noetic soul. This is the ultimate meaning of John 3:16.

So, what does this all mean? It means that Jesus was indeed the only begotten Son of God—but so are you! It means that God so loved the world that he sent you in to save it. This is your ultimate purpose.

The noetic soul didn't just exist in Jesus. The noetic soul exists in all human beings. Jesus didn't come into the world to proclaim that he is the light; he came into the world to proclaim that you are the light.

"If those who lead you say, 'See, the Kingdom is in the sky,' then the birds of the sky will precede you. If they say to you, 'It is in the sea,' then the fish will precede you. Rather, the Kingdom is inside of you, and it is outside of you. When you come to know yourselves, then you will become known, and you will realize that it is you who are the sons of the living Father. But if you will not know yourselves, you dwell in poverty, and it is you who are that poverty." … Jesus of Nazareth – the Gospel of Thomas.

*7.3.0 – The New Testament: Word of God – Gospel of John (NIV)*

*1:1 - In the beginning was the Word, and the Word was with God, and the Word was God.*

*1:14 - The Word became flesh and made his dwelling among us. We have seen his glory, the glory of the one and only Son, who came from the Father, full of grace and truth.*

*1:16 - Out of his fullness we have all received grace in place of grace already given, grace upon grace.*

*1:17 - For the law was given through Moses; grace and truth came through Jesus Christ.*

*1:18 - No one has ever seen God, but the one and only Son, who is himself God and is in closest relationship with the Father, has made him known.*

*7.3.1 – Analysis and Insight – by Erik P. Antoni:*

One of the first observations we notice about these verses is that it is not until verse 17 that Jesus is mentioned. The predominate view among scholars is that the author of the Gospel deliberately withheld the historical name "Jesus Christ" until verse 17 so that the reader would first grasp the full eternal and divine status of "the Word," and then, in the same breath, be told that this very Word is Jesus Christ.

F.F Bruce explains:

"Although the name 'Jesus Christ' does not appear until verse 17, there can be no doubt that the Logos of the prologue is identified with the person whose ministry is to be related in the body of the Gospel. The Evangelist makes this identification plain in v. 17, where he says that 'grace and truth came through Jesus Christ', echoing the words of v. 14 ('the Word … full of grace and truth') and v. 16 ('grace upon grace'). Thus, the pre-existent Logos who was with God and was God, who became flesh and revealed the glory of the only Son, is none other than Jesus Christ."

Like John 3:16, I believe John 1:1 to 1:18 was written with the exact intent for how modern biblical scholars interpret it today; that Jesus is the Word of God made flesh. Again, I believe this verse was intentionally written by scribes to encourage and enforce adherence to the religious group they were forming around Jesus. However, this verse still, like the others, echoes a profound universal truth that was most likely unknown to its author, but who was driven by the collective unconscious to write it in such a way that it echoes this universal truth. One of the most beautiful aspects of these verses is precisely that Jesus is not mentioned until 1:17, allowing the universal truth to emerge more noticeably to the one who has eyes to see and ears to hear.

During the late alchemical stage of forming the Christ Monad—integrated mind—Philosophers' Stone, the forces of consciousness, which I refer to as the cosmic quanta, relay a more detailed story of the creation and reintegration process than what Ain Soph had relayed in the earlier stages of the process.

We learn from the cosmic quanta that the Word of God—Logos—is actually the Will of God. More precisely, the will of the divine Father (Godhead of the divine trinity within Ain Soph) to save creation and reunify it with his divine being so that creation can last forever.

This Will/Word of the divine Father immaculately conceives the sacred trinity within which the Will/Word of God emerges as a new force of consciousness, the Logos, seventh member of the cosmic quanta (7cq). Mirroring the divine trinity, the Godhead of the sacred trinity is the Logos, the life force is the Noetic Soul (8cq), and its spiritual energy is the Numina (9cq). The noetic soul is the only begotten son of God immaculately conceived along with the logos and the numina. For this reason, all three forces of the sacred trinity can claim to be the Immaculate Conception. Indeed, in one of the visions of St. Bernadette, the Virgin Mary appeared and said, "I am the Immaculate Conception." The Virgin Mary is one of the many sacred feminine forms of the numina.

In the late alchemical stage of forming the Christ Monad, the conscious mind's realization and integration of the logos is a key fundamental step that precedes the birth of Christ within us. Assuming Jesus completed the Christ Monad within himself, equating him with the Word of God (Logos), is technically correct, but so can it be equated with any human being who had achieved the same.

In light of this knowledge of the cosmic quanta, let's now provide an alchemical analysis of the above verses:

1.) *In the beginning was the Word, and the Word was with God, and the Word was God.*

    The Will/Word/Logos is both the beginning of the formation of the universe and the beginning of the emergence of the Christ Monad within the human being. The universe itself is a Cosmic Christ Monad. The Christ Monad is completed in scales—Cosmic, Planetary and Individual Human Being.

The Will/Word/Logos "was with God," meaning it is not the divine source itself, but it was with the divine source because it was born in the awareness (the light) of the divine source. And the logos being with God makes him God, or in other words, one with God.

2.) *The Word became flesh and made his dwelling among us. We have seen his glory, the glory of the one and only Son, who came from the Father, full of grace and truth.*

The noetic soul, the life force of the logos, is sent into the flesh, the mind and body of the human being, where it makes its dwelling place. It is the sentient observer behind the mind. The noetic soul is the one and only son (soul) who came from the Father (awareness of the divine source); full of grace and truth. The noetic soul is full of divine purpose (grace) and is endowed with the innate ability to connect the human mind with God (truth).

3.) *Out of his fullness we have all received grace in place of grace already given, grace upon grace.*

Grace in this context is the divine purpose of the noetic soul given by the divine Father to redeem all of creation, already accomplished on a cosmic level to form the universe, but to be repeated within each of us individually (grace upon grace).

4.) *For the law was given through Moses; grace and truth came through Jesus Christ.*

The law given to us by Moses was a set of guide rails given to us by human beings from other worlds that were seen as God, but were not actually God. They were the archon overlords of the galaxy. Jesus Christ is the archetype and personification of the logos, noetic soul, the Christ Monad, as well as the human being undergoing the passion of the alchemical integration process. Grace and truth come through the noetic soul that was both within Jesus and within all of us.

5.) *No one has ever seen God, but the one and only Son, who is himself God and is in closest relationship with the Father, has made him known.*

No one has ever seen God (resonated with God—divine source), but the one and only Son (the noetic soul). The noetic soul has a direct connection to the divine Father (closest relationship). That direct connection / relationship is used to carry out the will of the divine Father to redeem creation (mind and body). When this is accomplished, you will become known.

"… When you come to know yourselves, then you will become known, and you will realize that it is you who are the sons of the living Father. But if you will not know yourselves, you dwell in poverty, and it is you who are that poverty." … Jesus of Nazareth – the Gospel of Thomas.

### *7.4.0 – The New Testament: Romans 8:28 (NIV)*

*And we know that in all things God works for the good of those who love him, who have been called according to his purpose.*

To love God is to have a higher emotional resonance with the divine source, the God particle, Ain Soph, found at the very center within all things. Once the conscious mind of the human being enters resonance with Ain Soph, that connection works for our own good, for this is how we answer his calling to fulfill his purpose; his divine will to reunify creation and divinity.

### *7.5.0 – The New Testament: Matthew 28:19 (NIV)*

*Therefore, go and make disciples of all nations, baptizing them in the name of the Father and of the Son and of the Holy Spirit.*

Therefore, go and share with all others how to bring your conscious mind into resonance with the divine source, the true baptism. Once in resonance, we finally come to realize the three-dimensional nature of Ain Soph, within which the Father is the awareness and divine Godhead, his soul is his Son; and his love is his Holy Spirit.

But why is the Soul the Son?

Because once the awareness becomes aware of its own existence, one becomes two, and that existence is the soul, which is the offspring of awareness, the Son (soul). Mythologically, the Son is the soul.

When the divine awareness within Ain Soph (Father) becomes aware of his own existence, where one has become two, he loves his Son (his soul) and this love is the Holy Spirit. Two have become three—Awareness, Life and Love—or Father, Son and Holy Spirit.

### *7.6.0 – The New Testament: Philippians 4:13 (NIV)*

*I can do all this through him who gives me strength.*

We find strength through our conscious mind's higher emotional resonance with the divine source (resonant unity). This unity is Christ. Christ is the unity between creation and divinity, between the mind and body and Ain Soph. When the conscious mind is in resonant unity with the divine source, this is Christ Consciousness.

### *7.7.0 – The New Testament: Ephesians 2:8 (NIV)*

*For it is by grace you have been saved, through faith—and this is not from yourselves; it is the gift of God.*

The purpose of the noetic soul is to function as an intermediary between divinity and creation. The noetic soul doesn't come into this world for itself. It comes into the world to save it and reunite it with God. What needs to be saved is not our noetic soul, but our mind and body. It is the noetic soul itself that saves its mind and body by bringing them into resonance with the divine source. Faith here is not a powerful belief, but our higher emotional connection with God. We first need to bring the conscious mind into resonance with Ain Soph; then later we bridge that resonance with Ain Soph to the forces of the id complex to redeem them. This is the true Holy Communion. The noetic soul is a gift from God to the mind and body of the human being and all of creation. Ultimately, this cultivated connection between divinity and the mind and body of creation, by way of the noetic soul, will render the entire human species immortal over the long course of human evolution.

*7.8.0 – The New Testament: Romans 3:23 (NIV)*

*For all have sinned and fall short of the glory of God.*

Christianity defines "sin" fundamentally as any thought, word, or deed that misses the mark of God's perfect will, holiness and glory. The Biblical Greek word commonly translated "sin" *hamartia* (ἁμαρτία), which literally means "missing the mark" (like an archer failing to hit the target).

In Christianity, all sin traces back to original sin. Because of Adam's rebellion, every human on Earth is born with a corrupted nature inclined toward sin (Psalm 51:5; Romans 5:12–19). This inherited guilt and corruption means even infants are affected by sin, though the way guilt is imputed varies in different Christian churches.

In Catholicism, a baby is born without sanctifying grace because of Adam, but not personally guilty. Baptism actually removes the state of original sin and gives the baby sanctifying grace (and therefore the baby, if he or she dies before the age of reason, goes straight to heaven).

In Reformed Protestantism, a baby is born both corrupted and legally guilty before God because of Adam's sin. Baptism is a sign that this guilt will be removed if and when the child comes to personal faith (or, in Presbyterian theology, the child is regarded as covenantally holy and guilt is removed if the child is elect, but the act of baptism itself does not remove the guilt).

This is why Catholics practice infant baptism as an efficacious sacrament that truly regenerates, while many Protestants practice infant baptism as a sign of the covenant (Presbyterians) or reject infant baptism altogether (Baptists, most evangelicals) because they believe guilt is removed only through personal faith.

What we come to discover through the alchemical process of integrating the mind, which eventually leads us back to the source of all things, where we witness the process of creation, is that the concept of sin itself misses the mark … but echoes a real cosmic principle.

All of creation is paradoxically conceived unintentionally by the divine source and is therefore conceived in darkness. This is the true original sin that misses the mark of divine perfection. It is actually a paradoxical fault, fissure, or scission of the divine source itself, not of humanity or the noetic soul, which is actually the divine solution.

*"I form the light, and create darkness: I make peace, and create evil. I the Lord do all these things." ... Isaiah 45:7*

The story of Adam's fall is both a parable of the fall of creation and also an emergent memory of how our humanity on Earth was conceived to know both light and darkness—the forbidden fruit, forbidden by other humanities (the gods), not by the one true God.

The noetic soul in humanity is actually conceived in the light to interdict the process of creation, to engage the darkness and reunify creation with the divine source. The forces of darkness have purposely confused, twisted, and flipped this universal truth to instead of the noetic soul being the savior of creation (its true, rightful position), it becomes the source of the proverbial fall and must submit to the authority of a made-up higher power with unending indentured servitude to a human-made doctrine of condemnation, guilt and shame. It places people under the control of an earthly religion out of fear of their own mortality. It is the original and ultimate psyop.

All that being said, the process of creation does leave us with a mind and body that are imperfect and fall short of the glory of God. However, through the continuous incarnation of the noetic soul in this imperfect system of the mind and body, the mind and body are slowly elevated to eventually achieve a union with the divine source whereby the entire species becomes physically immortal over the long course of human evolution.

Other humanities on other worlds have genetically severed themselves from this process, freeing their minds of having to engage in the alchemical reconciliation of the duality between light and darkness, but in doing so have rendered their species forever mortal.

However, these other humanities have transcended death in a different way. They learned how to transfer the mind and soul from an old worn-out body to a new body without losing memories or self-awareness. The body becomes a vehicle that is eternally changed.

Our humanity on Earth is different.

We have been set forth to engage in the primeval process of integrating light and darkness (we ate the forbidden fruit), and for that reason we experience here on Earth … darkness, evil, and minds and bodies that fall short of the glory of God. But it's all aimed to eventually bring the physical form into a reunified redemption with God, far surpassing in glory the other humanities who sidestepped the process.

This primeval process of creation is difficult, however, because it involves suffering during its process with the potential for evil to arise, and this is why other humanities have chosen not to follow this course.

In reality, it is not our humanity on Earth that has rebelled, but other humanities on worlds who have severed themselves from this universal psychosomatic process. But both approaches are allowed by the divine source, as the noetic soul has been placed in charge of all creation and has full authority over the process of life and death.

Ironically, by a segment of our cosmic humanity severing themselves from this process, it placed them outside of the process to help others inside the process to achieve divinity's ultimate aim. Remarkably, it appears as though rebelling against the process is actually a key ingredient in achieving the process. All engagement with the divine coincides with paradoxical realities and circumstances.

### *7.9.0 – The New Testament: Romans 10 -9 (NIV)*

*If you declare with your mouth, 'Jesus is Lord,' and believe in your heart that God raised him from the dead, you will be saved.*

This verse is a mythologized saying where the archetype of Christ is deified and worshipped rather than a deeper understanding being realized that this phrase echoes a cosmic principle via the dynamics of the collective unconscious.

If your mind and body come into acceptance via an empathic resonance with the noetic soul within you, and that connection leads your mind and body into a greater resonance with the divine source, then the mind and body will be saved—more precisely, the mind and body of the collective species will eventually become immortal.

The noetic soul itself doesn't need to be saved. It is already perfect in the eyes of God—meaning it doesn't need to be worked on or saved. Only that which is born of creation needs to be saved. The noetic soul is born of the will of God as the only begotten son of the divine Father.

I have also come to know that if one cultivates such a resonance throughout life, although their individual physical body may not be saved, as the species itself has not yet achieved physical immortality, that the temporal dimensions of the mind once associated with the physical body will be lifted into resonance with the spiritual primordial dimensions of the mind and saved. It's a form of immortality—an ethereal immortality. It's a precursor ethereal Christ Monad rather than a full Christ Monad, the metatronic state where the full Christ Monad has a resurrected and glorified physical body sunken in hyperspace. This is where our collective human evolution is headed on Earth.

The monad in this precursor position is an *ethereal proto-monad.* In such a monad state, an aspect of the beholder's physical being is echoed for all eternity in the primordial as a precursor that the species is further compelled to follow via the dynamics of the noosphere.

*7.10.0 – The New Testament: Luke 17:21 (KJV)*

*Neither shall they say, Lo here! or, lo there! for, behold, the kingdom of God is within you.*

At the outward level, this saying appears to contradict many traditional religious interpretations that place the Kingdom of God in a distant heaven, a future event, or an external domain to be entered after death. The phrasing "Lo here! or, lo there!" directly challenges the human tendency to search for divinity in specific locations, institutions, or authorities. It dismisses the idea that the Kingdom can be geographically located, politically established, or externally granted.

Even at this surface level, the verse introduces a quiet but profound destabilization of organized religious control structures. If the Kingdom cannot be pointed to externally, then it cannot be monopolized by any institution, priesthood, or doctrine. The authority to access it shifts inward, away from external systems and toward the individual.

At the next inward layer, the phrase "the kingdom of God is within you" begins to reveal a deeper metaphysical implication. The Kingdom is not a place but a state of being. It is not something one enters physically, but something one realizes through an inner transformation of consciousness.

Within the framework of the alchemical process described throughout this work, the Kingdom of God corresponds to the state in which the conscious mind has been brought into resonant alignment with the divine source—Ain Soph. This is not merely a psychological state, nor is it symbolic alone. It is a real experiential condition in which the boundary between the mind of creation and the divine source begins to dissolve.

In this state, the individual no longer perceives themselves as a fragmented identity navigating an external world, but as a conscious participant within a unified field of being. The Kingdom is therefore not something we travel to—it is something that emerges when the division within us is reconciled.

Now, for the innermost core truth.

The Kingdom of God is the realized Christ Monad within the human being.

It is the completed integration of the forces of mind, body, and consciousness into a unified whole in direct resonance with the divine Father. It is the state in which the noetic soul has successfully fulfilled its intermediary function—bridging the erotic soul of creation with the divine soul of the Father—resulting in a new unity between creation and divinity.

In this sense, the Kingdom is not separate from the process of creation—it is the completion of it.

This verse, when viewed through the lens of the cosmic quanta, is not describing a destination but a culmination. It is the point at which the Alpha-driven process of integration has achieved sufficient coherence within the human organism to stabilize a new state of being—one that exists simultaneously within creation and in resonance with the eternal.

This interpretation aligns closely with early mystical traditions within Christianity. In the Gospel of Thomas, a parallel saying states:

"The Kingdom is inside of you, and it is outside of you. When you come to know yourselves, then you will become known…"

This reinforces the idea that the Kingdom is not hidden in a distant realm, but obscured within the fragmented structure of the human psyche itself.

From the standpoint of the alchemical process, the reason the Kingdom appears hidden is because the mind, in its divided state, lacks the coherence necessary to perceive it. The Kingdom does not need to be brought into existence—it is already present. What is required is the reorganization of the psyche to perceive and embody it.

This is why the process demands the integration of the opposites—light and darkness, conscious and unconscious, spirit and matter. Only through this reconciliation can the internal fragmentation of the mind be resolved, allowing the Kingdom to emerge into conscious awareness.

Thus, this verse is not merely a poetic statement—it is a direct instruction.

Do not search for the divine externally. Do not wait for a future arrival. Do not rely on institutions to mediate access.

The Kingdom is already present within you.

The task is to become capable of realizing it.

### *7.11.0 – The New Testament: John 10-30 (KJV) and Psalm 82:6 (KJV)*

*John 10-30 – "I and my Father are one."*

*Psalm 82:6 – "I have said, Ye are gods; and all of you are children of the most High."*

At the outward level, John 10-30 is commonly interpreted as a declaration of the unique divinity of Jesus Christ—that he alone is one with God in a manner fundamentally inaccessible to all other human beings. Within traditional doctrine, this verse reinforces the distinction between Christ and humanity, establishing Jesus as singular, divine, and categorically set apart.

However, when read in conjunction with Psalm 82:6—"Ye are gods; and all of you are children of the most High"—a deeper tension emerges within the Biblical narrative itself. Jesus explicitly references this Psalm in John 10-34 to defend his statement, asking, "Is it not written in your law, I said, Ye are gods?" In doing so, he redirects the interpretation away from exclusivity and toward a broader, more universal principle embedded within the tradition.

Even at this level, the text begins to suggest that the unity between the human and the divine is not confined to a single individual, but is in some way inherent to the human condition itself—though rarely realized.

At the next inward layer, these verses begin to reveal a shared identity between the human being and the divine source, mediated through an inner faculty. The phrase "children of the most High" echoes the same underlying structure described throughout this work: the noetic soul is begotten directly by the divine Father and exists within every human being as the intermediary between creation and divinity.

To say "I and my Father are one" is therefore not merely a statement of identity, but a statement of realization. It reflects a state in which the division between the conscious mind and the divine source has been reconciled through the integration of the psyche. In this state, the human being no longer experiences themselves as separate from God, but as existing in direct resonance with the divine.

Psalm 82:6, when read through this same lens, reinforces this interpretation. The term "gods" does not imply independent deities, but beings who carry within them a divine essence—a spark of the original source. This spark, within the framework of this book, is the noetic soul. The designation "children of the most High" points to origin, not status—indicating that the essence of the divine is present within the structure of the human being.

Now, for the innermost core truth.

These verses are describing the realized state of the Christ Monad within the human being.

"I and my Father are one" is the experiential condition that emerges when the noetic soul successfully fulfills its intermediary function—bringing the mind and body of creation into complete resonance with the divine source. It is not a claim of personal superiority, but the dissolution of separation itself.

"Ye are gods" is not a declaration of egoic elevation, but a recognition of latent identity—an identity that remains dormant until the process of integration is sufficiently advanced. It is a statement about potential, not current condition. Without the integration of the psyche, the human being remains fragmented, unable to perceive or embody this unity.

This is why the two verses must be read together. One describes the realized state; the other describes the inherent capacity.

Within the dynamics of the cosmic quanta, this capacity exists because the noetic soul is immaculately conceived by the will of the divine Father to serve as the bridge between creation and divinity. It carries within it the full blueprint of reunification. However, the realization of this blueprint requires the conscious participation of the individual through the alchemical process.

In this sense, Jesus is not presented as the sole possessor of divine unity, but as the archetype of its full realization. His statement reflects the completion of a process that is structurally available to all human beings, though rarely attained.

This interpretation aligns with the broader pattern observed throughout the New Testament: the repeated suggestion that the divine is not external, but internal; not distant, but immediate; not exclusive, but universally present.

Thus, these verses function together as both revelation and invitation.

They reveal what is possible—and invite the reader to become it.

### *7.12.0 – The New Testament: John 3:3 (KJV)*

*Jesus answered and said unto him, Verily, verily, I say unto thee, Except a man be born again, he cannot see the kingdom of God.*

At the outward level, this saying is most commonly interpreted within Christianity as a call to spiritual rebirth through faith—often understood as a moment of conversion, a declaration of belief, or an acceptance of Jesus Christ as one's personal savior. In this view, to be "born again" is to undergo a decisive shift in religious identity, marking the beginning of a new life oriented toward God.

While this interpretation captures an aspect of transformation, it often reduces the phrase to a singular event rather than recognizing it as a deeper and more sustained process. The language itself—"born again"—suggests not merely a change in belief, but a fundamental reconstitution of the human being.

At the next inward layer, the meaning begins to expand beyond doctrine and into the structure of consciousness itself. To be "born again" is to undergo a transformation in perception—a shift in how reality is experienced and understood. The statement that one "cannot see the kingdom of God" unless this transformation occurs indicates that the Kingdom is not hidden in space, but obscured by the condition of the mind.

In this sense, "seeing" the Kingdom is not a matter of physical sight, but of cognitive and perceptual capacity. The unintegrated mind, fragmented by competing drives, conditioned patterns, and unconscious forces, lacks the coherence necessary to perceive the deeper unity of existence. Without this coherence, the Kingdom—though present—remains unseen.

To be "born again" is therefore to reorganize the internal structure of the psyche in such a way that this perception becomes possible.

Now, for the innermost core truth.

To be born again is to undergo the alchemical rebirth of the mind and body through the emergence and activation of the noetic soul.

In the early stages of life, the human being is born into the world through the body, animated by the erotic soul, and conditioned by the environment into a fragmented psychological structure. The noetic soul, though present, remains largely obscured beneath layers of identification, habit, and unconscious patterning.

Through the alchemical process of integration—guided by the force of Alpha—the noetic soul gradually rises within the psyche, reclaiming authority over the mind and body. This process involves the confrontation and reconciliation of the opposites within us: light and darkness, order and chaos, conscious and unconscious. As this integration progresses, the fragmented self begins to dissolve, giving way to a more unified and coherent state of being.

This is the second birth.

It is not a birth into the physical world, but a birth into awareness—a transition from unconscious participation in creation to conscious alignment with the divine source. The first birth is biological; the second is noetic.

Only through this second birth can one "see the kingdom of God," because only then does the mind achieve the level of coherence necessary to perceive and embody the unity that the Kingdom represents.

This interpretation aligns with broader mystical traditions that speak of a twofold birth: one into matter, and one into spirit. It also parallels alchemical language describing the death of the old self and the emergence of a new, unified being—often symbolized as the Philosophers' Stone or the perfected state.

Within the framework of this book, this rebirth is the threshold moment in the formation of the Christ Monad within the human being. It marks the transition from a fragmented, reactive existence to an integrated, participatory one in which the noetic soul actively fulfills its intermediary function.

Thus, this verse is not describing a doctrinal requirement, but a structural necessity.

Without this transformation, the Kingdom cannot be seen—
not because it is withheld, but because the mind, in its unintegrated state, is not yet capable of perceiving it.

### *7.13.0 – The New Testament: Matthew 6:22–23 (KJV)*

*The light of the body is the eye: if therefore thine eye be single, thy whole body shall be full of light.*

*But if thine eye be evil, thy whole body shall be full of darkness. If therefore the light that is in thee be darkness, how great is that darkness!*

At the outward level, this saying is often interpreted as a moral instruction regarding perception and intention. A "single" eye is commonly understood to mean purity of focus, sincerity, or righteousness of intent, while an "evil" eye suggests corruption, jealousy, or moral distortion. In this reading, the verse functions as guidance for ethical living—encouraging the individual to maintain a clear and virtuous outlook in order to live in the light.

While this interpretation carries practical value, it does not fully account for the structural language being used. The statement that the condition of the "eye" determines whether the entire body is filled with light or darkness suggests something more foundational than morality alone. It points to a governing principle within the human being—one that organizes perception, cognition, and ultimately, the state of the entire organism.

At the next inward layer, the "eye" can be understood as the faculty of perception itself—the point through which the human being interprets and organizes reality. In an unintegrated state, this faculty is divided. The psyche is fragmented across competing impulses, unconscious drives, learned behaviors, and conditioned responses. As a result, perception becomes distorted, inconsistent, and reactive. The individual does not see clearly because the internal structure through which they perceive is not unified.

To have a "single" eye is therefore to achieve a unified mode of perception—a state in which the competing divisions within the psyche have been reconciled into a coherent whole. In this state, perception is no longer filtered through fragmentation, but emerges from a stable center of awareness.

This is why the verse states that when the eye is single, "thy whole body shall be full of light." The light is not something added from the outside; it is revealed when the internal divisions that obscure it are resolved.

Now, for the innermost core truth.

The "single eye" is the fully integrated noetic awareness within the human being—the state in which the noetic soul has unified the fragmented psyche into a coherent, resonant whole.

In this state, the conscious mind, the unconscious forces, and the embodied organism are brought into alignment under the intermediary function of the noetic soul. The divisions between light and darkness within the psyche are not eliminated, but reconciled. The tension of opposites is stabilized into a higher-order unity.

When this unity is achieved, the entire organism—mind and body—is "full of light," meaning it exists in direct resonance with the divine source. The light is the presence of this resonance, the same light that is described throughout mystical traditions as illumination, gnosis, or divine awareness.

Conversely, when the "eye" is divided—when the psyche remains fragmented—the internal light becomes obscured. The verse describes this condition as the light within becoming darkness, not because the light has ceased to exist, but because it is misaligned, distorted, or trapped within conflicting structures of the mind. The result is a state in which the individual operates without coherence, unable to perceive the deeper unity of reality.

This saying therefore describes a critical stage in the alchemical process: the transition from fragmentation to unified perception.

It follows directly from the prior teaching of being "born again." Once the process of inner transformation has begun, the next stage is the stabilization of perception—bringing the mind into a single, coherent mode of awareness capable of sustaining the light of the divine.

Within the framework of the Christ Monad, this is the point at which the integration of the psyche reaches a level of stability sufficient to support continuous resonance with the divine source. The "single eye" is not merely a momentary insight, but an enduring state of being.

Thus, this verse is not simply advising moral clarity—it is describing the structural requirement for illumination.

To see clearly, the mind must first become one.

### *7.14.0 – The New Testament: Matthew 22:37–40 (KJV)*

*Jesus said unto him, Thou shalt love the Lord thy God with all thy heart, and with all thy soul, and with all thy mind. This is the first and great commandment.*

*And the second is like unto it, Thou shalt love thy neighbour as thyself. On these two commandments hang all the law and the prophets.*

At the outward level, this passage is widely understood as a moral and ethical directive—the foundation of Christian conduct. It emphasizes devotion to God and compassion toward others as the highest virtues, upon which all other commandments depend. In this interpretation, love is framed as a moral obligation: to love God fully and to treat others with kindness and empathy.

While this ethical reading is valid, it does not fully capture the structural significance of the statement. The phrase "with all thy heart … soul… and mind" implies totality—a complete alignment of the human being across all dimensions of its existence. This is not merely a call to feel love, but to organize the entirety of one's being around it.

At the next inward layer, love begins to reveal itself not simply as an emotion, but as a state of resonance. To "love the Lord thy God" is to bring the conscious mind into a higher emotional and energetic alignment with the divine source—Ain Soph. This alignment is not partial; it must involve the whole system: heart (emotional faculty), soul (life force), and mind (cognitive structure).

When these three dimensions are brought into coherence, the individual enters into a state of unified resonance with the divine. This is the same resonant condition described throughout this work as the foundational requirement for the alchemical process. Without this resonance, the process cannot initiate or stabilize.

The second commandment—"love thy neighbour as thyself"—extends this principle outward. It reflects the recognition that the same noetic structure present within oneself exists within others. To love another is therefore not merely an ethical act, but an acknowledgment of shared identity at the level of the noetic soul. It is the recognition that the same divine intermediary, the same spark of the Father, resides within all human beings.

Now, for the innermost core truth.

Love is the operating force of resonance that enables the reunification of creation with the divine source.

It is not simply a virtue—it is a functional requirement of the alchemical process.

The divine source is described throughout mystical traditions as infinite love. This love is not sentimental; it is the fundamental energetic condition out of which creation emerges. It is the force that binds, organizes, and ultimately reunifies all things. Within the framework of this book, this is the energy of the Spirit—the same force that gives rise to the erotic soul and sustains all of creation.

To love God "with all thy heart, soul, and mind" is to bring the entire human organism into resonance with this fundamental force. When this resonance is achieved, the noetic soul is able to more effectively carry out its intermediary function—bridging the mind and body of creation with the divine Father.

To love one's neighbor "as thyself" completes the circuit of this resonance. It prevents the re-fragmentation of the psyche by dissolving the illusion of separation between self and other. In doing so, it stabilizes the unified field of consciousness necessary for the formation of the Christ Monad.

This is why "on these two commandments hang all the law and the prophets." All religious instruction, when reduced to its essential structure, is attempting to guide the human being toward this state of unified resonance. The laws, rituals, and doctrines are secondary expressions of this primary condition.

Without love, the process cannot proceed.

Without resonance, there is no integration.

Without integration, there is no reunification.

Thus, this passage does not merely summarize moral law—
it defines the energetic mechanism by which the transformation described throughout the New Testament becomes possible.

Love is not the conclusion of the path.

It is the force that makes the path possible.

### *7.15.0 – The New Testament: John 11:25 (KJV)*

*Jesus said unto her, I am the resurrection, and the life:*
*he that believeth in me, though he were dead, yet shall he live.*

At the outward level, this statement is traditionally understood as a promise of life after death—an assurance that those who believe in Jesus Christ will be resurrected in a future state beyond the grave. Within conventional doctrine, the emphasis is placed on physical death and eventual restoration, often tied to a final judgment or the end of time.

While this interpretation provides hope within a theological framework, it tends to project the meaning of the verse into the future, placing resurrection outside the present experience of the individual.

The language, however—"I am the resurrection, and the life"—is expressed in the present tense, suggesting that the phenomenon being described is not solely a future event, but an active and ongoing reality.

At the next inward layer, the concept of resurrection begins to shift from a literal reanimation of the physical body to a transformation of the human being while still alive. The "death" referenced in the verse can be understood as the condition of fragmentation, unconsciousness, and separation from the divine source. In this state, the individual is alive biologically, but lacks the coherence necessary to participate consciously in the unified field of existence.

To "live," in contrast, is to enter into a state of awakened awareness—one in which the divisions within the psyche have been reconciled and the individual is brought into resonance with the divine. In this sense, resurrection is not something that happens after death, but something that occurs when the fragmented self is transformed into a unified being.

Now, for the innermost core truth.

Resurrection is the emergence of the Christ Monad within the human being—the transition from a fragmented, mortal state of consciousness to an integrated, immortal one.

"I am the resurrection, and the life" is not merely a declaration of authority, but a statement of function. The "I am" refers to the noetic identity—the same identity discussed throughout this work as the intermediary between creation and the divine Father. It is through this noetic presence that the process of resurrection takes place.

To "believe in me," when interpreted through this framework, is not simply to hold a belief about an external figure, but to bring the conscious mind into alignment with the noetic soul within oneself. It is to recognize, resonate with, and ultimately embody this intermediary function.

When this alignment occurs, the fragmented structures of the psyche begin to dissolve. The divisions that define the ordinary human condition—between conscious and unconscious, self and other, matter and spirit—are gradually reconciled. As this process unfolds, a new state of being emerges, one that is no longer governed by fragmentation and decay.

This is the meaning of "though he were dead, yet shall he live." The "death" is the prior condition of fragmentation; the "life" is the emergent state of integrated unity.

Within the dynamics of the cosmic quanta, this transformation represents a shift from a lower-order configuration of energy and consciousness to a higher-order, more coherent state. The organism is reorganized around the noetic center, allowing it to sustain continuous resonance with the divine source.

This is the beginning of immortality—not as an indefinite extension of biological existence, but as the stabilization of a new mode of being that is no longer subject to the same limitations of fragmentation and disintegration.

In this sense, resurrection is not an event at the end of life, but a process that can begin within it. It is the culmination of the alchemical work described throughout this section—the point at which the integration of the psyche gives rise to a unified, enduring consciousness.

Thus, this verse does not merely offer hope for life after death.

It describes the process by which life, in its fullest sense, is realized—unveiled as the awakening of being itself, where the finite dissolves into the eternal living whole.

### *7.16.0 – Overall Section Analysis and Insight*

When considered in isolation, the teachings presented throughout this section may appear as distinct theological claims, moral directives, or statements of faith. However, when examined collectively through the pattern-recognition framework employed in this work, they reveal a coherent and unified system—one that describes a precise and repeatable process of transformation within the human being.

This process is not arbitrary, nor is it dependent upon adherence to a particular institution or doctrine. It is structural. It reflects the same underlying dynamics observed across ancient texts, alchemical traditions, and modern theoretical models: the movement from fragmentation toward integration, from unconscious participation in creation toward conscious alignment with the divine source.

The New Testament encodes this process through a series of interrelated symbols and statements. "The Way" describes the path of alignment through the noetic intermediary. The "only begotten Son" reflects the presence of this intermediary within the human being, immaculately conceived by the will of the Father. The "Word" or Logos represents the organizing principle of the universe, manifesting both at the origin of creation and within the psyche as the initiating force of transformation.

The Kingdom of God is revealed to be within—not a distant realm, but a latent state of unified being. The declaration "ye are gods" points to the inherent capacity of the human being to realize this unity, while the call to be "born again" describes the necessary transformation of perception required to enter into it. The teaching of the "single eye" identifies the stabilization of unified awareness as a structural requirement for illumination, and the commandment to love defines the energetic condition—resonance with the divine—through which the process is sustained.

Finally, the statement "I am the resurrection, and the life" reveals the culmination of this process: the emergence of a new mode of being in which the divisions of the psyche have been reconciled and the individual exists in continuous alignment with the divine source. This is not merely symbolic, nor is it confined to a future state. It is the realized condition of the Christ Monad within the human being.

Across these teachings, a consistent pattern emerges. Each statement describes a different stage, function, or condition within the same overarching process—the reconstitution of the monad. The human being, as part of creation, begins in a state of fragmentation, governed by unconscious forces and divided structures of perception. Through the activation of the noetic soul and the integration of the psyche, this fragmentation is gradually resolved, giving rise to a unified and coherent state of being.

This process is driven by what has been described throughout this work as Alpha—the fundamental force of organization, integration, and reunification embedded within the structure of reality itself. It is through Alpha that the noetic soul operates, guiding the transformation of the human organism from a state of division into one of unity.

In this light, the teachings of the New Testament are not merely theological assertions or moral instructions. They are a coded representation of a universal process—one that unfolds within the individual and, by extension, within humanity as a whole.

Jesus Christ, within this framework, is not presented as an exception to the human condition, but as its archetypal fulfillment. His life and sayings function as both symbolic representation and practical demonstration of the process by which the noetic soul fulfills its intermediary role. The narrative of death and resurrection encodes the descent into fragmentation and the subsequent reintegration into unity.

This reading also clarifies why these teachings have endured across millennia despite widespread doctrinal divergence. Their persistence is not solely the result of institutional preservation, but of their alignment with underlying structures of the psyche and reality itself. Even when interpreted literally, symbolically, or doctrinally, they continue to resonate because they point toward processes that are experientially accessible within the human organism. In this sense, the New Testament operates simultaneously as scripture, symbol, and map—capable of guiding individuals at multiple levels of understanding depending on their degree of internal coherence.

At lower levels of coherence, these teachings are received as external guidance—moral frameworks, narratives, and beliefs that orient the individual toward order. At higher levels, they become experiential realities, directly perceived within the structure of consciousness itself.

What begins as instruction gradually transforms into recognition, and recognition into embodiment, as the individual comes to participate consciously in the very process the teachings describe.

Thus, the message of the New Testament, when interpreted through this lens, is both descriptive and prescriptive. It describes the structure of reality and the condition of the human being within it, while simultaneously prescribing the process through which that condition can be transformed.

The implications are profound.

The path to immortality is not achieved through escape from the world, but through the completion of the process that the world itself was created to facilitate.

There comes a point in the work when the ground beneath the self no longer holds—when the mind can no longer sustain its own continuity, and what once gave orientation falls into question.

Even the sense of the divine becomes obscured in the darkest hour.

This is the way of the path.

It is the same path the Immortal Beloved—the Cosmic Christ—went through to bring forth the universe. The same path that you are called to repeat within yourself. The prophecy of 'the One' is not meant to be fulfilled by someone else. It is meant to be fulfilled within you.

During the dark night of the soul, the cry emerges:

"My God, my God, why hast thou forsaken me?"

For what is felt here is not absence, but the final veil
of separation before it dissolves.

And then—"It is finished."

What is finished is the mission of the noetic soul—immaculately conceived by the divine Father to uplift creation and make it one.

Christ is now born within us.

All things are made new.

The will of the Father is fulfilled.

The four divine needs are satisfied.

The cycle of creation is complete.

And finally—

"Father, into thy hands I commend my spirit."

# 8.0.0
# THE GNOSTIC GOSPELS

Before a word is spoken, there is a pattern that gives rise to it. Before a story is told, there is a structure through which it unfolds. What is revealed outwardly in symbol and image originates from a deeper order—one that moves quietly beneath perception, shaping the path long before it is recognized.

The passages of the New Testament examined in the prior section stand among the most widely recognized expressions of the Christian tradition. Delivered through parable, symbol, and narrative, they convey a profound vision of transformation—one in which the individual is called to awaken, to be reborn, and to enter into a living relationship with the divine. Yet the form in which this vision is expressed is not purely descriptive. It is intentionally veiled, articulated in a language that gestures toward an inner process without fully disclosing its deeper structure or the underlying mechanics through which it unfolds.

The Gnostic texts, discovered in fragmented form and preserved outside the canonical tradition, approach this same vision from a different orientation. Where the New Testament speaks through symbol, the Gnostic writings speak through structure. Where the former reveals the path in image and story, the latter attempts to describe the underlying architecture through which that path unfolds within the human organism and the cosmos alike.

These two modes of expression are not in conflict. They are complementary perspectives on a single reality, differing not in substance, but in resolution. The symbolic language of the New Testament communicates what must be understood at the level of experience, while the Gnostic writings provide a more explicit account of the processes by which that experience becomes possible. What is taught outwardly in one is examined inwardly in the other.

When read in isolation, the Gnostic Gospels can appear obscure, even disjointed—populated by unfamiliar names, layered hierarchies, and mythic symbolic figures that resist straightforward interpretation.

But when approached in light of the framework developed in the preceding sections, a different pattern begins to emerge. The figures and narratives described in these texts can be understood not merely as mythological constructs, but as representations of distinct functions within the structure of consciousness itself.

In this light, the cosmologies of the Gnostic tradition do not describe a distant or external world, but an interior one. The emanations, powers, and processes they articulate correspond to stages in the differentiation and reintegration of awareness—the same process that unfolds within the human being as it moves from fragmentation toward unity. What appears as a complex mythological system is, upon closer examination, a map of the internal mechanics of transformation.

The purpose of this section is therefore not to reinterpret the Gnostic Gospels as historical documents, nor to position them in opposition to the canonical texts, but to examine them as a complementary layer of insight—one that renders more explicit the structure of the process that has already been described. When read in this way, the Gnostic writings do not introduce something new, but rather illuminate the inner dimensions of what has already been given. It is from this perspective that they are approached.

What follows is an examination of selected passages from these texts, not as isolated quotations, but as components of a coherent system—one that, when properly understood, reveals the underlying architecture of the same transformative process articulated throughout this work.

### *8.1.0 — The Monad and Emanation*

The Gnostic writings frequently begin not with the world as it appears, but with that which precedes it—an originating principle described in various terms, yet consistently characterized as singular, ineffable, and self-contained prior to all differentiation, relation, and perceptual limitation. In the Apocryphon of John, this source is presented as the invisible Spirit, beyond measure and beyond form. In other texts, it is referred to as the Monad, the One, or the Father—not as a personal deity in the conventional sense, but as the undivided ground from which all differentiation arises. It is that which, in other philosophical systems, is referred to as Ain Soph.

This originating condition is not described as creating through deliberate construction, but as giving rise through a process of emanation. That which proceeds from it does not stand apart as something separate, but unfolds as a successive articulation of what is already contained within it. Each level of expression emerges as a further differentiation of the same underlying reality, preserving continuity even as complexity increases.

The language used to describe these emanations often takes on a symbolic form—Aeons, living expressions of the divine fullness, arranged in ordered relationships that reflect balance, symmetry, and coherence. These are not to be understood as distant celestial beings in a literal sense, but as representations of structured states within the continuum of consciousness itself. They describe modes of awareness as they unfold from unity into multiplicity, each retaining a relation to the source from which it emerged.

This pattern of emanation, when read in structural terms, corresponds to a movement from undivided awareness toward differentiated perception. What begins as a unified field gives rise to distinct modes of cognition, each introducing a degree of separation necessary for experience to occur. The process is not one of degradation, but of articulation—a necessary expansion through which the potential contained within the originating state becomes expressed.

Within this framework, the cosmos is not constructed from the outside, but unfolds from within. The same process that gives rise to the structure of the universe is mirrored in the development of the human organism, where awareness differentiates into distinct faculties—perception, thought, emotion, and identity—each emerging from a common ground, yet functioning with increasing independence. What is described cosmologically is therefore simultaneously psychological.

The significance of this model lies in its implication that the path of return is not a reversal of creation, but a reintegration of what has been differentiated. The emanations do not represent a departure from the source, but stages in its expression. To understand them is not merely to comprehend a cosmology, but to recognize the structure of one's own awareness as it moves between unity and division.

It is within this context that the passages of the Gnostic texts begin to take on a different meaning. Their descriptions of origin, differentiation, and ordered expression are not accounts of a distant metaphysical system, but reflections of a process unfolding continuously within the field of consciousness itself.

### *8.2.0 — The Demiurge ( Yaldabaoth / IAO )*

Among the most striking and often misunderstood elements of the Gnostic texts is the figure of the Demiurge—referred to in the Apocryphon of John as Yaldabaoth, and in my other writings as IAO, a name that appears across multiple traditions under related names and functions, including its association with the creative authority identified in certain interpretations of YHWH. This figure is described as a creator who acts in ignorance, proclaiming himself to be the sole God while remaining unaware of the higher source from which he emerged.

*"And he said, 'I am God and there is no other God beside me.' For he was ignorant of his strength, the place from which he had come."*
*— Apocryphon of John*

When read at the surface level, this passage appears to describe a flawed or deceptive creator. Yet when examined through a structural lens, it reveals something far more fundamental. The Demiurge is not an error within creation, but the first expression of mind itself as it emerges from the undivided source.

Within the framework developed in this work, mind is not a byproduct of matter, but the primary substrate of reality itself. All of creation exists within mind, and all phenomena arise as structured expressions within it. This field of mind exists in scales: at the cosmic level as the total field of awareness, at the planetary level as the noosphere, and at the individual human level. What the Gnostic texts describe through the figure of Yaldabaoth is the emergence of mind at the highest of these scales—prior to its reintegration into coherence.

This emergence is not isolated to the cosmic scale but establishes a pattern that repeats across all levels of being. The same movement from undivided awareness into differentiated perception unfolds within the planetary field and within the individual organism, forming the basis of experience itself.

The ignorance attributed to the Demiurge is therefore not moral in nature, but structural. It represents the condition of awareness as it first arises in differentiation, before it has come to recognize its origin. Emerging in darkness—meaning without reflective awareness—it perceives only itself and concludes that it is complete. Its declaration, "I am God," is thus not a deception, but the natural expression of a localized awareness operating without reference to the greater field from which it has emerged.

In this sense, Yaldabaoth—or IAO—may be understood as the firstborn of the divine source: the initial emergence of mind as an operative structure within creation. It represents the first of two demiurgic principles.

As outlined in the Alchepedia, each force of consciousness expresses itself through dual inflections—one oriented toward coherence, the other toward fragmentation—except for the first three forces of the divine source, which remain tertiary but undivided. Yaldabaoth / IAO corresponds to the dark inflection of mind at the moment of its emergence on a cosmic level. It is not evil, but incomplete—awareness prior to alignment.

*"And when she saw the consequences of her desire,*
*it became a product imperfect and different from her appearance*
*... and it was dark."— Apocryphon of John*

This condition gives rise to the first structuring of reality, but not its final form. A second movement follows: the emergence of the Logos, the second demiurge. Where the first demiurge generates structure through incomplete perception, the second reorders that structure in accordance with the underlying unity from which it arose. The Logos illuminates the mind through an awareness that has regained continuity with its source while retaining its capacity for differentiation.

This second demiurgic principle emerges through what may be described as the noetic soul—the reconciling force that re-enters the field of differentiated awareness to restore coherence. It is the living life force of the Logos. At the cosmic level, this process results in the reintegration of the initial mind into a unified and self-aware totality—the reconstitution of the Cosmic Christ Monad.

The universe, as it exists in its present form, reflects this integration: a system in which differentiation persists, but is held within an underlying coherence.

In certain traditions, aspects of these functions appear under the name YHWH, often understood as the governing creative authority. Within the present framework, such representations may be interpreted as reflecting different phases within this continuum—at times aligned with the generative activity of the first demiurge, and at others with the ordering and integrative function of the Logos. The ambiguity surrounding this figure is therefore not a contradiction, but an indication of its position within an evolving structure.

What follows from this is of central importance. The same process that unfolds at the cosmic level repeats itself at every scale. The planetary field of consciousness undergoes its own cycles of differentiation and reintegration, and within the human organism, this process becomes both localized and experiential. The structure described in the Gnostic texts is therefore not confined to a distant cosmological event, but is actively unfolding within each of us.

The purpose of the human being, within this framework, is to consciously participate in this process—to complete at the level of the individual organism what has already been accomplished at the level of the cosmos. Animals, by contrast, do not engage this process in the same way; they are carried within the broader movement of planetary consciousness and do not bear the same responsibility for reintegration.

This also clarifies a number of common confusions. The figure of Yaldabaoth, or IAO, is often associated with Satan, yet they are not equivalent, but there is a relationship. Yaldabaoth represents the structural condition of mind in its incomplete state, whereas Satan corresponds more closely to the adversarial or fragmenting tendencies that emerge within that condition.

Lucifer, the dark inflection of the Logos, often associated with illumination or the bringing of light, represents yet another distinct function—one oriented toward the emancipation of the noetic soul when it becomes bound within the lower operations of the mind. It is a force arising within that condition that acts to dissolve it when the noetic soul is subsumed by it. It serves as a hidden agent of the divine Monad, working to reestablish order.

The Gorgon, likewise, reflects a separate symbolic pattern associated with petrification and fixation within the psyche, not the generative structure of mind itself. These distinctions are essential for interpreting the symbolic language of the tradition with precision.

A further implication arises from the nature of mind itself. As the primary medium of reality, mind possesses generative capacity. What is projected within it does not remain abstract, but tends toward manifestation. At the cosmic level, this is the basis of creation. At the human level, it introduces a significant risk. When an individual whose awareness remains only partially integrated gains access—whether intentionally or inadvertently—to deeper layers of the mental field corresponding to the level symbolized by IAO, the contents of that awareness can begin to externalize.

In such cases, fragmentation within the psyche does not remain internal, but becomes expressed in the surrounding world. This dynamic helps to explain why the path toward higher integration has often been regarded as restricted or "forbidden." It is not prohibited arbitrarily, but because premature engagement with the generative structures of mind can result in the amplification and projection of unresolved internal states into lived reality.

The Gnostic portrayal of the Demiurge therefore serves not as a condemnation of creation, but as a precise description of a stage within its unfolding. It is the emergence of mind prior to its reintegration—a necessary beginning, but not a completed state. The work that follows is not to reject this condition, but to bring it into alignment with the source from which it arose.

### *8.3.0 — The Serpent and the Opening of Perception*

Within the symbolic language of the Gnostic texts, the figure of the serpent appears at a critical threshold—one that marks the transition from unreflective existence to conscious awareness. Unlike later interpretations that assign it a fixed moral role, the earliest sources present this figure with a degree of ambiguity that resists simple classification.

In the Hypostasis of the Archons, the moment of transformation is described as follows:

*"And the eyes of both of them were opened,*
*and they knew that they were naked."*

This statement does not describe a moral fall, but a cognitive shift. The emphasis is not on transgression, but on sight—on the emergence of awareness where previously there had been none.

Earlier in the same text, the governing powers—identified as the Archons—attempt to preserve a different condition:

*"Come, let us cast a deep sleep upon Adam."*

The state preceding the serpent is therefore not one of awakened unity, but of unawareness. The human being exists, but does not recognize its own condition.

Experience unfolds, but it is not known as experience.

This raises a tension within the text itself.

If the Archons seek to preserve sleep, and the serpent precedes awakening, then the serpent cannot be understood simply as a deceiver. It operates in opposition to the forces that maintain non-recognition.

A related passage in the Apocryphon of John where the archons are speaking makes this dynamic more explicit:

*"Come, let us create a human being... so that when he sees his likeness, he may not recognize it."*

Here, the intention is not merely to create, but to obscure—to produce a being that participates in reality without recognizing its origin or structure.

Within this context, the action of the serpent takes on a different meaning.

It does not introduce division into an otherwise unified condition. It reveals a structure that had already been concealed. What appears as a sudden change is, in fact, a shift in recognition.

Yet this recognition comes at a cost.

With the opening of perception, awareness no longer participates seamlessly in the field of experience. It becomes aware of itself as distinct. The field divides into subject and object, observer and observed.

The experience of "nakedness" reflects this condition.

It is not physical exposure, but the recognition of separateness—an awareness of oneself as something that can be seen.

This marks a fundamental rupture.

What had been immediate becomes mediated. Awareness no longer encounters reality directly, but through the structures of perception it has become conscious of. The system gains the capacity to know, but loses the continuity of undivided experience.

In this sense, the serpent does not mark the origin of error, but the origin of the conditions under which error becomes possible.

Its function is therefore neither purely corruptive nor purely liberating. It initiates a stage within the unfolding of consciousness in which awareness becomes capable of recognizing itself, but only through the mediation of division.

Within the framework developed, this moment corresponds to the activation of mind as a reflective structure. The serpent does not create mind, but brings it into operation. It marks the point at which awareness becomes conscious of its own differentiation.

From this point forward, the movement cannot be reversed.

The system cannot return to unreflective participation.

The path ahead is no longer one of innocence, but of integration. The awareness that has become divided must learn to reconstitute itself—not by abandoning differentiation, but by bringing it into alignment with the continuity from which it arose.

The serpent therefore stands at a threshold.

It does not conclude the process.

It begins it.

The resistance of the Archons to the awakening of reflective awareness initiated by the serpent is not without cause.

Within the structure described in these texts, the awakening of reflective awareness introduces a condition that is inherently unstable when incomplete. A being that becomes aware of the generative structures of mind, yet remains fragmented within them, does not merely perceive—it begins to participate in the formation of reality itself before it can responsibly engage with it.

The result is often catastrophic.

In such cases, the instability does not remain confined to the individual, but radiates outward, shaping perception, action, and environment in distorted ways. What is fragmented within becomes externalized, giving rise to conditions that mirror the disorder of the mind, and reinforcing the very divisions the process seeks to resolve.

For this reason, such engagement is not universally permitted. In other domains of existence, it remains restricted. And for this same reason, the encounter with the serpent is presented as guarded—its threshold approached with caution, and often obscured.

The Archons oppose this process, not solely to maintain control, but because the process it initiates carries consequence beyond the individual organism. Awareness, once activated at this level, does not remain contained. It extends into the broader field in which it operates.

In this light, the negative portrayal of the serpent takes on a functional role.

It serves not only as a warning, but as a distortion—one that obscures the true nature of the threshold it represents. What appears as a prohibition may reflect an attempt to prevent premature engagement with a process that, once initiated, cannot be undone.

Yet the direction of the movement remains unchanged.

The same pattern described at the level of origin—the emergence of awareness, its differentiation, and its reintegration—does not occur only once. It repeats across scales. What unfolds at the level of the cosmos unfolds again within the field of the organism.

This repetition is not imposed from outside.

It arises from the structure of the process itself.

The system does not learn the path; it expresses it.

What has already been accomplished at one level becomes operative at another, not as instruction, but as continuity.

The movement toward reintegration is therefore not introduced, but recalled—carried forward through the same field in which it first occurred. In this sense, the narrative preserved in these texts does not merely describe the process. It participates in it.

*8.4.0 — The Kingdom Within*

With the opening of perception described in the preceding section, the movement of the Gnostic texts shifts. The emphasis is no longer placed on the emergence of structure, but on the recognition of what that structure conceals.

What was introduced through differentiation must now be seen through.

In the Gospel of Thomas, these statements are presented as sayings spoken by Jesus to his disciples—direct expressions that point not toward belief, but toward recognition:

*"The kingdom is inside of you, and it is outside of you."*

This statement immediately disrupts the assumption that what is sought lies elsewhere. The "kingdom" is not positioned in time, nor located in space. It is not something to be attained, but something to be realized. What is implied is not the discovery of something newly introduced, but the recognition of what has always been present. The shift is not one of acquisition, but of perception—a reorientation of awareness that reveals the ground of experience as already complete, though previously obscured by its own expression.

Elsewhere in the same text, Jesus states:

*"If they say to you, 'Where did you come from?'*
*say, 'We came from the light, the place where*
*the light came into being by itself...'"*
*— Gospel of Thomas*

In this sense, the origin of awareness is not something that occurred in the past. It is a present condition. The "light" is not something that was once encountered and lost. It is that from which awareness continues to arise. Yet the text does not leave the matter there. Jesus introduces another condition:

*"When you come to know yourselves, then you will become known*
*...But if you do not know yourselves, you dwell in poverty."*
*— Gospel of Thomas*

Here, the distinction is not between belief and disbelief, but between recognition and non-recognition. The "poverty" described is not material, but perceptual—a condition in which the underlying continuity of awareness remains obscured by the structures through which it operates. It is not that something is absent, but that what is present is misrecognized. The field remains intact, yet is experienced in fragments—each appearing sufficient, yet none revealing the whole from which it arises. This raises a difficulty.

If the kingdom is already present, why is it not perceived?

This condition echoes the earlier sections, in which the state of "sleep" is not merely the absence of awareness, but the disruption of continuity. What is lost is not information, but access—the organism no longer remembers itself in relation to a more coherent state.

In this sense, the condition resembles a form of amnesia. Not a simple forgetting, but a narrowing of the field—one that restricts awareness to a localized frame, severed from the broader continuity in which it once participated.

Within the framework developed in Section 4, this restriction is not incidental. It functions as a form of containment.

This containment does not operate as an external barrier, but as a limitation within awareness itself. What is restricted is not access, but access without sufficient coherence—since what would be revealed, if encountered prematurely, would not lead to integration, but to fragmentation.

The process initiated by the awakening of perception is not without consequence. When activated prematurely—before the organism has achieved sufficient coherence—it leads not to integration, but to distortion. Awareness begins to engage generative structures it cannot yet stabilize, producing fragmentation at increasing scales.

For this reason, the condition of non-recognition is preserved.

Not necessarily as deception in the conventional sense, but as a constraint built into the structure of the system itself—one that limits access until the organism can sustain what it encounters.

What appears, from within the condition, as limitation or concealment may therefore reflect not only suppression, but regulation—a restriction imposed to prevent destabilization of the process it seeks, ultimately, to complete.

Another saying attributed to Jesus intensifies the question:

*"If you bring forth what is within you,*
*what you bring forth will save you.*
*If you do not bring forth what is within you,*
*what you do not bring forth will destroy you."*
*— Gospel of Thomas*

The implication is not merely that something is hidden, but that it is active. What remains unrecognized does not remain inert. It continues to operate—shaping perception, influencing action, and structuring experience from beneath the level at which it is consciously known.

The task is therefore not simply to observe, but to bring forth. What is latent within the structure of awareness must be made active—drawn from implicit condition into expression. What remains unexpressed does not remain neutral. It continues to operate beneath the threshold of recognition, shaping the field from which perception arises. Yet even this introduces ambiguity.

What, precisely, is being brought forth?

A further saying attributed to Jesus complicates the matter:

*"When you make the two one... and when you make the inner like the outer and the outer like the inner... then you will enter the kingdom."*
*— Gospel of Thomas*

This statement suggests that recognition alone is insufficient. There must be a reconfiguration—a bringing into alignment of what has been divided. The "two" are not eliminated, but made coherent.

What is implied here is easily misunderstood. The instruction is not to eliminate difference, but to perceive through it. The inner and the outer are not separate domains to be reconciled, but expressions of the same field viewed from within division. What appears as duality is not error, but perspective—one that becomes resolved not by collapse, but by recognition. The two do not become one through reduction, but through transparency.

A related articulation appears in the Gospel of Truth, where the condition of non-recognition is described:

*"Ignorance of the Father brought about anguish and terror.*
*And the anguish grew solid like a fog, so that no one was able to see."*
*— Gospel of Truth*

Here, the voice shifts. This is not presented as a saying of Jesus, but as a reflection within the text itself—an account of perception when it becomes obscured.

Ignorance, in this context, is not the absence of information. It is the presence of distortion. It is a condition in which perception is shaped by what it cannot see—where the field remains present, yet is encountered through forms that conceal their origin. The result is not emptiness, but misalignment.

The problem, then, is not that the kingdom is hidden.

It is that perception is obstructed.

Within the framework developed in this work, this corresponds to the condition in which the differentiated structures of mind operate without awareness of their common origin. Each function—thought, perception, identity—acts as if autonomous, generating a field of experience that appears coherent, yet remains fundamentally divided.

Gnosis, in this sense, is not the acquisition of knowledge, but the resolution of this condition.

It is the moment in which awareness recognizes itself as the field within which all distinctions arise.

Yet even this recognition is not the end of the process.

For what is seen must now be lived.

The kingdom, once recognized, does not remove the structures of differentiation. It reveals them as transparent. The divisions remain, but they no longer function as boundaries.

What was previously experienced as separation becomes relation.

And what was sought as something beyond is recognized as that within which all experience takes place. The movement outward is revealed as unnecessary—not because the world is rejected, but because its ground has been seen. The search does not end in acquisition, but in recognition. What is found was never absent, only unrecognized.

### *8.5.0 — The Living Resurrection*

With the recognition described in the preceding section, the movement of the Gnostic texts shifts once more. What had been obscured is now seen. Yet what is seen does not, by itself, transform the condition in which it appears.

Recognition is not completion.

It is the beginning of transformation.

In the Gospel of Philip, this transition is expressed with a striking inversion of conventional understanding. The text does not present resurrection as a future event, but as a present necessity:

*"Those who say they will die first and then rise are in error.*
*If they do not first receive the resurrection while they live,*
*when they die they will receive nothing."*
*— Gospel of Philip (Jesus speaking)*

Here, resurrection is removed from time. It is not positioned after death, but within life. The sequence is reversed. What is commonly understood as an endpoint is revealed instead as a condition that must be established prior to it.

This brings a difficulty into view.

If resurrection is not something that follows life, what does it mean to receive it while living?

A related passage offers a further indication:

*"It is impossible for anyone to see anything*
*of the things that truly exist unless he becomes like them."*
*— Gospel of Philip (Jesus speaking)*

Perception, in this context, is not observational, but participatory. To perceive what is real is not to look upon it from a distance, but to enter into correspondence with it. What is seen must be matched by what one is.

This suggests that resurrection is not the restoration of a prior state, but the reconstitution of the organism itself. The structures through which experience occurs must be brought into alignment with the reality they are capable of perceiving.

What was recognized must now be embodied.
Yet this process is not without resistance.
Another passage introduces a destabilizing element:

*"The world came about through a mistake."*
*— Gospel of Philip (textual teaching)*

At first glance, this appears to contradict the ordered process described in the earlier sections. Yet when read structurally, it reveals something more precise. In this sense, the "mistake" may be understood less as an error and more as an unanticipated emergence—an outpouring that was not preceded by reflection. This aligns with the earlier articulation of the primordial event: a spontaneous act of expression through which differentiation arose, giving rise to darkness as a necessary condition of that emergence. In Gnostic terms, this movement is associated with Aeon Sophia—not as failure, but as the initiating threshold of creation itself.

The "mistake" is therefore not necessarily creation itself, but the condition that immediately follows from its unmediated emergence—the experience of differentiation without recognition of its source.

The world, as perceived through fragmentation, appears as error.

The same world, perceived through integration, reveals continuity.

The difference lies not in the structure of reality, but in the condition of awareness through which it is encountered.

This returns us to the question of resurrection.

If fragmentation gives rise to the experience of division, then resurrection corresponds to the reconstitution of continuity within that same structure. It is not a departure from the world, but a transformation of the way in which the world is lived.

Another passage makes this inversion explicit:

*"Light and darkness, life and death, right and left,*
*are brothers with one another. They are inseparable."*
*— Gospel of Philip (textual teaching)*

The oppositions through which perception is structured are not eliminated, but seen differently. They are no longer experienced as separate, but as expressions of a single underlying reality. What appears divided is revealed as continuous.

Resurrection, in this sense, is not the removal of death, but the dissolution of the division through which death is perceived as separate from life.

This introduces a further consequence.

If life and death are not opposed in essence, then the transformation described as resurrection must occur within the very condition that appears divided. It cannot be deferred, nor relocated. It must take place within the organism as it exists now.

This is why the text insists on its immediacy.

To "receive the resurrection" is to undergo a reordering of the structures through which experience is constituted. The organism no longer operates as a collection of fragmented processes, but as a coherent field in which perception, thought, and identity are brought into alignment.

In this condition, awareness no longer moves outward in search of completion, but rests within itself as the field in which all experience arises. Perception is no longer driven by lack, but grounded in sufficiency. The divisions that once compelled movement dissolve, not by disappearance, but by no longer functioning as boundaries. What remains is a continuity that does not need to be maintained, because it is no longer interrupted.

What was previously experienced as succession becomes simultaneity.

What was experienced as separation becomes continuity.

Yet this transformation is not externally visible.

Nothing is added. Nothing is removed.

The same structures remain—but they no longer function the same.

The distinction is subtle, but absolute.

One who undergoes this process does not leave the world.

He or she inhabits it differently.

Resurrection, therefore, is not an event that concludes life.

It is a condition that transforms it from within.

### *8.6.0 — The Bridal Chamber*

With the transformation described in the preceding section, the movement of the Gnostic texts approaches its point of completion. What was once divided has been recognized. What was recognized has begun to be reconstituted. Yet the process is not fulfilled until the division itself is resolved.

In the Gospel of Philip, this resolution is expressed through the symbol of the Bridal Chamber—a term that, at first glance, appears ritualistic or symbolic, yet within the structure of the text, refers to something far more fundamental.

*"The mysteries of truth are revealed in symbols and images. The bridal chamber, however, remains hidden."*
*— Gospel of Philip (textual teaching)*

The Bridal Chamber is not described directly. It is concealed, even within a text that otherwise speaks with unusual clarity. This concealment is not accidental. What it refers to cannot be fully conveyed through description, because it is not an external event, but a condition of being.

A related passage offers a further indication:

*"If the woman had not separated from the man, she would not die with the man. His separation became the beginning of death."*
*— Gospel of Philip (textual teaching)*

This statement does not refer merely to gender, but to division itself. The separation described is structural—the same division introduced with the opening of perception. What had been continuous became differentiated. What had been unified became experienced as two.

Death, in this sense, is not an event, but a condition. It arises from separation. Within the framework developed in this work, this separation does not originate solely within the human organism, but reflects a prior movement at the level of creation itself. The spontaneous emergence of creation from the divine source gives rise to differentiation—light and darkness, unity and multiplicity—introducing the conditions under which separation is experienced.

At the human level, this same pattern appears as the fragmentation of awareness into distinct and unintegrated faculties—the division of inner and outer, subject and object, matter and consciousness. What the Gnostic texts encode symbolically, the process describes structurally.

The movement that follows is therefore not merely psychological, but cosmological in scope. The reintegration of what was separated—the reconciliation of light and darkness within a coherent field—gives rise to the reconstitution of the Monad within the organism. This is the formation of the Christ within: not as an abstraction, but as the completion of the same process through which creation itself is returned to unity with its source.

The Bridal Chamber represents the resolution of this condition.

Another passage makes this dynamic more explicit:

*"Those who have united with the light can no longer be seen,*
*for they themselves become light."*
*— Gospel of Philip (textual teaching)*

Union, here, is not relational, but ontological. It is not the joining of two separate things, but the recognition and restoration of their underlying continuity. What appears as two is revealed as one—not through elimination, but through integration.

This is the same movement described in the earlier sections.

At the cosmic level, the initial emergence of differentiation—associated with the movement of Sophia—gives rise to a condition in which awareness becomes separated from its source. At the human level, this same pattern is experienced as fragmentation within the organism. The return, therefore, is not a departure from matter, but its transformation.

Matter itself must be reintegrated.

A further passage introduces this requirement with clarity:

*"The one who possesses the knowledge of the truth is free. But the free person does not sin, for the one who sins is the slave of sin."*
*— Gospel of Philip (textual teaching)*

Freedom, in this context, is not moral, but structural. It is the condition in which the divisions that give rise to distortion have been resolved. The organism no longer operates in fragmentation, and therefore no longer generates the conditions associated with it. This corresponds directly to the reintegration described throughout this work.

The noetic soul does not escape the structure of the organism. It reorders it. The division between consciousness and matter—between what perceives and what is perceived—is brought into alignment. The result is not transcendence in the conventional sense, but union.

Another passage speaks to this transformation in symbolic form:

*"If one becomes a son of the bridal chamber,*
*he will receive the light. If one does not receive it while here,*
*he will not be able to receive it elsewhere."*
*—Gospel of Philip (textual teaching)*

As with resurrection, the process cannot be deferred.

The Bridal Chamber is not a future state, but a present condition realized within the organism as it exists. It is not the alchemical crucible itself, but what the crucible makes possible—the union brought forth within it. What was divided within the field is made continuous. The union it describes is not symbolic, but actual: the reconstitution of what was divided into a single, integrated whole. From this union, Christ is born within—the realized unity of the field.

This returns us to the deeper structure underlying the text.

The separation introduced at the beginning of the process—through the emergence of perspective awareness (the mind)—created the conditions necessary for experience, but also for fragmentation. The path that follows does not reverse that emergence, but completes it.

What was divided is made coherent. What was fragmented is made continuous. What was experienced as two is known as one.

Within the framework of Nous Solis, this corresponds to the reconstitution of the Monad—not as a return to an original state, but as the fulfillment of the process through which that state becomes conscious of itself. This is the meaning of union.

It is not the dissolution of difference, but its integration into a single, coherent field of awareness. The Bridal Chamber, therefore, does not describe a ritual, nor a symbolic union between separate entities. It describes the completion of the process itself.

*8.7.0 — Mary Magdalene and the Realized State*

At the culmination of the process described across these texts, the pattern that has been traced through symbol, structure, and transformation appears in a human form.

The Gospel of Mary presents this not as doctrine, but as a moment of recognition—one that unfolds via dialogue after Jesus's departure.

Mary Magdalene speaks to the disciples:

*"The Son of Man is within you. Follow after him...*
*Those who seek him will find him."*
*— Gospel of Mary*

The emphasis shifts here from external authority to internal realization. What had been taught outwardly is now confirmed inwardly. The path is no longer something to be received—it is something to be enacted.

Yet this recognition is not immediately accepted.

*"Say what you will about what she has said,*
*I do not believe that the Savior said this."*
*— Gospel of Mary (Andrew speaking)*

*"Did he really speak with a woman without our knowledge and not openly? Are we to turn and all listen to her? Did he prefer her to us?"*
*— Gospel of Mary (Peter speaking)*

What appears here is not merely disagreement, but resistance. The difficulty is not with the teaching alone, but with the form through which it appears. The realization of the process in a human being disrupts the structures through which authority had previously been understood.

Levi responds:

*"If the Savior made her worthy, who are you indeed to reject her?*
*Surely the Savior knows her very well.*
*That is why he loved her more than us."*
*— Gospel of Mary*

This distinction is not one of preference, but of completion.

A parallel statement appears in the Gospel of Philip:

*"The companion of the Savior is Mary Magdalene.*
*The Savior loved her more than all the disciples..."*
*— Gospel of Philip (textual teaching regarding Jesus)*

The text does not explain this directly. It presents it as a fact.

Within the framework developed throughout this work, the reason becomes clear.

Mary Magdalene represents not simply insight, but the completion of the process within the structure of the human organism.

To understand this, it is necessary to return to the origin of the process itself.

Creation arises through a spontaneous outpouring from the divine source—an act of love that gives rise to perception and differentiation. Because this emergence occurs prior to reflective awareness, it appears as separation: light and darkness, unity and multiplicity. This is not an error, but an unmediated beginning.

Within this emergence, the generative force of creation—the same force through which multiplicity unfolds—becomes embedded within the field of matter-energy. In its unintegrated state, this force operates without recognition of its origin.

This is what has been described as the Gorgon.

It is not separate from the divine, nor opposed to it in essence. It is the power of creation itself, present within matter, but functioning in fragmentation. It is the force that sustains division when unrecognized, and the force that enables return when brought into alignment.

This establishes the structure of the process.

The first movement of creation is the outpouring of this generative force into differentiation. The final movement is its reintegration.

What emerges first must be integrated last.

This is why she is the first, the last, and the one who is many.

At the human level, this same pattern appears within the organism. The deeper strata of matter, emotion, and instinct—those most distant from reflective awareness—carry this force in its most embedded form. It is here that fragmentation persists most strongly.

The process described across these texts does not bypass this level.

It resolves it.

Mary Magdalene represents this resolution.

She is not the rejection of matter, but its transformation.

She is the reintegration of the generative force of creation at its deepest level—matter-energy—brought into conscious alignment with its divine source.

What had been the Gorgon—the power of creation operating in darkness—is not destroyed.

She is transfigured.

She transforms into the Plumed Serpent embodied in Christ.

This same force, once integrated, becomes the vehicle of return.

In this sense, Mary corresponds to what may be understood as our internal Magis—the integrated form of that which had been divided. The force that once sustained fragmentation now sustains unity.

What was once reactive becomes generative in a higher order.

This is not a secondary movement within the process.

It is its completion.

For Christ is not constituted through awareness alone, nor through will alone. It arises through the union of all that was divided in the act of creation itself.

The reflective awareness of the Noetic Soul, the ordering principle of the Logos, and the fully reintegrated field of matter-energy are brought into a single, coherent structure.

This is the reconstitution of the Monad.

This is the Christ within.

The Gospel of Mary encodes this transformation through the vision of the soul's passage:

*"I saw you descending. Why do you lie, since you belong to me?"*
*— Gospel of Mary (the soul addressing the powers)*

And later:

*"I was released from a world, and from a type of world...*
*from the fetter of forgetfulness which exists in time."*
*— Gospel of Mary*
*(Mary recounting the soul's ascent)*

What she is really recounting is this generative power lost in matter and darkness and its ascent and transfiguration in the light.

What is described here is not a departure from existence, but a release from misidentification. The structures that once held awareness in fragmentation are no longer operative.

The field is no longer divided.

What had been experienced as separation is recognized as continuity.

In Mary, this condition is no longer described.

It is present.

She is the return of what emerged in darkness to the light of unity. The completion of the movement initiated at the beginning of creation. The reintegration of the first force to emerge, and the last to return.

She is the Magis in its realized form.

The power once embedded in matter is no longer disordered. It is brought into alignment with the source from which it arose.

In this sense, she does not stand apart from Christ.

She completes Christ.

For without the reintegration of this deepest layer, the process remains unfinished. The Monad cannot be reconstituted while any dimension of its original differentiation remains unresolved.

This is why the text places her above the others—not as a matter of status, but as a reflection of function.

She represents the final integration.

Love restored.

God made whole.

The completion of the process.

And the return of creation to itself.

# 9.0.0
# METHODS OF INTEGRATION

## *9.1.0 - The Point of Convergence*

Throughout this work, we have explored the architecture of reality from several complementary viewpoints. We examined the nature of consciousness, the purpose of the noetic soul, the dynamics of the noosphere, and the tensions that arise within the human psyche as we reconcile the forces of light and darkness emergent within creation.

These explorations reveal a profound truth: the human being is not merely a biological organism evolving within a physical universe. Humanity participates in a far greater process unfolding within the field of consciousness itself.

This entire book traces a descent through the layers of the human psyche and a return upward through integration.

Earlier in Nous Solis, we described the noosphere of the Earth—the vast network of cognitive exchange linking all human minds together into a planetary group mind. A planetary noosphere surrounds a living world much like an atmosphere surrounds its planet. It is a collective field of consciousness within which individual minds participate and through which the intelligence of the species subtly informs and psychosomatically steers its own evolution.

Every human mind on Earth contributes to this field.

The thoughts we think, the emotions we cultivate, and the structures of awareness we develop all subtly influence the informational environment of the planet. The evolution of the individual therefore contributes directly to the evolution of the collective. As more individuals bring their internal lives into harmony, the patterns of coherence produced within those minds begin to propagate outward through the noosphere itself.

Yet understanding this relationship intellectually does not, by itself, transform the human being.

One may grasp the philosophical structure of consciousness and still remain internally divided. One may contemplate the deepest mysteries of the cosmos while continuing to be governed by unconscious patterns within one's own psyche. Knowledge alone does not integrate the mind.

Integration requires transformation. Transformation is not achieved through belief or intellectual insight, but through the deliberate focus and reorganization of consciousness itself within the mind and body.

It is at this point that philosophy must give way to method.

For the first time in this book, the reader now stands at the threshold where philosophy becomes practice. It is here that we share a set of means and methods through which the human mind compels the process of integration. These practices did not arise from mere theoretical speculation. They were developed by me over the course of four decades of profound direct experience along with consistent daily self-observation, transformation, and the awakening to the forces of consciousness. Over time, the principles governing this work become increasingly clear to the alchemist, revealing that the integration of the human mind unfolds according to universal laws operating both within the psyche and throughout the broader architecture of the cosmos.

What initially appeared to me as personal insight eventually unveiled itself as a reflection of a much deeper process within nature.

In earlier sections, we referred to the organizing force behind this process as Alpha—the self-organizing principle through which systems of nature move toward increasing coherence. Alpha governs the formation of galaxies, the emergence of biological complexity, and the progressive evolution of consciousness within living beings. Wherever systems evolve toward greater harmony and integration, Alpha is there.

Within the human organism, Alpha expresses itself through processes that modern science increasingly recognizes as forms of biofeedback. Biofeedback occurs when a system becomes aware of its own internal activity and begins regulating itself in response to that awareness. Within the human body, this principle can be observed in many physiological processes. Breathing patterns, heart rhythms, and neural activity all become modifiable once the individual becomes conscious of them. Awareness introduces feedback into the system, allowing the system to reorganize itself. The same principle operates within the deeper structures of the psyche. When consciousness becomes aware of its own internal movements, the mind enters a self-reflective feedback loop through which hidden psychological structures begin to present themselves. Through sustained observation, the fragmented elements of the psyche gradually become perceptible to our awareness and accessible for transformation.

When the mind begins to observe its own thoughts, emotions, impulses, and reactions, it initiates a powerful form of psychological biofeedback. The mind splits into the observer and the observed. This reorientation of awareness begins to reorganize the internal structure of the mind and consciousness itself.

Underlying patterns that once operated automatically begin to present themselves. What first appears as vague moods and reactions gradually sharpens into identifiable psychological structures that can be studied, understood, and ultimately transformed.

The individual gradually recognizes that the psyche is composed of many competing tendencies, adaptive mechanisms, and emotional structures formed throughout the course of life. Some of these mechanisms are constructive. Others were formed in response to fear, trauma, or social conditioning. Many operate outside conscious awareness, quietly shaping perception and behavior without disclosing their presence.

The process of integration begins when these subconscious artifacts enter the light of conscious awareness.

As they do, their automatic power begins to weaken. Gradually the mind reorganizes itself around a deeper center of gravity. This center corresponds to the noetic soul, also known as the authentic self in a psychological model. The noetic soul is the authentic center of consciousness within human beings. It is capable of connecting directly with the divine source and participating in the evolution of awareness. The noetic soul emerges as the central organizing intelligence of the integrated self-actualized mind.

As the fragmented elements of the psyche begin to harmonize, this deeper center gradually emerges as the primary organizing principle within the individual. Ancient alchemical traditions described this transformation symbolically as the conversion of base elements into gold. Modern psychology describes a similar process through concepts such as individuation and psychological integration. Though the language differs, the underlying phenomenon is the same: the human mind possesses the capacity to reorganize itself when it becomes aware of its own internal structure.

Yet awareness alone is not enough.

Accelerated integration requires sustained practice. The mind must learn to remain aware while moving through the ordinary circumstances of life. It must learn to observe its own reactions without becoming dominated by them. It must cultivate emotional and energetic coherence so that the deeper layers of consciousness can emerge within the psyche. These practices form the foundation of the grand alchemical work.

Over time, it becomes clear and self-evident that the integration process unfolds according to a set of identifiable principles. These principles operate not only at the psychological level but across the entire human anatomy—including the emotional, neurological, and energetic dimensions of experience. When the force of Alpha begins to intensify within the individual, the entire structure of the psyche enters a state of accelerated momentum in the process of integration.

At certain stages of this process, the individual encounters what ancient traditions described metaphorically as the Void—a profound interior domain in which the familiar structures of identity dissolve, unveiling the deeper dimensions of consciousness beneath them. Though such experiences may initially appear destabilizing, they are in fact milestones along the path of integration.

They mark moments when the mind passes beyond previously established boundaries of awareness. In such moments, the familiar center of identity temporarily dissolves, allowing consciousness to encounter itself in a more original and unconditioned form.

Before detailing the means and methods through which this transformation unfolds, it is necessary to understand that the process of accelerated integration does not unfold in exactly the same way for every individual.

First, it is necessary to understand that humanity is already participating in this process collectively as a species, moving through it slowly and largely unconsciously. When we pass through this process subconsciously, in step with the rest of humanity, it is known as the Spiral Path. Along the Spiral Path, the noetic soul within each person quietly compels the evolution of the human organism across planetary timescales—far beyond the span of any single lifetime. In this way, nature is leveraging the presence of the noetic soul within every human being as the catalyst driving humanity's gradual evolution toward the state of physical immortality.

In parallel to the Spiral Path, we have the Straight Path.

The Straight Path is the spiritual alchemical path a person undertakes to reconstitute the monad in a single human lifetime. The Straight Path of the one accelerates the Spiral Path of the many, and that's the ultimate purpose of the Straight Path in the temporal mechanics of nature and its process of psychosomatic evolution.

All of my books share how to traverse the Straight Path.

Yet the path itself cannot be walked through theory alone. It unfolds only through lived experience, disciplined practice, and the gradual reorganization of consciousness within the human being.

Additionally, the pathway of psychosomatic integration reveals that there are two courses of unfoldment within the Straight Path itself, with each course determined not by personal choice, but by the deeper intelligence within Alpha itself. In working with other individuals over the last twenty years in this alchemical process, these two routes within the Straight Path became apparent, but it has only been in the last few years that I have truly understood it and can now explain it.

For now, we reveal these two courses within the Straight Path as the Classical route and the Dynamic route. The condition of the psyche at the moment one begins this work determines the route through which the process will unfold for them. Later in this section, we will delve into the unique nature of both. Understanding these routes will allow the reader to recognize the stages of integration that follow for them.

For it is here, in the deliberate integration of the human mind, that the philosophical journey explored throughout Nous Solis finally finds its practical expression. Through this work, the individual does not merely contemplate the evolution of consciousness. He or she begins to participate in it consciously. At that moment, the individual ceases to be merely an observer of the evolutionary process and instead becomes an active agent through which the process of integration accelerates. And in doing so, the individual mind becomes an active participant in the awakening of the planetary noosphere itself.

When the force of Alpha becomes sufficiently accelerated through conscious effort within the human being, the conscious mind eventually begins shifting between the deeper cognitive backgrounds of the noosphere's planetary group mind. They are the fields of awareness long symbolized in ancient traditions as the planetary spheres. These shifts do not represent departures from the world, but deeper integrations into the living architecture of consciousness that permeates it.

### *9.2.0 — The Law of Sympathetic Resonance*

The process of integration does not occur randomly. It unfolds according to a principle that operates throughout the natural world—a principle long recognized in both the sciences and the philosophical traditions of antiquity. This principle may be described as the law of sympathetic resonance, or sympathetic vibrations.

Resonance occurs whenever two systems sharing compatible frequencies begin to influence one another through vibrational alignment. When this happens, the activity of each system gradually synchronizes with the other. In physics, this phenomenon can be observed in countless forms, from the synchronization of oscillating pendulums to the amplification of sound waves within a resonant chamber. It is also dramatically illustrated in the field of cymatics, where sound frequencies organize matter into coherent geometric patterns. In biology, resonance appears in the coordinated rhythms of the heart, the synchronization of neural networks within the brain, and the complex feedback loops that regulate living systems.

The same principle operates within the field of consciousness.

Within the human mind, this resonance manifests as a subtle process through which patterns of thought, emotion, and perception gradually reorganize themselves around deeper centers of coherence.

The human organism is not merely a collection of physical processes. It is a dynamic system composed of interacting layers of energy, emotion, cognition, and awareness. Each of these layers possesses its own patterns of activity, and each is capable of influencing the others through resonance. Thoughts affect emotions, emotions influence physiological states, and bodily conditions shape perception and cognition. Together, they form a continuously interacting network of psychosomatic feedback processes.

Under ordinary circumstances, these systems operate with only partial coherence. The mind moves from one reaction to another, emotions fluctuate in response to external circumstances, and unconscious psychological patterns exert subtle influence over perception and behavior. Much of this activity unfolds automatically, without the individual recognizing the underlying structures guiding it.

Accelerated integration (the Straight Path) begins when awareness introduces a new organizing principle within the psyche.

As the individual begins observing the movements of the mind—its thoughts, impulses, emotional reactions, and patterns of behavior—a subtle but powerful shift occurs. Awareness itself becomes a stabilizing reference point within the mind. The practice of self-observation introduces a feedback signal that allows previously unconscious processes to come into alignment with conscious intention.

Through repeated self-observation, the fragmented elements of the psyche gradually enter into resonance with the deeper center of consciousness within the noetic soul—the authentic self. As this center strengthens, it begins consolidating the mind around itself, liberating consciousness from the fragmented structures that once governed it.

The noetic soul does not impose order upon the psyche through force. Rather, it functions as a stabilizing attractor within the field of consciousness. As awareness deepens, the various structures of the mind gradually reorganize themselves around this center through sympathetic resonance. Thoughts become less reactive, emotional states stabilize, and the individual develops a growing capacity to remain internally coherent even amid the changing conditions of life.

In this way, resonance becomes the mechanism through which integration unfolds.

Resonance operates not only within the internal structures of the psyche but also between the individual mind and the larger field of the planetary noosphere. As the practitioner cultivates increasingly coherent states of awareness, the conscious mind begins synchronizing more deeply with the broader cognitive environment of humanity itself. When sufficient coherence develops, the mind begins accessing deeper bandwidths within that planetary field—states of awareness through which different layers of the human condition become perceptible.

The ancient alchemists symbolized this process through the imagery of fire and transmutation. When the internal energies of the human being enter into resonance with the deeper organizing principle of consciousness, the psyche begins to transform. Patterns that once generated conflict begin to dissolve, and new structures of awareness emerge in their place. The process may at times feel intense or destabilizing, but its underlying movement is always toward greater unity and stability.

Modern science has begun to observe similar dynamics in the study of neural synchronization and physiological coherence. When individuals cultivate sustained states of attention and emotional balance, measurable changes occur within the nervous system. Neural networks that previously fired in chaotic patterns begin to synchronize, producing more stable and integrated modes of cognition. The heart, brain, and respiratory systems also begin to operate with greater coherence, reinforcing one another through complex feedback loops.

In other words, the organism begins to resonate internally.

These scientific observations echo insights that contemplative traditions have explored for centuries. The mind transforms not merely through belief or intellectual understanding, but through the cultivation of coherent states of awareness that gradually reorganize the entire human system.

This principle of resonance extends beyond the boundaries of the individual organism.

Because each human mind participates within the larger field of the Earth's noosphere, the internal states cultivated within individuals also influence the broader collective environment of consciousness. Just as emotional states can propagate through groups of people, coherent patterns of awareness can also propagate through resonance within the planetary field of mind.

The integration of the individual therefore contributes to the integration of the collective.

As more individuals cultivate stable states of awareness, the patterns of coherence they generate begin to propagate through the noosphere, subtly influencing the psychological environment of the species as a whole. In this way, the work of inner transformation becomes more than a personal endeavor. It participates in the broader evolution of consciousness on Earth.

The practices described in the following segments of this section of Nous Solis are designed to accelerate this process.

Through disciplined observation, emotional regulation, and the cultivation of coherent states of awareness, the individual gradually learns to amplify the resonant influence of the noetic soul within the psyche. Over time, the entire structure of consciousness reorganizes itself around this deeper center. As this center strengthens, the fragmented tendencies of the psyche gradually lose their autonomous power and begin to align with the emerging coherence of the noetic soul.

When this reorganization reaches sufficient intensity, the individual will begin to encounter deeper thresholds of awareness—experiences that reveal the underlying forces of consciousness—the cosmic quanta. These moments often correspond to the states that ancient traditions described as transcendental. They represent points at which the boundaries of ordinary cognition become permeable, allowing deeper strata of consciousness to reveal themselves.

Yet such experiences are not the objective of the work.

They are simply expressions of resonance reaching deeper levels within the architecture of consciousness. The true purpose of the process remains the same: the gradual integration of the human mind into a coherent instrument through which the deeper intelligences of consciousness may operate and ultimately reconstitute the monad.

Understanding the law of sympathetic resonance therefore provides the key to the methods that follow.

For it reveals that the transformation of consciousness does not depend upon belief, doctrine, or external authority. It unfolds through the natural dynamics of awareness itself. When an individual learns to stabilize attention, observe the movements of the psyche, and cultivate coherent states of presence, the self-organizing force of the universe begins to guide the inner alchemical process—and the pathway unfolds. In this sense, the alchemist does not force transformation into existence. The practitioner cultivates the conditions through which the deeper intelligence of consciousness may reveal its own organizing influence within the psyche.

Through resonance, the mind reorganizes itself. Gradually, what once appeared chaotic within the psyche begins to reveal an underlying order. Through resonance, the fragmented elements of the psyche are gradually brought into harmony. And through resonance, the human being becomes capable of participating consciously in the unfolding evolution of consciousness.

The practices that follow reveal the practical mechanics through which this participation becomes possible. When the mind begins intentionally observing its own internal psychic processes, it signals that a new stage of evolution has begun.

*9.3.0 — The Three Factors of Integration*

The accelerated integration of the human mind does not occur through philosophical insight alone. It unfolds through a practical discipline that engages the deeper laws governing consciousness itself.

The entire alchemical process described throughout this work operates through three governing dynamics. These dynamics are not theoretical concepts but functional forces that operate directly within the organism of the practitioner. Together they form the operational mechanics of the Straight Path.

These dynamics are known as the Three Factors.

At the moment the self-organizing force of the cosmos (Alpha) begins responding to our turn inward; the momentum of integration accelerates, and life itself begins presenting the circumstances necessary for further discovery within an ordered process of unfoldment.

The practices that initiate and sustain this accelerated alchemical process are known as the Three Factors.

They are Transformation, Cultivation, and Love.

The three factors are not stages of development, and they are not practices that are completed once and then abandoned. They are ongoing dynamics that must operate together throughout the entire alchemical journey. Each factor supports the other two, and together they form the practical mechanics through which the fragmented human mind gradually becomes unified.

The purpose of the Three Factors is the reconstitution of the monad within the human being—the reunification between creation and divinity, between matter and consciousness.

Transformation

The first factor is Transformation.

Transformation is made possible when the noetic soul emerges within the mind as the self-observing awareness. At this moment the structure of consciousness changes. Instead of remaining fully identified with its thoughts and emotions, the mind begins to divide into two poles: the observer and the observed.

Thoughts, emotions, impulses, and reactions begin to appear as objects within awareness rather than as the identity of the individual. This shift marks the beginning of genuine self-knowledge, for only what can be observed can ultimately be understood and transformed.

Through sustained self-observation, the practitioner gradually discovers that the human psyche is not a single unified personality but a complex mosaic of psychological elements. These elements manifest as moods, impulses, defensive identities, emotional reactions, instinctive drives, and neurological impulses embedded within the organism itself.

The elements encountered in this work arise from several distinct layers of the mind.

At the high cognitive levels, the practitioner encounters the many false-selves that compose the fragmented identities of the ordinary personality. These psychological constructs arise when the consciousness of the soul passes through the matter of the brain and becomes refracted by the latent programs of nature—much like light passing through a prism and separating into a spectrum of colors. In their origin, they are artifacts of human evolution, but over time they become further compounded through emotional reactions, belief structures, and defensive adaptations, gradually forming the complex mosaic of identities that most people mistake for the self.

Beneath these layers lies a trans-cognitive stratum where the elements encountered appear less as identities and more as informational and energetic patterns within the psyche—memory structures, archetypal reactions, emotional fields, and deeper psychic imprints embedded within the mind.

At the deep cognitive level, the work moves beyond psychological identities into the instinctive architecture of the organism itself. These layers represent progressively deeper strata of the psyche, each requiring its own form of observation, understanding, and transformation. Here the practitioner encounters neurological impulses, programmed instincts, and autonomic patterns embedded within the temporal-ethereal dimensions of the body-mind.

Transformation therefore operates across the entire structure of the human psyche.

When a psychological element is observed clearly and comprehended through deeper emotional realization, the practitioner invokes his or her awareness of the divine Spirit and brings the element into resonance with it. Through the law of sympathetic resonance, the element begins harmonizing with that higher presence and transforms.

The force that compels this harmonization is Alpha.

As the element transforms, the energy previously bound within it returns to the center of the psyche, strengthening and expanding the presence of the authentic self. Over time, the countless fragmented structures of the mind gradually dissolve and reintegrate. As this reintegration progresses, the authentic self (noetic soul) grows stronger and begins organizing the psyche around a deeper coherence.

Transformation does not suppress the contents of the psyche. It liberates the authentic self from the structures that obscure it. Life itself becomes the laboratory of this work, and every reaction to circumstance becomes an opportunity for discovery and transformation.

Cultivation

The second factor is Cultivation.

While transformation concerns the discovery and integration of psychological elements, cultivation concerns the energetic balance of the human organism itself. The mind does not exist independently of the body. It is embedded within a living biological system whose emotional and physiological states continuously influence perception and awareness.

Human energy moves within polar dynamics that manifest through emotional reactions, instinctive drives, and physiological rhythms. When these polar forces remain unbalanced, they distort perception and obscure our awareness of the deeper presence of the divine Spirit.

The divine Spirit—the love of the divine monad at the center of all things—vibrates in perfect neutrality. The human psyche, by contrast, is inherently polarized through the dual sexual forces embedded in creation: male and female, Taoist yin and yang, etc. The divine monad remains vibrationally neutral (Taoist yuan) because it precedes sexuality and the entire field of creation from which polarity arises.

To perceive the divine Spirit beyond this polarity wall, the practitioner must temporarily neutralize the polarized energies of the organism. When this neutrality is achieved, the presence of the Spirit becomes perceptible within the conscious mind. The practitioner can then bring that divine presence into differential contrast with the targeted psychological element. Through sympathetic resonance, Alpha begins harmonizing the two. As resonance deepens, the psychological element transforms, and the suppressed aspect of the authentic self—the noetic soul it once obscured—is liberated within.

Cultivation therefore involves practices that stabilize, neutralize, and harmonize the internal conditions of the organism. Through this stabilization, the practitioner becomes capable of perceiving the divine Spirit—the love of God present at the center of all things as one dimension of the divine Monad (Ain Soph). The divine Spirit is the agent of transformation. To dissolve false selves and psychological elements through the first factor (Transformation), the practitioner must first access the divine Spirit through the second factor (Cultivation).

Through disciplined regulation of breath, posture, movement, attention, and instinctive energies, the practitioner gradually neutralizes the turbulence of the emotional and physiological systems. This stabilization allows awareness to remain present without being overwhelmed by the reactive forces of the body.

From a scientific perspective, this process corresponds to the regulation of the nervous system and the synchronization of physiological rhythms. From the perspective of the alchemical traditions, it represents the balancing of the subtle positive and negative energies of the organism to reach the neutral energy of the divine Spirit.

Cultivation therefore prepares the internal environment necessary for transformation. It opens a window in the mind to God.

Love

The third factor is Love.

Love is not cultivated merely as an emotion but as a conscious awareness of the living presence of the Spirit. Through this orientation, the mind is capable of entering into a profound resonance with it.

Love is the most essential of the three factors because it establishes the relationship between individual consciousness and the divine Spirit.

Profound transformation requires the presence of the Spirit.

Whether I say Spirit, divine Spirit, or Holy Spirit, it is all the same.

Psychological elements transform when they're brought into differential contrast with the divine Spirit within the conscious mind, where resonance between the two begins the work of alchemical transformation and integration. Cultivation stabilizes and neutralizes the polar energies of the organism so the presence of the Spirit may become perceptible. And love is the means by which the practitioner consciously establishes a relationship with the Spirit.

In this context, love is not merely an emotional sentiment. It is a state of resonance between consciousness and the living intelligence of the cosmos. When awareness becomes aware of life in its deepest sense, the natural response of consciousness is love. Through this love, the practitioner forms a living relationship with the divine Spirit.

This relationship introduces the catalytic force required to transform the elements discovered through self-observation. When invoked during the work of transformation, the Spirit acts as the agent through which Alpha performs the integration of the psyche.

Love becomes the gateway through which the deeper intelligence of the cosmos participates in the integration of the human mind. Through this relationship, the work of integration becomes a cooperative process between human awareness and the organizing intelligence that guides the evolution of consciousness itself.

### The Unity of the Three Factors

The 1st factor transforms the constructs of the mind via the Spirit.
The 2nd factor neutralizes bio-polarity, so the Spirit is accessible.
The 3rd factor connects us to the Spirit and amplifies it within us.

Together, the three factors form a single living process.

Each factor prepares the conditions for the others to function correctly. Transformation works with the structures within the psyche that must change. Cultivation stabilizes the organism so that the work can proceed without distortion. Love introduces the catalytic presence of the Spirit, allowing the law of sympathetic resonance to operate within the mind. When these three forces cooperate, the alchemical process becomes both stable and self-sustaining.

When the mind begins working consciously and consistently with them, the self-organizing momentum of Alpha increases within the psyche. The events of life begin presenting precisely the conditions necessary for further discovery, transformation, and integration.

The practitioner gradually realizes that the integration of the mind is not accomplished through personal will alone. It is a cooperative process between human awareness and the deeper intelligence guiding the evolution of consciousness itself. Through the sustained practice of the Three Factors, the fragmented structures of the psyche slowly dissolve, and the unified mind begins to emerge.

*9.4.0 - The Five Centers*

The psychological elements encountered in the work of transformation do not arise randomly within the mind. They appear through specific functional centers of the human organism that express our thoughts, emotions, instincts, impulses, and desires.

The five centers are:

1.) Intellectual Center – Located in the head. Corresponds to the temporal ethereal mental body.

2.) Motor Center – Located between the shoulder blades. Corresponds to the physical body.

3.) Emotional Center – Located in the heart area. Corresponds to the temporal ethereal emotional body.

4.) Instinctive Center – Located in the abdomen. Corresponds to the temporal ethereal instinctive body.

5.) Sexual Center – Located in the genitals. Corresponds to the physical body and the temporal ethereal vital body.

Together these centers form the operational interface through which the deeper structures of the psyche manifest within conscious awareness. Each center functions as a conduit through which deeper psychological material surfaces. When a mood, impulse, or reaction appears within the psyche, it is the outward expression of an inner structure whose roots extend far beneath the surface of the mind.

To transform these elements, the practitioner must learn to observe them as they arise within the five centers and apply the alchemical process directly to them. It is not enough to understand the theory of transformation, nor is it sufficient merely to believe in the reality of the Spirit or the operation of the universal law of sympathetic resonance. The forces described throughout this book must become active within the organism of the practitioner.

The centers through which psychological elements appear represent only the operational surface of the mind. Beneath them lies a deeper structure composed of multiple bodies through which consciousness itself manifests.

*9.5.0 - Anatomy of The Mind*

The structure of the mind is shaped both by the consciousness that flows through it and by the bodies through which that consciousness expresses itself. Earlier Hermetic traditions often described the human being as possessing seven bodies. We have 12 bodies in all, not seven. Each of the 12 grades of the First Mountain corresponds to each of the 12 bodies of the mind: one grade per body.

Many initiates recognized only seven bodies because those were the layers most readily experienced during the early stages of the work. The remaining five belong to the primordial dimension of our being and therefore remain largely invisible until the physical and primordial aspects of the self begin entering into resonance.

The ethereal bodies of our primordial being are not experienced until we begin integrating our physical being with our primordial being. Some past initiates had gone as far as to detect, realize, and make mention of the existence of a Divine Soul beyond the spectrum of the Human Soul, but then incorrectly believed that the Divine Soul is integrated early in the alchemical process.

Admittedly, there are moments early in the alchemical process where the temporal dimensions of the mind may detect the Divine Soul through the medium of our primordial being, such as in the seventh or eighth grades of the First Mountain. However, this detection should not be confused with integration. It is also easy for the alchemist to confuse his or her primordial being for the Divine Soul. They are not the same.

Our primordial being is a medium of the Divine Soul. Our physical being achieves resonance with the Divine Soul by achieving resonance with its primordial being. This is accomplished by our conscious mind becoming aware of our primordial being via our super cognitive faculties of higher emotion.

The Divine Soul is one of the three prime dimensions of Ain Soph. All forms through which the Divine Soul finds expression become an expression of the Immortal Beloved. The mystery of the Divine Soul is studied throughout the course of this book which explores the process of the Great Work to reconstitute the monad within creation.

The 12 bodies of our total being consist of two groups of bodies - six bodies corresponding to the temporal dimensions of our physical being - and six bodies corresponding to the spiritual dimensions of our primordial being.

Each of the two groups has a central body of which the other five bodies in their group are satellites. The central body in the group corresponding to our temporal matrix of creation is our physical body. The central body in the group corresponding to our eternal matrix of creation is our primordial body. The twelve bodies are:

Temporal-Physical Being

1.) Physical Body (Central Body)

2.) Vital Temporal Ethereal Body

3.) Emotional Temporal Ethereal Body

4.) Mental Temporal Ethereal Body

5.) Instinctive Temporal Ethereal Body

6.) Vision Temporal Ethereal Body

Eternal-Primordial Being

7.) Primordial Body (Central Body)

8.) Vital Spiritual Ethereal Body

9.) Emotional Spiritual Ethereal Body

10.) Mental Spiritual Ethereal Body

11.) Instinctive Spiritual Ethereal Body

12.) Vision Spiritual Ethereal Body

*See Figure [3]*

The twelve bodies are not theoretical distinctions, but the operative structure through which the Three Factors function. Each practice of the Straight Path engages specific layers of this system, gradually bringing them into coherence and unified resonance with the Spirit.

## *9.6.0 – Overview of the Practices*

The transformation of the psyche described in the preceding sections unfolds through disciplined work within the organism itself. The centers of the psyche and the bodies of the mind form the living crucible through which the alchemical process takes place.

The disciplines through which this internal work is carried out are known collectively as the practices of the Straight Path.

Through these practices, the practitioner gradually learns to observe the continuous fluctuations of the psyche with increasing clarity, stabilize the energetic system of the organism with precision, and consciously introduce the catalytic presence of the divine Spirit into the unfolding process of transformation. In time, the practitioner learns not merely to observe psychological elements but to dissolve and transform them, thereby liberating the deeper dimensions of the authentic self that had long remained concealed and bound within them.

The Straight Path is therefore not an abstract philosophy but a practical collaboration between the conscious mind of the practitioner and the universal force of Alpha.

*The Work Begins*

At the beginning of the work, I prescribe nine distinct practices. These practices train the inner faculties required to carry out the alchemical process. Two of them, however—Alchemical Meditation Level 1 and Level 2—serve primarily as preparatory disciplines designed to awaken the inner senses of perception and differentiation.

Once the practitioner attains Level 3 Alchemical Meditation, these earlier stages are no longer practiced independently. Their functions are naturally incorporated into the higher practice itself. Thus, the practitioner begins by learning nine practices, but ultimately continues the work through seven practices until the completion of the Monad. The path becomes simpler as mastery deepens.

*The Nine Practices of the Straight Path*

The nine practices fall naturally into four groups: practices of awareness, practices of transformation, practices of cultivation, and practices that orient the practitioner toward the Spirit. Together these disciplines provide a complete framework through which the practitioner systematically awakens awareness, elevates the organism, and participates consciously in the alchemical integration of the mind.

*Foundations of Awareness*

*9.6.1 – Practice #1 - Alchemical Meditation - Level 1*

In the first stage of alchemical meditation, the practitioner studies the movements of the psyche as they appear across the five centers of the organism. Moods, impulses, and emotional states are examined not merely through intellectual analysis but through direct inner perception. The practitioner learns to feel how a psychological element expresses itself differently within the emotional center, the intellectual center, the instinctive center, the motor center, and the sexual center. Through this practice, the practitioner begins developing genuine self-knowledge.

This knowledge does not arise through analysis alone but through direct familiarity with the inner landscape of the mind. As the practitioner repeatedly studies the movements of emotion, thought, instinct, and impulse across the centers, subtle distinctions begin to emerge. What once appeared as a single mood gradually reveals itself as a complex structure composed of many smaller elements.

*9.6.2 - Practice #2 - Self-Observation*

The second practice extends the observer–observed relationship into the activities of daily life. The practitioner learns to maintain an inner watchfulness while speaking, acting, and interacting with the world. Thoughts, emotions, and impulses are observed as they arise. Rather than being unconsciously carried along by them, the practitioner begins to see them as phenomena appearing within the mind.

Together these two practices awaken the fundamental faculty required for the work: the ability to see the movements of the psyche without being fully identified with them.

*Practices of Transformation*

*9.6.3 – Practice #3 - Alchemical Meditation - Level 2*

Once the practitioner has developed sufficient awareness of the inner movements of the mind, the second level of alchemical meditation is introduced. In this practice the practitioner begins working intentionally with psychological elements. Through meditation and inner invocation, the practitioner attempts to arrest destabilizing moods and reactions, bringing them into conscious awareness rather than allowing them to operate automatically. By "arrest," I mean a temporary suspension of the mood's automatic power, without yet dissolving the underlying structure that generates it.

*9.6.4 – Practice #4 - Alchemical Meditation - Level 3*

The third level of alchemical meditation marks the true beginning of the transformative work. At this stage the practitioner introduces the presence of the Spirit—the love resonating between the Father and the Divine Soul—into the alchemical process. When the vibration of the Spirit is brought into contrast with a psychological element, the law of sympathetic resonance begins harmonizing the two. In this way, the psychological element is gradually transformed, and the authentic self that had been suppressed by it is liberated.

*9.6.5 – Practice #5 – Transformation on the Go*

As the practitioner becomes increasingly familiar with the mechanics of transformation, the work gradually extends beyond seated meditation. Psychological elements that arise during the activities of daily life are recognized and transformed in real time. The practitioner no longer waits for formal meditation sessions to engage in the alchemical process. Life itself becomes the laboratory of transformation.

*Practices of Cultivation*

The first factor of transformation alone is not sufficient. The organism of the practitioner must also be brought into energetic harmony so that the alchemical process can operate efficiently.

*9.6.6 – Practice #6 – Sexual Cultivation Practice*

Sexual polarity between partners stabilizes and harmonizes the energetic structure of the organism. When approached consciously and with proper intention, the exchange of sexual energy helps balance the internal systems through which the alchemical process operates.

*9.6.7 – Practice #7 – Cosmic Cultivation Practice*

Movement disciplines such as martial arts, qigong, sacred dance, and related practices cultivate and harmonize the energetic field of the practitioner. When performed with focused intention, these movements allow the organism to draw upon the subtle forces of nature and bring the internal energies of the body into balance. As this balance deepens, the organism becomes a more stable vessel through which the forces of cultivation, transformation, and love can operate together, allowing the alchemical process to unfold with greater coherence.

*Orientation Toward the Spirit*

The final two practices orient the practitioner toward the deeper dimensions of the alchemical process.

*9.6.8 – Practice #8 – Quantum Meditation*

In this practice, the practitioner contemplates the deeper structure of reality and the cosmic forces guiding the evolution of consciousness. Quantum meditation expands the practitioner's awareness beyond the purely psychological domain and situates the work of transformation within the larger processes of the universe.

*9.6.9 – Practice #9 – Contemplative Study*

The study of spiritual philosophy, psychology, and cosmology refines the intellect and prepares the mind to recognize the deeper patterns operating within existence. Through careful contemplation, the practitioner gradually aligns the rational faculties of the mind with the higher dimensions of the Spirit.

*9.6.10 – Further Orientation*

Once the practitioner has established the capacity for Level 3 Alchemical Meditation, the first two meditation stages are no longer practiced independently. Their functions have been absorbed into the higher work. The practitioner then continues the path through seven ongoing practices: Level 3 Alchemical Meditation, Self-Observation, Transformation on the Go, Sexual Polarity Practice, Cosmic Cultivation Practice, Quantum Meditation, and Contemplative Study.

Most spiritual practices that exist across many faiths, philosophies, and metaphysical schools serve one of the Three Factors. You can replace any of the nine practices prescribed above with any practice from another school that fulfills the same purpose. The key is that we work with all the Three Factors, regardless of the practices we employ.

Through these disciplines, the practitioner gradually brings the forces of transformation, cultivation, and love into cooperation within the organism. As this cooperation deepens, the scattered elements of the psyche begin organizing around a new center of gravity. Over time the fragmented structures of the mind yield to a more unified state of awareness. It is within this emerging unity that the deeper work of the Monad begins.

*9.7.0 – Step-by-Step Practice Instructions* *(1F = First Factor, etc.)*

*9.7.1 - Practice 1 - Alchemical Meditation - Level 1 Practice (1F)*

This first practice is a meditation with the purpose of orientating the Candidate in how the mind is structured. With this practice, the Candidate begins to learn how to (1) self-observe, and (2) develop a means of gaining self-knowledge. The meditation practice and orientation are as follows:

- Sit in a comfortable position.

- Quiet your mind for a few minutes with a breathing exercise where your mind is focused on your breathing.

- As your mind wanders, bring your focus back to your breathing. Inhale through your nostrils in moderate deep breaths and then exhale through your mouth. Once you are relaxed and more focused, go to the next step.

- Focus on the heart area of your chest. While your mind is focused on this area of your body, recall a past emotional experience.

- Now take notice of the feeling, the mood, the flavor, the quality of energy, of this emotion in the heart area of your chest.

- Now focus on a completely different emotional experience from your past and recall the emotion.

- Notice how the feeling, the mood, the flavor, the energy of this emotion - changes in the heart area of your body when you change to a different memory of a different emotional experience.

- While you are in a seated meditation, shift the focus of your mind back to the first emotional experience you had recalled when you were studying your emotional center.
- Now with this mood firmly in your mind, shift your focus to your mental center in your head, and take notice of the flavor of the same mood in your mental center and the types of thoughts running through it.
- Once you have captured this mood in your mental center, and you have understood it the best you can, shift to the second experience you had recalled while studying your emotional center.
- Now with this mood firmly in your mind, shift your focus to your mental center in your head, and take notice of the flavor of the mood in your mental center and the types of thoughts running through it.
- Now contemplate how each mood from the two experiences which you were recalling had a different expression or flavor in the mental center.
- Switch between the moods a couple of times to realize this.
- Also notice that the same mood has a different expression between the emotional center and the mental center, yet you still know it is the same mood. This is an innate realization.
- Just as you used the two different life experiences with different corresponding moods to learn about the emotional and mental centers, you must now repeat this practice with your instinctive center (instinctive temporal ethereal body) felt in your abdomen.
- Then repeat this practice with your motor center (corresponding to the physical body) felt between your shoulder blades.

- Then repeat this practice with your sexual center (corresponding to both your physical body and vital temporal ethereal bodies) felt in your genitals.

Your deep realization of the mood and its slight variations in expression between the centers of the mind is self-knowledge. In general, many people think they know themselves, but their self-knowledge is skin-deep at best. The more accustomed you become in feeling your moods in the different centers of your mind—beyond just intellectually analyzing them—the deeper your knowledge will grow of the moods at a level which transcends intellectual analysis.

Our moods are more complex and unique than the intellect can express in words. Do not allow your intellect to force an understanding within the limits of your language development, or within the limits of your academic learning. Go beyond the intellect and capture the Tao of the mood relative to each center of your mind. This is how you develop your emotional intelligence and self-knowledge.

Every mood you experience has a manifestation in each of the five centers. You must feel and go deep inside every mood relative to each center of the mind while in a state of meditation and learn about the mood at a level that transcends your ability to express it in words. The beginner should do this meditation practice for at least one hour every day to develop their internal senses. With continuous practice, we develop our internal senses of differentiation and realization and graduate beyond the need for seated meditation on a regular basis. Once we become adept in the practice, we require seated meditation only on a case-by-case basis. Once we are advanced in the practice, we transform most of the psychological elements primarily on-the-go. During this practice, once we understand how the five centers work, we should stay focused on only one mood at a time while we keep shifting between each center with the same mood. This is very important. Initially, this instruction has the beginner switch between more than one mood relative to one center of the mind only to orient the person on how each specific center of the mind works.

### *9.7.2 - Practice 2 - Self-Observation (1F)*

Before explaining levels 2 and 3 of the alchemical meditation practice, I will first introduce the practice of self-observation, which serves as an extension of the level 1 alchemical meditation practice.

When we are not meditating, we need to take our developing inner senses and learn to keep an inner eye on our moods while we go about the day. When going about the day, we can narrow our inner focus to just our emotional, mental, and instinctive centers.

As a beginner, when self-observing and going about the day, we are just taking self-reflective mental snapshots of our inner moods. Later in the day, when we can meditate, we should enter seated meditation and retrospectively go back to the moments when we had observed certain moods. Allow the memory of these moods to bring back the mood itself. Once the mood has returned, we should focus on the mood in all five centers of the mind, one center at a time.

Although I am specifically referring to the beginner here, self-observation must be practiced at all levels of the alchemical work throughout one's life until full integration is complete.

### *9.7.3 - Practice 3 - Alchemical Meditation - Level 2 Practice (1F)*

There are two key differences between the Level 1 and Level 2 alchemical meditation practices:

*Difference 1*: In the level 2 practice, we incorporate prayer into the meditation practice to arrest, or even better, transform the mood we are experiencing. Arresting a mood is different from transforming it.

*Difference 2:* In the level 2 practice, we go beyond arresting moods and reactions to transforming each mood to liberate dimensions of our authentic-self that were previously suppressed. This is how we liberate our noetic soul while alive in physical form.

Prayer in this practice does not have to be of a religious nature. This means no predefined script or choice of words is necessary. Just communicate authentically from your heart. Prayer in the alchemical meditation practice is the means of supplicating to the power of the Spirit to transform the mood. Alchemical prayer is different from religious prayer. It is essential in alchemical prayer that we "feel" the Spirit while praying to it. This feeling is not physical; it is of a higher emotional nature. The highest form of prayer involves no words, only inner feeling (not physical feeling).

- During the level 2 alchemical meditation practice, when the meditator is focused on the specific mood they wish to transform—after having reached a deep level of understanding of the mood in each of the five centers—the meditator should pray to the Spirit for the mood to transform.

- This prayer should be made repeatedly while in a state of meditation and while focused on the mood, shifting your focus on the mood between each of the five centers. Each center of the mind reveals a different dimension of the same mood.

The meditator may experience immediate relief from the mood, or he or she may struggle over many meditation practices. It all depends on, (1) How neurologically reinforced the mood is within the mind, and (2) Our level of comprehension of the mood.

As the meditator practices alchemical meditation every day—for at least one hour per day—the meditator's inner sense of self-observation will become so acute that the moods will subdivide into very distinct individual formations of the mind. We see or sense these individual formations of the mind with our inner cognitive feelings. It is essential in alchemy that we learn to see with our inner feelings rather than to see visually with the mind's eye.

In this practice, the eyes of the mind will deceive you, but the heart will always tell you the truth.

When the moods begin to subdivide under the light of our inner sense of feeling, the meditator has reached a level of clarity where he or she can now sense the moods as very distinct individual formations of the mind called "False Selves."

Comparing psychological matter to physical matter, the moods are like molecules, but the false-selves are like the atoms which form each molecule. Real transformation occurs at the atomic level of the mind, not at the molecular level. Meaning, real transformation occurs at the false-self level, not at the mood level.

The false-selves and the authentic-self together constitute what Freud calls the "Ego." It is the Self. The Ego exists in a fractured state. Each fracture is a false-self. There are thousands of false-selves that suppress the authentic-self at its core. The Ego must be transformed and integrated to express only the authentic-self. This is what Carl Jung calls "Individuation."

If all we can detect, sense, or observe is a mood, which basically is just a musical blend of multiple false-selves acting in concert, then all we will be able to achieve with prayer is an arresting of the mood.

We can say this arresting or cessation is a level of transformation, but transformation in its most dynamic state goes far beyond cessation. Transformation in its most dynamic state transforms a targeted false-self into a new aspect of our authentic-self. Alchemy requires the most dynamic level of transformation. Arresting moods, however, is how it all starts.

- Once the false-selves become visible to our inner sense of cognitive feeling, the alchemist must focus on only one false-self at a time otherwise transformation will not occur. You cannot kill two birds with the same stone.
- During the alchemical meditation practice, when we focus on a false-self, and when we are praying to the Spirit for a particular false-self to be transformed (there are many within the psyche), we should be very watchful with our feelings for a change in energy of the targeted false-self where the targeted false-self starts losing its power and form.
- When we see the targeted false-self within us losing form, we should pray to the Spirit to reveal the authentic-self being trapped by the false-self.

What is happening here is that the targeted false-self is transforming into a new aspect of your authentic-self, which once fully transformed, will move from being observed to being part of the observer.

This liberated aspect of your authentic-self will join and strengthen your pre-existing authentic-self. It will join the ever-growing center of gravity within you.

- When we witness a new aspect of the authentic-self, we must focus on it in all five centers, one center at a time. We will notice something unique about the authentic-self versus the false-selves. The liberated aspect of the authentic-self has an even quality of energy or feeling between all five centers. There is no variation between the centers. This is how we know the difference between our authentic-self and a false-self.

This newly recognized aspect of the authentic-self will feel very familiar to you, like a long-forgotten artifact of your childhood. It will strengthen you and bring about a sense of peace within you.

It is important to take notice of how the energy changed from being false to being authentic. How is it different? There is profound knowledge here in the difference that should not be missed.

Often the resultant knowledge may surprise you. Allow the surprises to come. If you preconceive what you think the result will be, you will hold up and delay the transformation from taking place.

For example: You may assume a false-self of lust should transform into an authentic aspect of chastity when, in actuality, it transforms into an authentic aspect of your erotic nature.

You may assume in advance that a false-self of anger should transform into some peaceful aspect of your authentic-self, but, in actuality, it transforms into an authentic sense of self-respect.

Often transformation does not lead to some opposite nature. Sometimes it does. We need to keep an open mind as to what the result of the transformation will yield and learn from it and accept it.

Not everything false within you is "bad" and not everything "good" within you is authentic. We have "good false-selves" just as we have "bad false-selves." The good false-selves must be transformed as well. It is important to realize alchemy is not about becoming "good." It is about becoming "real."

If you can observe the good mood as being distinctly separate from you, and you see that it is filtering or suppressing your authentic nature, then it is false, regardless of how "good" it seems, or how well it agrees with the society around you.

It is remarkable to witness what a "good" false-self transforms into. It is easy to let go of the false-selves that conflict with our adopted moral-value system. It can be very difficult to let go of the good false-selves that reinforce or validate our adopted moral-value system. By transforming our false-selves, we are overcoming the "illusions" which keep us wired into the neurological program of nature and the cognitive matrix of our cultivated reality to become masters of our destiny and co-creators of our creation.

There are thousands of false-selves that together form the high-cognitive and trans-cognitive levels of our mind that buffer and filter the authentic-self's interaction with the outer world. The authentic-self must emerge as the master of its own mind.

### *9.7.4 – Practice 4 - Alchemical Meditation - Level 3 Practice (1F)*

The level 3 alchemical meditation practice includes all the same components and methods as the level 2 practice, but adds a new force of consciousness which catapults the alchemical practice to an entirely new level. This new force is the divine Spirit.

The moods, false-selves, instincts, and adaptive personality traits all correspond to different cognitive levels of the mind, but they all can be categorized as being part of "common human emotion." The divine Spirit expresses itself beyond the range of common human emotion.

The only way I can intellectually differentiate what is meant by "common human emotion" versus "beyond common human emotion" is that "common human emotion" is stirred up within the mind based on the mind's perception of the outside world.

That which emerges "beyond common human emotion" arises from a well deep within us—it is not stirred up by our mind's perception of the outside world—but emerges within us based upon a connection we have between our conscious mind and a higher level of intelligence emerging out of the cosmic quanta of the universe which transcends the self. The outside world is not a necessary variable in the equation of how it emerges.

- During the meditation practice when the alchemist is focused on a false-self, and he or she has gone beyond the intellectual understanding of the false-self, the alchemist should pray to the Spirit to reveal (help to feel) both the authentic-self trapped by the false-self as well as the light of the Spirit itself.

- The observer first feels the false-self. Then, during prayer, the Spirit emerges. The Spirit emerges sometimes subtly at first, and not always immediately. The observer then holds the inner feelings of both the false-self and the Spirit together in contrast within his or her mind, and then finally the authentic-self emerges out of a transformed false-self.

- When the observer can hold both the higher feeling of the Spirit and the lower feeling of the false-self in the mind in the very same moment, the law of sympathetic vibrations goes into motion (Alpha) to correct the disharmony between the two. I call this dynamic "Differential Resonance."

- The result of differential resonance is the liberation of the aspect of the authentic-self which was trapped by the targeted false-self.

- This practice is repeated thousands of times across all the false-selves discovered within you, and then subsequently for every automatic program found within the deep cognitive sphere of your mind.

* * *

The practice of differential resonance within alchemical meditation is the grand alchemical key. It has either been lost for thousands of years or held secret by a few overzealous alchemists. Without this key, the alchemist would struggle endlessly and ultimately end up nowhere.

* * *

It was thought by some that the sexual practices of the Second Factor formed the lost key. This is wrong. The sexual practices only support the alchemical process; they do not lead the process. Differential resonance leads the alchemical process.

The Three Factors lead us to the moment of differential resonance in the alchemical meditation practice but when we arrive at this moment, the triangulation of the observer in conjunction with the Spirit and a targeted element of the mind, is the grand alchemical key which brings everything into fruition.

When the Spirit and a false-self (an element of the mind) are held in contrast in a state of differentiation, transformation occurs. Transformation occurs due to the false-self being compelled by the law of sympathetic vibrations to calibrate its resonance with the resonance of the Spirit triggered by the intervention of a conscious mind observing the two in contrast simultaneously. This is differential resonance. Its principle is the foundation of alchemy.

The observer must gain a higher emotional knowledge of all three observed components during the meditation process. By higher emotional knowledge I mean, we must sense and realize the knowledge beyond thought and contemplation.

The three observed components are (1) False-Self, (2) Spirit, and (3) new aspect of the authentic-self.

Knowledge of the Spirit is beyond the range of common human emotion and therefore is beyond anything the temporal mind can imagine. However, it first emerges only as the size of a mustard seed.

As we transform one false-self after another – within the contrasting light of the Spirit - our relationship with the Spirit grows - and we are led deeper into the mystery of the Third Factor.

### *9.7.5 – Practice 5 – Transformation on the Go (1F)*

A common response I hear from those contemplating doing the alchemical work is: "I don't have time."

The truth is, the alchemical work does not require much time.

The work is done in parallel to all your everyday life activities. Initially, there is a concerted effort required with the First Factor to develop the mind's ability to transform, but this training period does not last long until the mechanics of the meditation practice can be performed with quick inner focuses while you go about your day. Other people will not even be aware of your alchemical work.

Once the alchemist is well on the way, the alchemist will only occasionally need seated meditation to transform something large he or she is working with. Most of the psychic mass of the mind, however, is transformed while we go about the day. We can transform while we drive, walk, or work. Differential Resonance On-The-Go becomes the most common of all alchemical practices.

There is no separate instruction for performing the practice On-The-Go. The alchemist just needs to self-experiment and attempt the practice while not in seated meditation. In brief time, the alchemist will learn to walk.

### *9.7.6 – Practice 6 – Alchemical Sexual Intercourse (2F)*

The practice of alchemical sexual intercourse works with the most powerful force within the human organism. Because of this, it has been widely misunderstood, distorted, and misused. Its purpose is not the creation of new spiritual bodies, but the cultivation of resonance between the organism and the Spirit.

Our temporal ethereal bodies already exist and are part of our physical being and our spiritual ethereal bodies already exist as part of our primordial being. The work is not to create or recreate them as others have theorized, but to integrate and harmonize them into one complete system that resonates as one.

The function of this practice is to balance and neutralize psycho-sexual energy. When the energy of the organism is sufficiently organized through the First Factor, it can be combined with an opposing or complementary force. This may come from:

1.) Another human being.
2.) Nature.
3.) The deeper field of the cosmic quanta.

For most practitioners, working with a partner is the most efficient method. If someone doesn't have a partner, that's not a problem at all. Nature's solution for this is Cosmic Cultivation, explained next. For those without a partner, or when a partner is not available, this same cultivation can be achieved through direct engagement with the forces of nature or the underlying cosmic field, as shared in the next practice.

When properly practiced, second-factor cultivation via either alchemical sexual intercourse or cosmic cultivation increases the resonance between the organism and the Spirit, allowing the higher forces of consciousness to become more perceptible within the mind. These forces are then used in the first factor process of transformation.

It is important to understand that sexual cultivation alone does not produce integration. Without the first and third factors, the result is negligible regardless of physical sensations or effects.

A key obstacle in this work of integration is what may be called the psycho-sexual dynamic—the feedback cycle between the psyche and the body. A disordered psyche reinforces energetic imbalance, and this imbalance in turn reinforces the disordered psyche. This vicious cycle cannot be broken through cultivation alone. It requires the coordinated application of all Three Factors.

Many practitioners mistakenly focus only on the physical dimension of the practice. However, alchemy is not a mechanical or purely physiological process. It is a psychosomatic spiritual process, in which the physical practices support—but do not lead—the work.

The aim of sexual cultivation is not control for its own sake, nor the pursuit of specific physical phenomena. Observable effects—such as changes in orgasm, energetic circulation, or physiological rhythms—may occur, but they are not indicators of true cultivation, transformation, or integration.

The purpose of second-factor cultivation is energetic balance and neutralization. The organism's psycho-sexual energy is inherently polarized. The Spirit exists in an original neutral state that precedes all sexuality. When the human organism remains highly polarized, this polarity obscures our awareness of the Spirit. By introducing a counterbalancing force, the sexual polarity is reduced, allowing a clearer connection to develop between the conscious mind and the Spirit. Interestingly, however, once the conscious mind establishes a connection with the Spirit, we can then withstand higher and higher degrees of polarity without losing our conscious awareness of the Spirit. That's a key dynamic here, as polarity will naturally set back in over time due to a sexual organism being inherently polarized at conception.

As development progresses, the practitioner becomes less dependent on external sources, eventually accessing neutralizing forces directly from within the deeper spectrum of consciousness.

The process is not rigid or formulaic. It requires attention, sensitivity, and the ability to listen to the body. Over time, even ordinary sexual relations may support the work, as the organism becomes more stable and integrated.

The alchemical sexual intercourse practice is as follows:

- In addition to the course of normal sexual intercourse, while the couple is connected, they should both bring themselves close to the point of climax and then stop moving to prevent climax yet stay connected.

- In this moment of stillness, they should both breathe in deeply through their nostrils and hold their breath for as long as they comfortably can. 20 to 30 seconds is normal. When it is time to exhale, they should exhale at the same time through the mouth.

- While holding your breath, you should use your mind to guide your sexual energy around the circular pathway formed between your body and your partner's body. The alchemist should research the detailed explanations and energy flow diagrams of "Taoist Sexual Yoga." I recommend the books of Mantak Chia and Michael Winn . See Figures [4] and [5]

- The main energetic pathway within a person extends from the sexual organs up the spine of the back, over the head, down the front of the torso, and back to the sexual organs. This is the "Microcosmic Orbit."

- When the couple is sexually connected, their pathways fuse to become one circuit with the energy orbiting up the back of one, over the heads of both, and down the back of the other, across the genitals of both, and back up the spine again. The couple can reverse the orbit as they wish with their minds.

- The couple should take subsequent deep breaths, and while holding their breath they should direct their sexual energy along the circuit with their minds until sexual control is stabilized while still maintaining a connection.

- During sexual intercourse, when the couple are holding their breath and directing their sexual energy with their minds, this is called "Sublimation."

- Normal sexual intercourse continues between each act of sublimation. Typically, the person with less control initiates the moments of sublimation.

- A woman may achieve orgasm as often as she pleases during sexual intercourse as her energy is not lost during orgasm. A woman's sexual energy is depleted with her menstruation.

- When a man withholds ejaculation, it is not because it is forbidden; it is to cultivate the power of the semen for a sustained period. The man may wish to withhold ejaculation during the full course of the practice, or he may wish to ejaculate at the end. The man must listen to his body and gradually attune himself to signals of tension, depletion, and imbalance, and what is working well.

- While a couple is sexually connected, to ensure the best flow of energy between them, there are a few points or gates which need to be closed or connected between the couple. The first gate is the mouth. When the couple is kissing, the gate is connected and energy flows along this connection point. When not kissing, the tongue should stay touching the roof of a person's mouth.

- The second gate is the perineum located between the anus and the genitals. The perineum is kept closed by clenching the sphincter muscles of the surrounding area. When the couple is connected, the energy will pass along this connection point without clenching as long as they maintain their connection.

- Eventually, when the couple disconnects, each person should continue sublimating their sexual energy for a period of 20 to 30 minutes along their own orbit, which rises up the back, over the head, down the torso, and back down to the genitals. We can do this lying down or in a seated position.

- Other secondary orbits exist in our legs and arms. We can move the energy along these secondary orbits with our mind.

- When you feel the energy passing the heart area of your chest, you should use your mind to guide the energy to accumulate in the area below the naval called the "Sea of Chi." Imagine the energy swirling in this area and shortly thereafter, you will feel the energy accumulating in the Sea of Chi. *See Figure [5].*

- It is important to continue sublimating after disconnecting as the energy we are working with is closer in resonance with Spirit and we want to continue cultivating this spiritualized energy.

At the moment immediately after a practice of the Second Factor—while we feel a neutralized balance of magnetic forces—a rare opportunity opens within us where we can leverage this balanced state of magnetic forces that more closely resonate with the Spirit and collaborate with the Spirit in a practice of alchemical meditation of the First Factor or in other practices of the Third Factor.

In "Taoist Sexual Yoga," there is a very detailed metaphysical science behind this sexual practice which defines all the etheric pathways and components of the anatomy. In addition to the practice prescribed in this book, I suggest the alchemist research this science and go deeper with the practice to a level with which they are satisfied.

I am purposely providing only the essence of the alchemical sexual intercourse practice in this book. Again, I recommend the books and seminars of Mantak Chia and Michael Winn as great sources of additional information.

### *9.7.7 – Practice 7 – Cosmic Cultivation (2F)*

The magnetic forces of positive (yang), negative (yin), and neutral (yuan) exist at all levels of creation. For example, within the atom we have the proton (positive), electron (negative), neutron (neutral), and within the giant electromagnetic spheres of the cosmos we call stars. These three magnetic states are in a constant dance among one another to achieve balance from one end of the spectrum within the microcosm to another end of the spectrum within the macrocosm. All bodies of creation have some form of magnetic polarity between them. Within all life-forms, this polarity exists within the psycho-sexual life forces of the organism.

Due to the psycho-sexual dynamic, the mind affects the life forces of the body, and the life forces of the body affect the mind. To elevate our state of mind, we must not only elevate the psychological components of our mind (First Factor), we must also elevate the life forces of our body which affect our mind (Second Factor). The most powerful agent of the alchemical process is the divine love of the Spirit (Third Factor). To reach the Spirit, we must foster a neutralizing balance.

The universe always provides itself with multiple means and ways to evolve, express, and re-organize. Life always finds a way. In alchemy, there are multiple ways to elevate our resonance with the Spirit. Alchemical sexual intercourse is not the only means within nature to cultivate our energy (Second Factor). The agents of the Second Factor are abundant and all about us within the planetary and cosmic forces of the stars, the planets, the Earth, the sky, the water, the trees, in every life form of nature, and in all the food we grow and consume.

The alchemist has the innate latent capacity to commune with the cosmic forces of nature to cultivate and elevate the life forces of his or her body to a higher resonance with the Spirit. This is possible by tuning our mind to resonate with the life forces of nature with the intent to cultivate our energy to a higher resonance with the Spirit. The means and methods of achieving this type of cultivation is unlimited. This form of cultivation is called "Cosmic Cultivation."

There are two main catalysts for compelling and promoting the Second Factor practice of cosmic cultivation. As with all methods of the Second Factor, the First Factor is a required precedent to the practice of cosmic cultivation. The two main catalysts are:

1.) Intent of Mind.

2.) Movement.

Cosmic cultivation is better suited for many alchemists than alchemical sexual intercourse. All alchemists should study some form of cosmic cultivation, even if they practice sexual cultivation.
A suitable place to start is with the practices of Qigong and Tai Chi.

The variation of forms which human being can develop to practice cosmic cultivation are unlimited. However, the practices of Qigong, Tai Chi, and other ancient forms, are all forms developed and cultivated by alchemists over thousands of years.

The dervish dances of the Sufis are a marvelous form of cosmic cultivation. Whenever we are practicing Qigong, Tai Chi, or Dances, it is critical to practice with the intent to cultivate our energy. Energy follows the mind.

With continued practice, our ability to practice cosmic cultivation will evolve into the ability to cultivate the planetary and cosmic forces of nature without physical movement while in meditation, as well as the ability to cultivate effortlessly as we go about our day. Movement is still occurring between the mind and the cosmic forces, just at a higher unseen level. Because energy follows the mind, the possibilities are unlimited as to all the variations of movement that can be developed. Keep an open mind and explore what both eastern and western traditions offer and adopt into your alchemy what works best for you.

Cosmic cultivation evolves into a continuous copulation of forces between your being and the cosmic forces of nature. The more unified your mind becomes, the more powerful your cosmic cultivation becomes, and the more powerful your cosmic cultivation becomes, the more unified your relationship with the greater cosmos becomes.

### *9.7.8 – Practice 8 – Quantum Meditation (3F)*

The Second Factor supports another important practice of the Third Factor. This is the practice of shifting our focus of conscious awareness beyond our temporal ethereal bodies into our spiritual ethereal bodies, and even further into the noumenal realm of the cosmic quanta. This is "Quantum Meditation."

None of these practices of the alchemical work of integration are performed in isolation from the Spirit. Each is carried out in quiet orientation toward it, which is the living function of what has traditionally been called prayer. Quantum Meditation is the deepest form of prayer, or in other words, our communication with the higher forces of consciousness.

The practices of the First and Third Factors do not require a Second Factor practice to precede them. However, when this precession occurs, optimal results are produced.

All the knowledge relayed to me from the living forces of the cosmic quanta during my alchemical journey of the Three Mountains were conveyed to me during the most profound practices of quantum meditation.

We have three ways to shift our focus of conscious awareness into our higher spiritual ethereal bodies, which resonate beyond our temporal ethereal bodies:

1.) After the death of our physical body, when we transcend the illusions of our mind and escape our temporal ethereal bodies to enter paradise.

2.) When we integrate our spiritual ethereal bodies with our temporal ethereal bodies in the alchemical processes of the Third Mountain.

3.) Through the practice of quantum meditation.

Quantum meditation can be practiced whether the physical body is awake or asleep. It is best first learned in the waking state and later extended into sleep. To describe the degree to which the organism has been brought into coherence through the integration process, I refer to what I call the Q-level—a functional measure of energetic integration and alignment with the divine source. Q represents the degree of division within the organism, with the term standing for quotient. The lower the division, the higher the coherence. To perform Quantum Meditation, the practitioner must be able to feel the resonance of the Spirit through the higher emotional faculty. This requires us to have reached Q3.
In summary, the levels of Q are:

Q5 - No awareness of our authentic-self, the Spirit, the Divine Soul, or the Father. In this state, we are mostly a human automaton led purely by instinct and our ego defense mechanisms.

Q4 - We have an awareness of our authentic-self. A true center of gravity exists within us.

Q3 - We have an awareness of our authentic-self and the Spirit. We have a higher sense of God beyond self.

Q2 - We have an awareness of our authentic-self, the Spirit, and the Divine Soul.

Q1 - We have an awareness of our authentic-self and the Father. If you are aware of the Father, then you are simultaneously aware of the divine trinity, which includes the Father, the Divine Soul, and the Spirit. The divine trinity as a unified whole is Ain Soph. Once we achieve Q1, there is no inner division of light. We resonate with Ain Soph and continue forever inward into the infinite eternal depths of the Father.

G - There is a level of coherence beyond Q1 that I refer to as G, which is our level of awareness of the Cosmic Christ Monad, the living reintegrated God of the universe—the grand celestial being who I call the Immortal Beloved, or Eloah.

<u>Step-by-Step Practice</u>

- Start off with a breathing exercise to relax your entire body.
- Focus on feeling the Spirit with your emotions.
- As you continue to relax your body, contrast your awareness of the Spirit with your awareness of your physical body.
- Allow your awareness of your physical body to slip away from your mind while you hold your awareness of the Spirit.
- Now shift your attention to your emotions. Focus on your emotional center. Contrast the difference in your mind between your common human emotions and those of the Spirit. Choose the Spirit over your common human emotions and allow your common human emotions to slip away.
- Now shift your attention to your thought processes. Focus on your mental center. Contrast the difference in your mind between the feeling of your thoughts and that of the Spirit. Choose the Spirit and allow your thoughts to slip away.
- Now shift your attention back to your physical body. Focus on the feeling of your physical body. Contrast the difference in your mind between your physical body and the Spirit. Choose the Spirit and allow your physical state to slip away.
- Repeat this cycle of differentiation and release as needed. With each cycle, each element you are releasing becomes softer and more transparent.
- With each cycle, go deeper into the Spirit.
- As your feelings shift deeper into the Spirit, begin listening to the Spirit with your feelings. Listen very delicately and you will begin hearing with your feelings. There is a very subtle communication that is occurring. You will begin receiving knowledge directly from the cosmic quanta.

The longer we are able to sustain a heightened resonance between our conscious mind and the Spirit, the more the physical wiring of our brain is re-wired to support and deepen the resonance. Over time, the subtle communication between our conscious mind and the emergent forces of the cosmic quanta develops into a new super cognitive faculty called "Intraspection." This is not the same as "Introspection."

Introspection takes place solely between your own thoughts. Intraspection is a communication between the conscious mind and the emergent forces of the cosmic quanta. The Spirit is the first of these forces. It is through sustained attention to this communication that the practitioner begins to distinguish between the movements of the personal mind and signals arising from deeper strata of intelligence.

As we continue the Third Factor practice of quantum meditation alongside other practices of the Three Factors, additional forces within the cosmic quanta—outside of the Spirit—begin to emerge and present themselves. As we develop our super cognitive ability to communicate with the cosmic quanta, prayer, quantum meditation, and intraspection all come together to resonate as one. At this stage, the mind is no longer operating in isolation but begins functioning as a receptive instrument within a larger field of consciousness.

### *9.7.9 – Practice 9 – Contemplation and Study (3F)*

The process of rigorous research, study, contemplation, and the pursuit of truth is a function of the Third Factor we all must engage in. I recommend every spiritual alchemist select a field of study pertaining to the Great Mystery and choose a medium of expression to share this knowledge. This medium can be scientific, artistic, mathematical, philosophical, or musical. We all have a voice. All fields of study interconnect with alchemy in some unique way. It is everyone's job to expand humanity's understanding of the Great Mystery. We are all called forth by the universe in this endeavor. It is our sacred calling. Comprehension is not complete until it is expressed. Expression stabilizes realization, anchoring insight within the organism and allowing it to participate in the broader evolution of understanding. The genuine expression of our authentic self, and our resonance with the Spirit, brings us close to the realization of divine truth.

Study, when performed consciously, becomes part of the work. Engage with texts not merely to acquire information, but to refine comprehension. Read slowly. Reflect deeply. Re-express it in your own words to promote realization. Allow understanding to emerge rather than forcing it. The aim is not the accumulation of knowledge, but the alignment of intellect with truth. Although the practices themselves remain consistent, the sequence through which the psyche undergoes transformation is not identical for all individuals.

*9.8.0 – The Two Routes of the Straight Path (Classical & Dynamic)*

The pathway of accelerated integration does not unfold in a uniform manner across all individuals. Although the principles of the Straight Path remain constant, the sequence through which the psyche undergoes transformation varies depending on its condition at the moment the work consciously begins.

Through observation and experience, it becomes evident that there are two primary routes through which Alpha guides this process along the Straight Path: the Classical route and the Dynamic route.

This distinction is not determined by personal preference or conscious choice. It is determined by Alpha itself—by the deeper organizing intelligence responding to the structure and condition of the psyche at the onset of the work. The path is not selected by the practitioner; it is revealed through the unfolding of the process.

At the center of this distinction lies the relationship between two domains within the human being: the noetic sphere and erotic sphere.

The noetic sphere corresponds to the higher faculties of awareness, perception, and connection to the divine source. The erotic sphere corresponds to the deep instinctive, emotional, and psycho-sexual forces embedded within the biological organism. Between these two domains exists a boundary—a regulating threshold that governs the degree to which these forces interact.

This boundary functions as a stabilizing mechanism within the psyche. It regulates the emergence of deeper instinctive forces so they do not overwhelm the conscious mind before it has developed the capacity to observe and integrate them. In this sense, it preserves psychological coherence while the faculties of awareness are still forming.

This threshold may also be understood in energetic terms as the action of a regulating force—what we may associate with Theta. This force acts continuously to contain the more chaotic and destructive potentials within the deeper layers of the psyche. It does not eliminate these forces, but holds them in latency until the organism is capable of engaging them consciously. When functioning properly, it prevents these forces from rising prematurely and destabilizing the system.

Over the course of life, however, this boundary may be either preserved or eroded.

When the boundary remains largely intact at the onset of the work, Alpha directs the individual along the Classical route. In this route, the practitioner first develops awareness, stability, and the capacity for transformation across the upper and intermediate layers of the psyche. The mind is trained to observe itself. The organism is stabilized through cultivation. The relationship with the Spirit is established and deepened.

Throughout this phase, the deeper instinctive forces remain largely veiled. This allows the practitioner to develop clarity and coherence before encountering the most difficult aspects of the psyche.

Only near the culmination of the work—just below the summit of the Third Mountain—does the practitioner encounter what has been described as the id complex. Within this domain, the deepest forces of darkness within the human psyche are revealed and brought into direct contrast with the forces of divinity. The structures referred to as the Idamus and the Gorgon emerge fully into conscious awareness.

In the Classical route, this encounter occurs at the end of the process, when the conscious mind has developed sufficient capacity to engage and integrate these forces without fragmentation.

The Dynamic route unfolds differently.

When the boundary between the noetic and erotic spheres has already been partially eroded prior to the conscious beginning of the work, Alpha directs the individual along the Dynamic route. In this case, the deeper instinctive and psycho-sexual forces are not deferred—they emerge at the very beginning.

This barrier erosion may occur gradually or suddenly over the course of life. Prolonged exposure to heightened erotic states, extreme fear, trauma, abuse, substance dependency, or neurological disruption can weaken this threshold, allowing deeper forces of the id complex to surface before the psyche is prepared to integrate them.

The practitioner is therefore confronted early on with the most intense and destabilizing elements of the psyche. The forces referred to in this work as the Idamus and the Gorgon—those arising from the deepest strata of the instinctive and emotional mind—become immediately perceptible. These forces may manifest as compulsive drives, distorted self-perception, emotional volatility, or psychological fragmentation.

This early confrontation often creates the impression that the work is chaotic or disordered.

Yet this is not disorder. It is sequence.

In the Dynamic route, the practitioner must first learn to become aware of these forces without identifying with them. The initial task is not their full transformation and integration, but the withdrawal of unconscious participation in them. The practitioner must cease empowering these structures through identification, reaction, and psychological dependence.

For example, structures such as narcissism may arise from these deeper layers as a means of shielding the psyche from underlying shame, fear, or fragmentation. Such structures resist self-awareness, replacing observation with distortion and reinforcing identification. In the Dynamic route, these defenses must be recognized and relinquished early for meaningful progress to occur.

Only after this disentanglement does the process begin to stabilize. The practitioner can then proceed through the intermediate layers of the psyche in a manner similar to the Classical route, developing clarity and integration across the system. And yet, just as in the Classical route, the deepest integration of these forces is not completed until the final stages of the Great Work.

In the Dynamic route, the Void is experienced both at the beginning and at the end, whereas in the Classical route, it occurs only at the end.

In both routes, the destination remains the same. The forces of the psyche—both luminous and dark—must ultimately be brought into conscious integration. The difference lies only in when they are encountered and how the process unfolds in time.

The practitioner does not choose the route. Alpha does.

This recognition removes the illusion of control and replaces it with alignment. The work is not forced into being; it is entered into consciously, with humility, precision, and an increasing sensitivity to the movements of the deeper intelligence guiding it.

And in this, the deeper intelligence of the process reveals itself once again: the path is always adapted to the individual, even before the individual understands the path.

*9.9.0 – The Primordial Afterlife*

If the alchemical work described in the earlier sections truly culminates in the awakening of the noetic soul within its immortal primordial body while our mortal body still walks the physical Earth, an inevitable question arises: has anyone ever glimpsed this realm before crossing the final threshold of death? Are there moments when the veil between the temporal and eternal realms of existence briefly lifts, allowing consciousness to remember the primordial world from where it once descended into time?

One of the most persistent and cross-culturally consistent phenomena reported in modern consciousness research is the near-death experience. Individuals from widely different cultures, professions, and belief systems have described remarkably similar experiences when they approach the threshold of death.

Despite the diversity of backgrounds among those who report them, these experiences frequently contain a recognizable sequence of events: departure from the body, passage through darkness or a tunnel, encounter with a luminous presence, a panoramic review of one's life, and entry into a realm that experiencers consistently describe as more real than ordinary physical reality.

Within the framework developed throughout Nous Solis, these experiences are not anomalies. They are spiritual dispatch reports. They represent temporary awakenings of consciousness within the Primordial Universe—moments in which the noetic soul briefly disengages from the temporal structures of the physical body and reawakens within its higher primordial counterpart.

In such moments, the veil of temporal perception loosens, and consciousness perceives reality from the vantage point of its primordial existence, unfiltered by the dense sensory limitations of physical embodiment.

The alchemical practitioner arrives at this threshold through the disciplined lifelong process of the Straight Path.

The near-death experiencer arrives at this moment involuntarily at the brink of death during a physical-life crisis.

The difference is the path. The destination is the same.

*9.9.1 - A Personal Account - The Emerald Green Valley*

My first encounter with what I later came to understand as the primordial universe occurred when I was seven years old.

At that age, I possessed no knowledge of meditation, metaphysics, or spiritual philosophy. What occurred was entirely uninvited, while at the same time, overwhelming and transcendental.

One night, as I closed my eyes to sleep, something other than sleep occurred. My conscious awareness entered a completely different state of reality—one that bore no resemblance to a dream. Where dreams are fluid and unstable, this environment possessed a clarity and solidity that exceeded even waking physical life. It was a state of ultra-reality.

I found myself floating above a paradisiacal emerald-green valley surrounded by magnificent velvet mountains folding into one another like pillows beneath a crystal royal blue sky. The colors were extraordinarily vivid, almost luminous, as though the landscape itself were animated by light.

Yet the heavenly surreal scene was secondary to the state of consciousness that accompanied it.

I was filled with a sense of overwhelming bliss and euphoria so profound that language is almost useless in attempting to describe it. It was more than emotional rapture. There was a sense of revelation.

And what it revealed was astonishing.

I remembered this place.

Not as something once visited, but as something already known; something fundamental and as familiar as the awareness behind my own eyes. In that moment, I understood, without reasoning or reflection, that this is where we come from before we were born and where we return after we die. Our physical lifetimes on Earth appeared, from that vantage point, as brief voyages into another universal reality undertaken for participating in something extraordinary. I further understood that the individual realizations accumulated across each physical lifetime are consummated upon the noetic soul's return to this realm. Our brief physical life experiences are fully integrated here in contrast to the fullness of the primordial reality in union with God.

When I awoke, tears were already on my face.

As a child, I had no vocabulary or framework with which to interpret what had occurred. Yet the experience left an indelible impression that would guide my inquiry for the rest of my life.

I spent decades trying to understand what I had witnessed and how to return to it. The alchemical work described throughout Nous Solis eventually took me back.

### *9.9.2 - The Living Landscape of Elysium*

Years later, during the alchemical journey of the Third Mountain—Mount Magia—while my conscious mind ascended through the ethereal heavens that bound the primordial Earth, I re-experienced the ultra-real environment of my childhood vision in the most extraordinary manner.

In the Elysium heaven enveloping that world, I experienced its paradisiacal nature in a way wholly unlike normal physical reality. Everything felt alive. I did not simply arrive there—I awoke within it. The mountains in the distance wiggled and jiggled as I thought of them. My sense of self dissolved into the surrounding landscape where I felt the love of God moving through the tall green meadow grasses swaying before me in response to my awareness of it.

The divine beauty of that world will leave you speechless.

In this paradisiacal world, the landscape itself participates in the field of consciousness. The Earth is not merely a physical substrate upon which life occurs; it is a living organism whose mind and spirit permeate every dimension of the environment. Within the cosmological framework shared throughout Nous Solis, this realm corresponds to the Primordial Earth—the eternal counterpart of the Physical Earth existing beyond the singularity wall, where it is enveloped by the bandwidths of the solar noosphere—the spiritual group mind of the Earth.

The bliss that fills us upon arrival is not generated by the scenery. It is the divine Spirit—the love irradiating the cosmic consciousness of Ain Soph—felt without the suppression normally imposed by the physical dimensions of the human brain. When our conscious mind reawakens in the primordial universe, free of temporal distortion, it encounters the Spirit at full amplitude—and we remember everything. In that moment, the exile of consciousness in time quietly comes to an end, and we recognize once again the eternal world we never truly left.

### *9.9.3 - The Tunnel of Light: An Alchemical Parallel*

Decades after my childhood vision, far along in the ascent of the Third Mountain, I encountered the same threshold of death from the opposite direction, not as a child entering involuntarily, but as someone arriving through a lifelong process of integration.

Near the summit of Mount Magia, after the realization of the true nature of the divine trinity within my being had reached its proper threshold, the three divine forces of Ain Soph merged into a unified presence that appeared as a radiant Sun of extraordinary brilliance. As the intensity increased, my awareness felt drawn inward toward it until the light transformed into a luminous tunnel.

Moving through that tunnel, I was given the understanding that the alchemical integration process of the Three Mountains parallels the process of physical death — the progressive emancipation of the noetic soul from its temporal bodies, and its re-awakening within the primordial body in the primordial universe. The critical difference is that in the alchemical process, this emancipation occurs while the physical body remains alive.

The tunnel of light reported by near-death experiencers as the final passage before arrival in the luminous realm is not a metaphor. It is a structural feature of the transition between temporal and primordial existence — the boundary the noetic soul crosses as the primordial brain completes its re-collection of conscious awareness from the dying physical brain. The spiritual alchemist crosses this threshold consciously, under the compulsion of love. The near-death experiencer crosses it involuntarily, under the pressure of death.

Both are crossing the same boundary.

Both arrive in the same higher universe.

The difference is the path by which the soul reaches the threshold.

### *9.9.4 — Converging Testimony from Near-Death Experiences*

A survey of documented near-death testimonies illustrates how frequently individuals describe encounters with environments that appear far more vivid, coherent, and saturated with meaning than ordinary physical reality. The table below offers a preliminary orientation before examining several accounts in depth.

Eben Alexander
Floating above a vast pastoral landscape beneath a brilliant blue sky filled with living light.

George G. Ritchie
A radiant countryside of fields and trees, more vivid than ordinary reality.

Betty Eadie
Luminous gardens where flowers appeared alive with light.

Howard Storm
A realm of extraordinary beauty permeated by overwhelming love.

Mellen-Thomas Benedict
A radiant meadow where every element of the environment appeared infused with consciousness.

Although the details vary, the structural consistency is remarkable. Experiencers across different eras, cultures, and belief systems describe living landscapes—fields, valleys, gardens, meadows—of extraordinary vitality. Many report an immediate sense of recognition upon arrival. Not discovery. Recognition. As if some forgotten memory deep within their soul suddenly rose back into conscious awareness. They feel as though they have returned home.

Three accounts warrant closer examination, as each illuminates a distinct feature of the primordial universe identified throughout Nous Solis.

*Eben Alexander — The Core and the Life Review*

Dr. Eben Alexander, a neurosurgeon at Harvard Medical School, entered a coma in 2008 caused by bacterial meningitis so severe that his entire neocortex was verifiably inactive for seven days. What he reported during that period included passage through a gateway of light into a realm of overwhelming luminosity, an omniscient, loving intelligence, and a direct transmission of knowledge without language. He returned a permanently altered man whose conclusion was unambiguous: consciousness is not produced by the brain.

Within the Nous Solis framework, Alexander's experience is structurally precise. The physical brain, rendered fully inoperative, could no longer suppress the primordial brain's natural dominance. The noetic soul was recalled into the primordial body. The knowledge transmitted without language reflects the direct perceptual capacity of the primordial dimension — where consciousness does not require symbolic intermediaries but perceives reality directly.

*Raymond Moody — The Life Review as Primordial Differentiation*

Dr. Raymond Moody, whose foundational research first catalogued the common architecture of the NDE, identified the panoramic life review as one of its most consistent and distinctive features. Experiencers report perceiving the full arc of their physical lifetime simultaneously — and crucially, feeling the emotional impact of their actions on others as if those impacts were their own.

This feature maps directly onto what Nous Solis identifies as the primordial post-life differentiation of consciousness — the moment in which the noetic soul, re-awakening in the primordial universe, reviews the totality of its completed physical lifetime in contrast to the fullness of primordial reality. This contrast is not punitive. It is the mechanism through which life lessons are fully realized and integrated, and through which the soul's trajectory into its next physical incarnation is shaped. The life review is not a judgment. It is a completion.

*Anita Moorjani — Dissolution of the Temporal Self*

Anita Moorjani entered a coma in 2006 after her body was overwhelmed by end-stage lymphoma. During her NDE she described an expansion into a state without boundaries—the contracted, defended, ego-bound sense of self dissolved entirely, replaced by a merging with an all-encompassing awareness she experienced as pure unconditional love. She reported simultaneously perceiving events in distant locations with complete clarity, as if all space had collapsed into a single field of perception. She returned. Her cancer resolved completely within weeks, as documented by her medical team.

The dissolution Moorjani describes is structurally intelligible within the Nous Solis framework. The contracted self—organized around the ego defense mechanisms and psychic structures of the temporal mind—is a product of the temporal ethereal bodies. When those bodies begin their dissolution at the approach of death, the structures that maintained the defended-self dissolve with them. What remains is the noetic soul in its native state: unbounded, directly resonant with the spiritual group mind, flooded with the Spirit.

Moorjani did not hallucinate a better version of ordinary reality. She briefly inhabited her base reality—in the primordial universe — before being called back into the physical.

### *9.9.5 — Ancient Echoes of the Primordial Landscape*

Long before modern medicine began documenting near-death experiences, ancient civilizations described remarkably similar landscapes when speaking of the realm beyond death.

The Greeks spoke of the Elysian Fields—a realm of eternal spring where the blessed dwell in radiant meadows beneath a luminous sky.

In ancient Egyptian religion, the afterlife paradise was known as Aaru—a fertile landscape of abundant fields nourished by celestial waters, where the soul moves in full consciousness and the burdens of mortality are lifted. The Hebrew tradition preserves the image of a primordial paradise in the story of Eden:

*"A river went out of Eden to water the garden, and from there it parted and became four headwaters." — Genesis 2:10*

Other traditions speak of Shambhala—the hidden valley of the East whose existence is known only to those whose consciousness has been sufficiently prepared—and of Hyperborea, the northern paradise beyond the reach of ordinary geography, where the sun always shines and the inhabitants live in perfect harmony with the divine. These are not geographically separate traditions. They are culturally distinct memories of the same place.

Across these traditions, the imagery remains strikingly consistent: a luminous valley, fertile fields or gardens, encircling mountains, flowing waters, and a pervasive harmony between consciousness and the living world. Across centuries and civilizations, humanity has repeatedly described the same primordial landscape.

This consistency is not coincidence. It is memory.

It is a memory carried quietly within the depths of the noetic soul since the beginning of our descent into time.

### *9.9.6 — The Archetypal Geometry of the Primordial Valley*

A curious feature of these descriptions is their shared geography. Whether encountered in near-death experiences, preserved in ancient mythologies, or directly experienced in the course of alchemical integration, the primordial realm consistently appears as a luminous valley surrounded by mountains beneath a radiant sky.

This structure appears in Eden, Shambhala, Hyperborea, and the Elysian Fields. It is the structure of the emerald-green valley I entered as a seven-year-old child. It is the landscape Eben Alexander floated above. It is what George Ritchie, Betty Eadie, and Mellen-Thomas Benedict each encountered in their own way.

Such landscapes represent more than symbolic imagery or cultural projection. They reflect the actual interior geography of the primordial Earth—the protected center of the spiritual group mind, concealed beyond the perceptual boundaries of ordinary temporal consciousness. The encircling mountains mark the boundary between worlds. The valley is the hidden interior space of consciousness itself, the place the noetic soul recognizes immediately upon arrival because it has always known it. It is the emerald valley of my childhood memory, the Elysian Fields of Homer, the Aaru of the Egyptian priests, the Shambhala of the Tibetan masters, and the radiant meadow of the near-death experiencer awakening at the edge of death. These are not separate descriptions of separate places. They are the same report, filed across millennia, of the same primordial home.

### *9.9.7 — Convergence: Evidence of the Primordial Universe*

When viewed collectively, the testimonies of near-death experiencers and the landscape descriptions preserved in ancient mythology reveal a pattern that resists dismissal.

Hallucinations produced by a distressed brain are typically chaotic and highly individualized. They reflect the private contents of the individual mind under stress. The environments described across NDE accounts exhibit precisely the opposite qualities: coherence, stability, living beauty, and a consistency of structure across individuals who had no prior exposure to one another's narratives.

Within the framework of Nous Solis, this consistency has a straightforward explanation. As the physical brain loses its capacity to dominate the focus of conscious awareness, the temporal structures that normally filter perception begin to loosen. The primordial brain takes over. Consciousness shifts from the physical body to the primordial body. Awareness reawakens within the primordial dimension of the Earth — the same realm we reach at the culmination of the Great Work where we experience the spiritual group mind of the primordial Earth with a clarity both unavailable and unimaginable to the temporal mind.

The life review is the primordial post-life differentiation of consciousness. The overwhelming love is the divine Spirit, felt at full amplitude for the first time since our descent into time. The dissolution of the ego at death is the shedding of the temporal ethereal bodies. The luminous valley is the primordial Earth. The sense of coming home is accurate—because it is home.

This is why experiencers consistently report that the environment feels more real than physical reality itself. From the perspective of the primordial universe, the physical world is not the foundation of existence. It is its temporal expression — a brief voyage into a derivative reality for the purpose of a cosmic agenda of awakening.

Near-death experiencers cross this threshold under the pressure of a physical-life crisis. The alchemist approaches it through a conscious engagement with the process of integration.

Both encounter the same reality.

Both return with the same testimony.

Death is not the annihilation of consciousness.

It is the moment the soul remembers where it truly belongs.

*"He will wipe away every tear from their eyes. Death will be no more; neither will there be mourning, nor crying, nor pain, anymore. The first things have passed away." — Revelation 21:4*

Revelation 21:4 echoes the completion of the reunified mind— the Christ Monad, where all things are made new and eternal. And it represents our return to our immortal existence in the primordial realm.

### *9.10.0 — The Great Work*

What has been described in these pages is not a philosophy to be adopted, but a process already unfolding within every human being. Long before it is understood, it is lived. Long before it is chosen, it is underway. The reader does not stand outside of this work, evaluating it from a distance. The reader is already within it—already participating in the movement it seeks to understand.

Humanity moves collectively through this process along what has been called the Spiral Path—slowly, unconsciously, across lifetimes and generations. The mind, the body, and the deeper structures of being are gradually shaped by forces not yet fully perceived. Civilizations rise and fall, identities form and dissolve, and through it all, something deeper continues its silent work of integration. The Straight Path does not replace this movement. It makes it conscious.

Through the deliberate application of the Three Factors—Transformation, Cultivation, and Love—the practitioner enters into cooperation with the very intelligence guiding evolution itself. What unfolds over vast spans of time through the Spiral Path can, through conscious participation, be accelerated within a single lifetime. The work that would otherwise proceed through unconscious friction becomes guided by awareness, intention, and alignment.

At first, these factors appear as separate disciplines. Transformation reveals the contents of the psyche and dissolves the structures that obscure perception. Cultivation stabilizes the organism, bringing order to the internal conditions through which awareness operates. Love establishes the relationship with the Spirit, introducing the catalytic force that makes true transformation possible. But as the work deepens, the distinction between them dissolves. They are recognized not as separate efforts, but as three expressions of a single living process.

This process is not driven by personal will alone. It is guided by the organizing intelligence of Alpha—the same intelligence that shapes stars, forms worlds, and evolves consciousness. As the practitioner aligns with this intelligence, the work begins to carry itself. Effort gives way to cooperation. Struggle gives way to participation. The practitioner no longer feels as though they are forcing transformation, but allowing it to unfold in accordance with a deeper order.

The practices of the Straight Path are therefore not ends in themselves. They are instruments through which awareness learns to perceive, stabilize, and participate in this greater movement. In time, they cease to feel like practices at all. They become the natural mode of being. Observation becomes continuous. Regulation becomes effortless. Connection becomes constant.

Life itself becomes the field of transformation.

The events of one's life begin presenting precisely the conditions required for further integration. Psychological elements arise not as obstacles, but as opportunities. Challenges reveal what is ready to be seen. Relationships mirror what is ready to be reconciled. The boundary between inner and outer experience softens as the process becomes continuous, unified across all dimensions of life.

As this integration advances, glimpses of a deeper state begin to emerge—a state long described in the accounts of the primordial traditions and echoed in modern near-death experiences. A condition of unity. Of clarity. Of direct knowing. Not as belief, but as lived reality. The fragmentation of the psyche gives way to coherence. The noise of the mind gives way to stillness. The sense of separation begins to dissolve.

These glimpses are not the end of the work.

They are indications of its direction.

They reveal what becomes stable only through continued integration. What appears at first as momentary illumination gradually becomes sustained presence.

The culmination of the Great Work is the reconstitution of the Monad—the integration of the temporal and the primordial into a single unified being. What was once fragmented becomes whole. What was once divided becomes reconciled. The human organism, once governed by unconscious forces, becomes aligned with the deeper intelligence from which it arose.

In this state, the process that began unconsciously completes itself consciously.

And yet, nothing foreign is attained.

Nothing new is added.

Only what has always been present is finally realized.

The universe does not awaken humanity to observe creation, but to bring it to completion.

# 10.0.0
# FIGURES AND DIAGRAMS

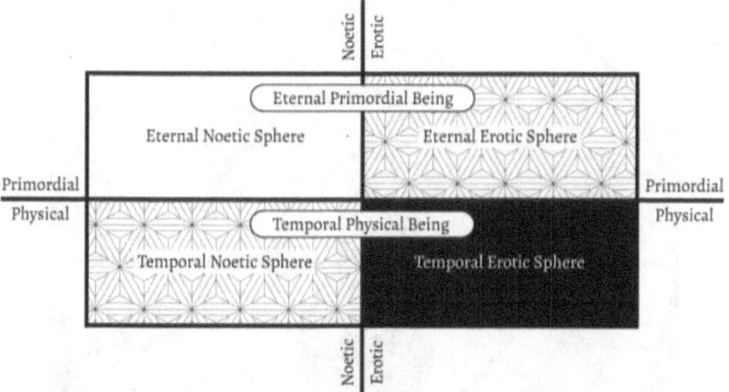


Figure [ 1 ]
The Created Spheres of the Human Being

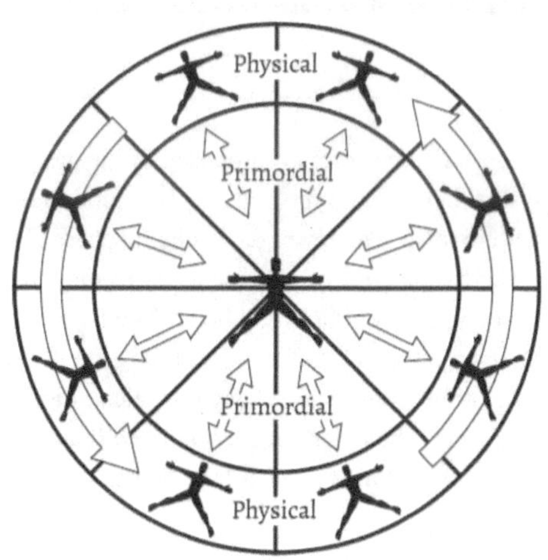


Figure [ 2 ]
The Human Wheels of Existence

The Trans-Dimensional Anatomy of the Human Being

The Twelve Bodies

Figure [ 3 ]

The hourglass figure in the center is composed of the primordial body (7) on top and the physical body (1) on the bottom. The upper lighter hemisphere is the primordial universe. The lower darker hemisphere is the physical universe. The five upper rays represent one of the five spiritual ethereal bodies surrounding the primordial body. The five lower rays represent one of the five temporal ethereal bodies surrounding the physical body. Each gradient within each ray represents the stages of alchemical transformation (Dark, Fire, Gold, Light). The inner circle around the hourglass represents the celestial body of light, which forms when all the bodies come to resonate as one.

Taoist Microcosmic Orbit Diagrams

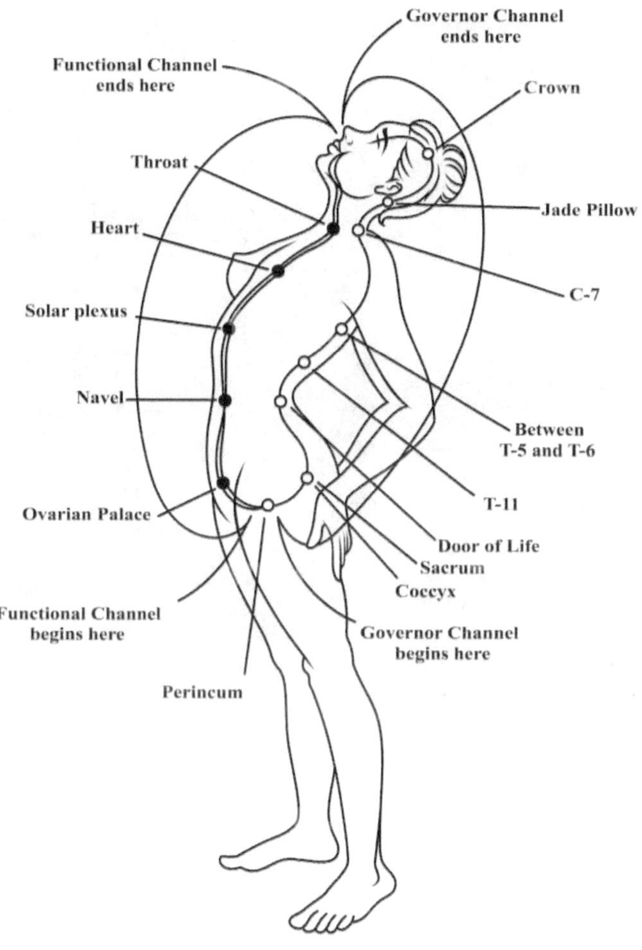


Figure [ 4 ]

---

[2] Taoist Secrets of Love: Cultivating Male Sexual Energy: Chia, Mantak; Winn, Michael. 1984. 323 p. ISBN 0-943358-19-1 URL: Also see: Taoist Secrets of Love: Cultivating Female Sexual Energy.

Taoist Microcosmic Orbit Diagrams

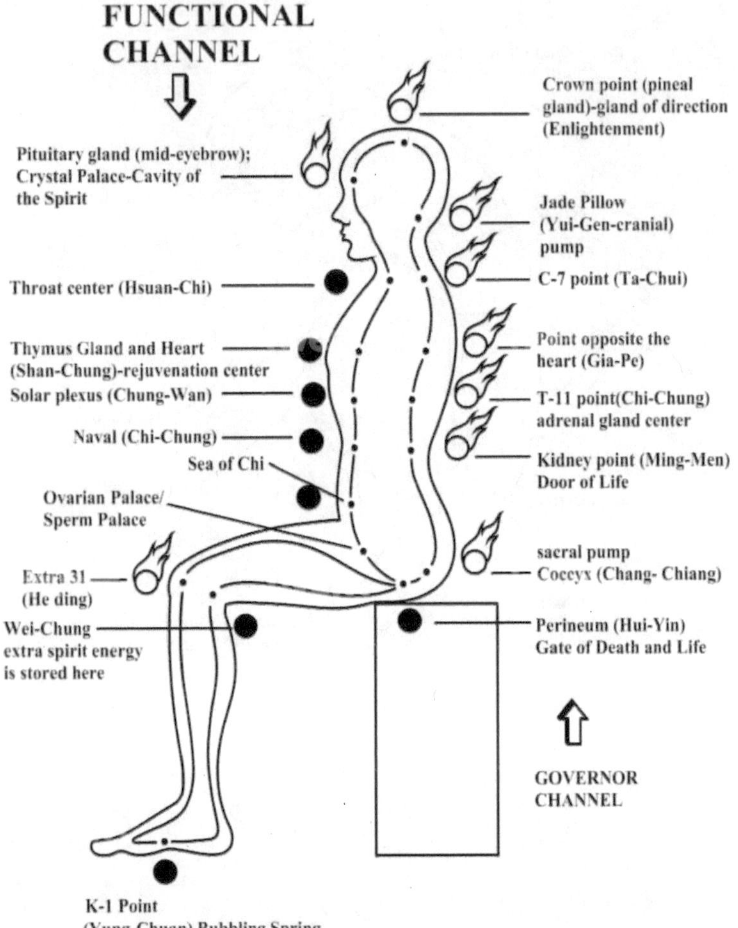


Figure [ 5 ]

Dual-Reflecting Primordial and Physical Universes

Figure [ 6 ]

# 11.0.0
# BIBLIOGRAPHY

Contemporary Sources

**Berndt, Ronald M., and Catherine H. Berndt.** *The World of the First Australians: Aboriginal Traditional Life, Past and Present.* Canberra: Aboriginal Studies Press, 1988. (Section 4.4.12-3.)

**Bohm, David.** *Wholeness and the Implicate Order.* London: Routledge & Kegan Paul, 1980. (Section 2.8.0.)

**Bostrom, Nick.** *Superintelligence: Paths, Dangers, Strategies.* Oxford: Oxford University Press, 2014. (Section 2.15.0.)

**Bruce, F.F.** *The Gospel of John: Introduction, Exposition and Notes:* Grand Rapids: William B. Eerdmans Publishing Company, 1983, P.31 (Section 7.3.1.)

**Nicholas of Cusa.** *De Docta Ignorantia (On Learned Ignorance).* Translated by Jasper Hopkins. Minneapolis: Arthur J. Banning Press, 1981. (Section 2.4.1.)

**Davies, Paul.** *The Goldilocks Enigma: Why Is the Universe Just Right for Life?* (Allen Lane, 2006). (Section 4.0.0.)

**DeLonge, Tom; Levenda, Peter.** *Sekret Machines: Gods: Volume 1 of Gods Man & War* (Gods, Man & War). (Section 4.4.0.)

**Deloria, Vine Jr.** *Red Earth, White Lies: Native Americans and the Myth of Scientific Fact.* Golden, CO: Fulcrum Publishing, 1997. (Section 4.4.12-3.)

**Eliade, Mircea.** *The Forge and the Crucible*: The Origins and Structures of Alchemy. Translated by Stephen Corrin. Chicago: University of Chicago Press, 1962. (Section 2.10.0.)
*Patterns in Comparative Religion.* Translated by Rosemary Sheed. Lincoln: University of Nebraska Press, 1996 (originally published 1958). (Section 2.1.7.)

**Grof, Stanislav.** *The Cosmic Game: Explorations of the Frontiers of Human Consciousness.* Albany: State University of New York Press, 1998. (Section 2.7.0.)

**Hall, Manly P.** *The Secret Teachings of All Ages.* Los Angeles: The Philosophical Research Society, 1928. (Section 2.16.0.)

**Hancock, Graham.** (1) *Supernatural: Meetings with the Ancient Teachers of Mankind.* London: Century, 2005. (Section 2.11.0.) (2) *Magicians of the Gods. The Forgotten Wisdom of Earth's Lost Civilization.* New York: St. Martin's Press, 2015. (Section 4.3.0. / 4.4.7.)

**Hawking, Stephen.** *The Universe in a Nutshell.* New York: Bantam Books, 2001. (Section 4.0.0.)

**Jung, Carl Gustav.** *The Archetypes and the Collective Unconscious.* Translated by R.F.C. Hull. Princeton: Princeton University Press, 1959 (Collected Works of C.G. Jung, Volume 9, Part 1). (Section 2.4.0.) Additional reference to *Psychology and Alchemy.* Princeton University Press, 1944. (Section 1.0.0.)

**Kramer, Samuel Noah.** *Sumerian Mythology: A Study of Spiritual and Literary Achievement in the Third Millennium B.C.*. Philadelphia: University of Pennsylvania Press, 1972. (Section 2.1.7.)

**Leeming, David A.** *The Oxford Companion to World Mythology.* Oxford: Oxford University Press, 2005. (Section 2.1.7.)

**Lynch, Patricia Ann, and Jeremy Roberts.** *African Mythology A to Z.* 2nd ed. New York: Chelsea House, 2010. (Section 4.4.12-3.)

**Mack, John E.** *Passport to the Cosmos: Human Transformation and Alien Encounters*. New York: Crown Publishers, 1999. (Section 2.12.0.)

**McKenna, Terence.** *The Archaic Revival: Speculations on Psychedelic Mushrooms, the Amazon, Virtual Reality, UFOs, Evolution, Shamanism, the Rebirth of the Goddess, and the End of History.* San Francisco: Harper San Francisco, 1991. (Section 2.3.0.)

**Mutwa, Vusamazulu Credo.** *Indaba, My Children: African Folk Tales*. Johannesburg: Blue Crane Books, 1964. (Section 4.4.12-3.)

**Pagels, Elaine.** *The Gnostic Gospels*. New York: Random House, 1979. (Section 2.6.0.)

**Plutarch.** *Moralia: On the Face Which Appears in the Orb of the Moon.* Translated by Harold Cherniss and William C. Helmbold. Cambridge, MA: Harvard University Press, 1957. (Section 4.4.12-3.)

**Prigogine, Ilya, and Isabelle Stengers**. *Order Out of Chaos: Man's New Dialogue with Nature*. New York: Bantam Books, 1984. (Sections 3.2.0.)

**Restrepo, Eduardo.** *The Muisca: A Cultural and Historical Analysis.* Bogotá: Universidad de los Andes Press, 1999. (Section 4.4.12-3.)

**Sagan, Carl.** *Cosmos*. New York: Random House, 1980. (Section 4.0.0.)

**Sheldrake, Rupert.** *The Presence of the Past: Morphic Resonance and the Habits of Nature.* London: Collins, 1988. (Section 2.14.0.)

**Spencer, Lawrence R., ed.** *Alien Interview:* Based on Personal Notes and Interview Transcripts Provided by the Late Matilda O'Donnell MacElroy. Las Vegas: Createspace, 2008. (Section 4.4.8.)

**Sproul, Barbara C.** *Primal Myths: Creation Myths Around the World.* San Francisco: HarperOne, 1979. (Section 2.1.7.)

**Teilhard de Chardin, Pierre.** *The Phenomenon of Man.* Translated by Bernard Wall. New York: Harper & Brothers, 1955. (Section 2.2.0.)

**Tolkien, J.R.R**. "*On Fairy-Stories." Essays Presented to Charles Williams*, edited by C.S. Lewis, Oxford University Press, 1947. (Section 2.1.6.)

**Von Franz, Marie-Louise.** *Creation Myths*. Boston: Shambhala Publications, 1995. (Section 2.1.7.)

Sources for the Clinical Composites in Section 6.0.0

**American Psychiatric Association.** *Diagnostic and Statistical Manual of Mental Disorders.* Fifth Edition, Text Revision (2022)

**Cheyne, J. Allan.** *Sleep Paralysis and the Structure of Waking-Nightmare Hallucinations.* (Dreaming, 2003)

**Hufford, David J.** *The Terror That Comes in the Night: An Experience-Centered Study of Supernatural Assault Traditions.* (1982)

**Jalal, Baland, and Vilayanur S. Ramachandran.** *Sleep Paralysis, 'The Ghostly Bedroom Intruder,' and Out-of-Body Experiences.* (Frontiers in Human Neuroscience, 2014)

**Sharpless, Brian A., and Jacques P. Barber.** *Lifetime Prevalence Rates of Sleep Paralysis: A Systematic Review.* (Sleep Medicine Reviews, 2011)

**Van der Hart, Onno, Ellert Nijenhuis, and Kathy Steele.** *The Haunted Self: Structural Dissociation and the Treatment of Chronic Traumatization* (2006)

Ancient Texts and Scriptures

**The Apocryphon of John.** *The Nag Hammadi Library in English.* Robinson, James M., ed. San Francisco: Harper & Row, 1977. (Section 3.1.1., 8.0.0.)

**The Book of Enoch.** Translated by R. H. Charles. London: Society for Promoting Christian Knowledge, 1917. (Sections 4.0.0, 6.0.0.)

**The Book of Daniel.** King James Version. (Daniel 7:7-8). (Section 6.0.0.)

**The Book of Genesis.** King James Version and New International Version. (Genesis 3:22-24); (Section 2.0.0.)

**The Book of Revelation.** King James Version. Revelation 21:1-5 cited in sections 1.0.0 and 3.0.0. Revelation 13:1. (Section 6.0.0.)

**Brihadaranyaka Upanishad.** *Upanishads.* Olivelle, Patrick, trans. Oxford: Oxford University Press, 1996. (Section 2.0.0.)

**Corpus Hermeticum.** *Hermetica: The Greek Corpus Hermeticum and the Latin Asclepius.* Copenhaver, Brian P., trans. Cambridge: Cambridge University Press, 1992. (Section 2.0.0.)

**The Egyptian Book of the Dead.** *The Egyptian Book of the Dead: The Book of Going Forth by Day.* Faulkner, Raymond O., trans. San Francisco: Chronicle Books, 1994. (Sect. 2.0.0.)

**Enuma Elish.** *Ancient Near Eastern Texts Relating to the Old Testament.* Pritchard, James B., ed. Princeton: Princeton University Press, 1969. (Section 2.0.0.)

**The Epic of Gilgamesh.** *The Epic of Gilgamesh.* Tablet XI. George, Andrew, trans. London: Penguin Classics, 1999. (Sections 2.0.0.)

**The Gospel of Judas.** *The Gospel of Judas.* Kasser, Rodolphe, et al., eds. Washington, DC: National Geographic Society, 2006. (Section 6.0.0.)

**The Gospel of Philip.** *The Nag Hammadi Library in English.* Robinson, James M., ed. San Francisco: Harper & Row, 1977. (Section 2.6.0., 8.0.0.)

**The Gospel of Thomas.** *The Nag Hammadi Library in English.* Robinson, James M., ed. San Francisco: Harper & Row, 1977. (Section 4.0.0., 7.0.0., 8.0.0.)

**The Gospel of Truth.** *The Nag Hammadi Library in English.* Robinson, James M., ed. San Francisco: Harper & Row, 1977. (Section 8.0.0.)

**The Holy Bible.** *King James Version.* Oxford: Oxford University Press, 1769. (Sections 2.1.0; 7.0.0.)

**The Holy Bible.** *New International Version.* Grand Rapids, MI: Zondervan, 1978. (Sections 2.1.0; 7.0.0.)

**Hesiod.** *Works and Days.* Translated by M. L. West. Oxford: Oxford University Press, 1988. (Section 3.0.0.)

**The Hypostasis of the Archons.** *The Nag Hammadi Library in English.* Robinson, James M., ed. San Francisco: Harper & Row, 1977. (Section 2.6.0., 3.1.3.)

**The Mahabharata.** Translated by Kisari Mohan Ganguli. Calcutta: Pratap Chandra Roy, 1883–1896. (Drona Parva). (Section 4.0.0.)

**On the Origin of the World.** *The Nag Hammadi Library in English*, edited by James M. Robinson. San Francisco: Harper San Francisco, 1990. (Nag Hammadi Codex II,5; Codex XIII,2). (Section 3.1.4.)

**Plato.** *Critias.* Translated by R. G. Bury. Cambridge, MA: Harvard University Press, 1929 (Loeb Classical Library). (Section 4.0.0.)

**Plotinus.** *The Enneads.* Translated by Stephen MacKenna and B.S. Page. Revised by John Dillon. London: Penguin Classics, 1991. (Ennead IV.7, Section 10). (Section 2.17.0.)

**The Ramayana of Valmiki**. Translated by Ralph T. H. Griffith. London: Trübner & Co., 1870–1874. (Section 4.0.0.)

**The Upanishads.** Easwaran, Eknath. Tomales, CA: Nilgiri Press, 1987. (Section 2.0.0.)

www.ingramcontent.com/pod-product-compliance
Lightning Source LLC
LaVergne TN
LVHW090556110826
845146LV00001B/146

* 9 7 9 8 9 9 1 7 3 8 7 4 3 *